Lecture Notes in Control and Information Sciences

Edited by A. V. Balakrishnan and M. Thoma

For further listing of published volumes please turn over to inside of back cover.

Lecture Notes in Control and Information Sciences

Edited by A.V. Balakrishnan and M. Thoma

46

Time-Scale Modeling of Dynamic Networks with Applications to Power Systems

Edited by J. H. Chow

Springer-Verlag Berlin Heidelberg GmbH

ISBN 978-3-540-12106-0   ISBN 978-3-540-39543-0 (eBook)
DOI 10.1007/978-3-540-39543-0

2061/3020-543210

JOE H. CHOW, Editor

Contributors:

BOZIDAR AVRAMOVIC, Systems Engineering for Power, Inc.

JOE H. CHOW, General Electric Company

PETAR V. KOKOTOVIC, University of Illinois

GEORGE M. PEPONIDES, M/A-Com Linkabit, Inc.

JAMES R. WINKELMAN, General Electric Company

To Doris

PREFACE

Reduced order modeling is often the point of departure in the study of large scale systems. It is commonly assumed in large scale system literature that the models of the systems have been given, the subsystems and their hierarchies defined, and the information exchange patterns already determined. The focus is then on the design of stabilizing or optimal controls in a decentralized manner. The questions as to how the subsystems and their hierarchies are defined, and how the reduced models can help a control engineer to design simple and robust controls remain to be answered.

This monograph develops a modeling methodology for a class of large scale systems with network structure. The methodology provides analytical tools to reveal the time-scale properties and replace heretofore heuristic means for defining decompositions into subsystems and control hierarchies. This time-scale methodology is motivated by the fact that responses of varying speeds are commonly observed in power systems and many other interconnected systems. The physical basis of the methodology is the relationship between time-scales and weak connections. For dynamic networks which include models of electrical circuits, mass-spring systems, torsional systems of turbine-generators and multi-market economies, weak connections necessarily give rise to time-scales. Thus the first task in the modeling procedure is to identify weak connections as subsystem boundaries. Then in the short term, the fast dynamics are modeled with the decoupled local subsystem models. The second task is to develop an aggregate model representing the interaction of subsystems. This aggregate model is to be used in long term studies because then the interactions through weak connections are significant. The same idea is implicit in existing empirical techniques for coherency-based equivalencing of power systems and aggregation of economic models.

A natural tool for analysis of asymptotic time-scale properties is the singular perturbation method, which is introduced in Chapter 2, extended in Chapter 3, and used throughout the monograph. Dynamic networks and the electromechanic model of power systems are described in Chapter 4. Both linear results (Chapters 3 to 6) and nonlinear results (Chapters 7 and 8) are illustrated at two levels: at the conceptual level by simple RC-circuits and at the more realistic level by models of real power systems. For reasons of space, the largest power system example contains only 48 machines. However, the time-scale methodology developed had already been applied to power systems as large as 400 machines and 1700 buses. The computation takes advantage of sparsity and the fact that only a small number of eigenvalues and eigenvectors are needed.

The monograph is written for a broad audience of systems and control engineers. The background assumed does not exceed the basic linear system theory covered in most undergraduate programs. In addition to its use by practicing engineers, the monograph can also serve as a text for a graduate course in power system modeling. Individual chapters can be used to supplement more general system and control theory courses.

The research topic leading to the monograph was inspired by Les Fink (Systems Engineering for Power) and Kjell Carlsen (Electric Utility Systems Engineering Department, GE), who continued to stimulate us throughout the research period. Discussions with Jean-Pierre Quadrat (INRIA, France), Jure Medanic (Pupin Institute, Yugoslavia) and many colleagues on the staff of the Coordinated Science Laboratory, University of Illinois, and EUSED had greatly contributed to this monograph. Special thanks are due to Jane Cullum (Thomas J. Watson Research Center, IBM) whose eigensolution algorithm extends the applicability of our methodology to very large power systems. The research was supported by a U.S. Department of Energy, Electric Energy System Division, contract with GE and a National Science Foundation grant to the University of Illinois. We also thank Janice Nolan, Holly Powers and Jean Fellos of the EUSED Word Processing Center for patiently typing many revisions of the manuscript.

Joe H. Chow
Schenectady, New York

October 1982

CONTENTS

CHAPTER 1

TIME-SCALES IN INTERCONNECTED SYSTEMS

1.1 Long and Short Term Dynamics

Dynamics of different speeds are frequently observed in models of large scale interconnected systems. In power systems, the concept of dynamic energy balance [51] has been developed to model machine oscillations in different time-scales. With an appropriate partition of a power system into areas, the motion of the center of angle associated with each area is much slower than the "synchronizing" oscillations between any two machines in the same area. A physical interpretation of this phenomenon is that the connections between the machines within an area are strong while those between the areas are weak [9]. Thus, the machines within the same areas interact on a short term basis. On a long term basis when these fast oscillations have decayed, the machines in the same area move together, that is, they are "coherent" with respect to the slow modes. These slow dynamics, which are represented by the area centers of angle, are due to the interactions between groups of machines through the weak connections which have become important in the long term.

The same reasoning can be used to interpret the time-scales that occur in many other physical systems. Simon and Ando [50] offered several examples, including the following:

> "Consider a building whose outside walls provide perfect thermal insulation from the environment. The building is divided into a large number of rooms, the walls between them being good, but not perfect, insulators. Each room is divided into a number of offices by partitions. The partitions are poor insulators. A thermometer hangs in each of the offices. Suppose that at time t_0 the various offices within the building are in a state of thermal disequilibrium - there is a wide variation in temperature from office to office and from room to room. When we take new temperature readings at time t_1, several hours after t_0, what will we find? At t_1, there will be very little variation in temperature among the offices within each single room, but there may still be large temperature variations among rooms. When we take readings again at time t_2, several days after t_1, we find an almost uniform temperature throughout the building; the temperature differences among rooms have virtually disappeared."

In this example, Simon and Ando attributed the difference in time-scales of the temperature dynamics to the differing strength of connections which are the insulators: the poor insulation of the partitions implies a rapid decay of temperature differences between the offices in the same room, while the good insulation renders the settling of the temperature differences between the rooms much slower.

Another example of a system with multi-time-scales occurs in economics [39]. In a large economy, commodities are naturally classified into strongly interacting groups in which the price variations of one commodity have substantial influence on the demand of the other. The commodities in a group form a "subeconomy." If the subeconomies are weakly connected, then in the short run, we only need to study the isolated subeconomies. The prices of the commodities in each subeconomy will reach a local equilibrium in which the prices of the commodities are proportional to each other. This equilibrium is a necessary condition for Lange's law of composition of goods [29]. It is analogous to "slow coherency" in power systems [4]. In the long run each subeconomy is represented by a single aggregate price which is used to study the interaction between subeconomies.

The time-scale separation is also observed in stochastic models [26]. In a system described by a finite state Markov chain, the interactions are the transition probabilities. If we group the states into classes along the weak connections, then in the short run the probability that a process will remain in the same class is high. The probability that a process will leave a class is significant only in the long run. Thus, over shorter periods of time, it is sufficient to model the system with isolated classes of states by neglecting the weak connections. For longer periods of time when the transition between classes of states becomes more probable, each class is aggregated into a single state and interconnected with the weak connections which have now become important. Such Markov chain models occur in queueing network models of computer and communication systems [12,40,46]. Discretized models of multi-dam hydro power systems also appear in the form of a weakly connected Markov model.

In the monograph we consider those interconnected systems which can be modeled as dynamic networks. They include power systems, electrical circuits and mass-spring systems. We will not deal with Markov models, although the techniques for the separation of their time-scales [26,40] are very similar to those for dynamic networks.

1.2 Reduced Order Modeling

An intuitive reduced order modeling procedure common to all the systems that we have discussed in the previous section consists of the following steps [50]:

1. Classify all the variables into a small number of groups.

2. Study the interactions within the groups as though the interactions among the groups did not exist.

3. Define indices representing groups and study the interaction among these indices without regard to the interactions within each group.

The coherency-based aggregation method [27,41] used in reduced simulations of power systems is an example of such a procedure. The indices are the centers of angle of the areas or groups of states which are found from coherency. In transient studies where the relative stability of the machines on the first "swing" is of concern, it is sufficient to simulate only the synchronizing oscillations within an area. For a longer term study, only the centers of angle for the areas need to be simulated.

Many issues have to be resolved to make these intuitive steps into a mathematical procedure. For example, what kind of systems is the procedure applicable to? Why do the weak connections give rise to time-scales? How do we find the weak connections or groups in a large scale system? What are the indices representing the groups? How do we model the slow and fast dynamics? How accurate are the reduced models? How can we improve on the reduced models? Are they applicable to nonlinear systems? These questions will be addressed by this monograph.

We consider a class of large scale systems which we call dynamic networks. For our purpose, a dynamic network consists of non-storage branches connecting storage nodes. Models of dynamic networks include RC-circuits, mass-spring systems, power systems and torsional systems for turbine generators. They can be linear as well as nonlinear.

The main tool in our analysis is the singular perturbation technique. The large body of literature on singular perturbations [28] assumes that the small singular perturbation parameter has already been identified, and the model is in the explicit form whose time-scales are easily recognized. Real systems modeled with physical variables often fail to be in the explicit form. We show that two-time-scale systems reducible to the explicit form have the conservation and equilibrium properties [37]. For nonexplicit models, a transformation can be constructed based on these properties to obtain the slow and fast variables.

The physical interpretation of the slow and fast variables comes from the concepts of aggregation and coherency. For a dynamic network, we define an area partition and aggregate the states in each area into a center of inertia variable. We show that the condition under which the center of the inertia variables are aggregable depends on the connections between the areas only. Under the same condition the states in the same areas are coherent with respect to the aggregate modes. Of particular importance is slow coherency [3], that is, the states in the same areas are coherent with respect to the slowest modes. In this case the slow variables are the aggregate variables and the fast variables are the differences between the states in the same area.

When would a system have slow coherency? A sufficient condition is that the areas be weakly connected. In the short term the weak connections can be neglected and the fast dynamics are modeled by the decoupled local models. In the long term, the weak connections become important and represent strong coupling between the aggregate variables. We will illustrate slow coherency and weak connections with several real power system models.

The singular perturbation analysis is also applicable to nonlinear dynamic networks [37]. The time-scale properties due to weak connections are independent of linearity assumptions - the aggregate variables are slow, while the difference variables are fast.

This method which encompasses the analytical tools of singular perturbations and weak connections, and the physical tools of aggregation and coherency is referred to as the time-scale modeling methodology. For applications to large scale systems, we develop a coherency grouping algorithm [3] to identify the areas. Schemes to correct for weak connections are developed to provide for improved accuracy.

1.3 Preview of the Chapters

The remainder of the monograph is organized into four parts: Chapters 2 and 3 present the necessary background and techniques of singular perturbations; Chapters 4 and 5 present the coherency-based aggregation method for dynamic networks; Chapter 6 relates the results in Chapters 2 to 5 to develop the time-scale modeling methodology; and Chapters 7 and 8 are extensions of the methodology to nonlinear systems. A more detailed synopsis of the chapters is given as follows.

Chapter 2 is an introduction to singular perturbations. It discusses the separation of time-scales and the slow and fast subsystems of a singularly perturbed system in explicit form. Eigenvalue and state approximations in terms of the singular perturbation parameter for both well-damped and oscillatory systems are given. Chapter 3 discusses the identification of time-scales in systems with small parameters via the equilibrium and conservation properties. A transformation which decouples the slow and fast variables in a general two-time-scale system is developed. Several other forms of singularly perturbed systems are analyzed.

Chapter 4 characterizes dynamic networks and introduces the area concept and the notion of the external and internal connections. Then it derives the aggregation condition and shows that it depends on the external connections only. Furthermore, the aggregate model preserves the dynamic network structure. Chapter 5 relates the aggregation condition to coherency and develops an algorithm to identify coherent areas.

Chapter 6 uses the singular perturbation and aggregation results to develop the time-scale modeling methodology. It shows that if the areas are weakly connected, the aggregate model is in a slow time-scale. The fast model decouples into the local models which describe the dynamics within the areas. Eigenvalue approximation is illustrated with several power system examples.

Chapter 7 extends the linear results in Chapters 3 to 6 to nonlinear dynamic networks. It discusses the time-scale separation in nonlinear systems. For nonlinear dynamic networks it shows that the aggregate variables are slow and the difference variables are fast. It develops a nonlinear time-scale modeling methodology, which is illustrated in Chapter 8 with reduced transient simulations of power systems.

CHAPTER 2

SINGULAR PERTURBATIONS AND TIME-SCALES

2.1 Introduction

Models of large scale systems involve interacting dynamic phenomena of widely differing speeds. In power systems, for example, voltage and frequency transients range from intervals of seconds (voltage regulator, speed governor and shaft energy storage) to several minutes (prime mover fuel transfer times and thermal energy storage) [32]. Simplified models of such systems are often based on the assumption that during the fast transients, the slow variables remain constant and that by the time their changes become noticeable, the fast transients have already reached their quasi-steady states. Then the only variables used for short term studies are the fast variables, while the slow variables are considered as constants. In long term studies, the model is formed by the slow variables and the quasi-steady states of the fast variables.

This common practice is mathematically inconsistent because it treats the time-varying quasi-steady states as constants, that is, it neglects their derivatives. Instead, a rigorous approach to this type of model simplification is to treat it as a two-time-scale singular perturbation problem. The perturbation parameter ε is the ratio of the time-scales of the slow and fast phenomena. This approach is asymptotic in the sense that as $\varepsilon \to 0$, the results tend to the exact results. This chapter presents a brief introduction to the singular perturbation method, which will be extended in Chapter 3 and applied to dynamic networks and power systems in Chapters 6, 7 and 8.

In Section 2.2, we introduce the explicit singular perturbation form and examine, in two time-scales, the limit as $\varepsilon \to 0$. We discuss a basic theorem which establishes the validity of a lower order two-time-scale approximation for a wide class of nonlinear systems. In Section 2.3, we prove this theorem for linear time-invariant systems by employing a decomposition into fast and slow subsystems. The subsystem decomposition is illustrated in Section 2.4 with an RC-circuit example having well-damped fast modes and with a mass-spring system example having poorly damped oscillatory fast modes.

Most of the results in the singular perturbation theory apply to the explicit form discussed in this chapter. In Chapter 3, we show how other important forms of singularly perturbed systems can be reduced to the explicit form.

2.2 The Explicit Singular Perturbation Form

In the quasi-steady state approach it is assumed that the state variables of an n-th order system are divided into r "slow" states y and n-r "fast" states z, and the full scale model is written as

$$dy/dt = f(y,z,t), \qquad y(t_0) = y_0, \qquad\qquad (2.2.1)$$

$$dz/dt = G(y,z,t), \qquad z(t_0) = z_0 . \qquad\qquad (2.2.2)$$

The only states used for long term studies are y, while the differential equations for z are reduced to algebraic or transcendental equations by formally setting dz/dt=0. The quasi-steady state model is thus

$$dy_s/dt = f(y_s,z_s,t), \qquad y_s(t_0) = y_0, \qquad\qquad (2.2.3)$$

$$0 = G(y_s,z_s,t). \qquad\qquad (2.2.4)$$

An inconsistency of this approach is that the requirement that z_s must be constant, as implied by $dz_s/dt=0$, is violated by (2.2.4) which defines z_s as a time-varying quantity. The initial condition for z_s had to be dropped in (2.2.4), since there is no freedom to satisfy it. Furthermore, if this simplified model fails to provide a good approximation of the actual solution y(t) and z(t), there is no provision for improving the approximation.

We now derive the explicit singular perturbation form of (2.2.1), (2.2.2) which removes the quasi-steady state inconsistency and allows an improvement of the approximation by two-time-scale expansions. Assuming that t is properly scaled for the slow phenomena, let us introduce a new time variable τ and scale it for the fast phenomena. For example, if t is in minutes, τ can be in seconds. The ratio of the time-scales, in this case 1/60, is in general a small positive parameter ε, which is the main tool for our asymptotic analysis. The new time variable is defined by

$$\tau = (t - t')/\varepsilon, \qquad\qquad (2.2.5)$$

and its initial instant τ=0 is chosen to correspond to a particular instant t' in t time-scale.

The wider the separation of the time-scales, such as seconds and hours, the smaller ϵ will be. On the other hand, the smaller ϵ is, the larger τ will be for a given $(t-t')$ interval. In the limit as $\epsilon \to 0$, even a short interval in t is "stretched" to an infinite interval in τ. When t is sufficiently large, the fast phenomena have adequate time to reach their steady states. This, however, does not contradict the assumption that $(t-t')$ is sufficiently short for considering the slow variables as constants. Thus, the limit of $\epsilon \to 0$ is equivalent to the quasi-steady state assumption, but without its inconsistency. Since it is known that the dynamics of the states z are $1/\epsilon$ times faster than those of y, that is, dz/dt is about $1/\epsilon$ times larger that dy/dt, we can rescale G as

$$g = \epsilon G \qquad\qquad (2.2.6)$$

such that f and g are of the same order of magnitude. The model (2.2.1), (2.2.2) then becomes

$$dy/dt = f(y,z,t), \qquad y(t_0) = y_0 , \qquad\qquad (2.2.7)$$

$$\epsilon dz/dt = g(y,z,t), \qquad z(t_0) = z_0, \qquad\qquad (2.2.8)$$

which we call the explicit form [28].

In the limit as $\epsilon \to 0$, this model (2.2.7), (2.2.8) defines the quasi-steady states $y_s(t)$, $z_s(t)$ as

$$dy_s/dt = f(y_s,z_s,t), \qquad y_s(t_0) = y_0, \qquad\qquad (2.2.9)$$

$$0 = g(y_s,z_s,t) \quad . \qquad\qquad (2.2.10)$$

Although this is the same model (2.2.3) and (2.2.4), its origin and meaning are different. The crucial difference is that $dz_s/dt \neq 0$, as required by (2.2.10), is not contradicted by $\epsilon(dz_s/dt)=0$ which is now due to $\epsilon=0$ and not to $dz_s/dt=0$. To obtain the fast parts of y and z, we rewrite (2.2.7), (2.2.8) in the fast time-scale τ

$$dy/d\tau = \epsilon f(y,z,t' + \epsilon\tau), \qquad\qquad (2.2.11)$$

$$dz/d\tau = g(y,z,t' + \epsilon\tau), \qquad\qquad (2.2.12)$$

and again examine the limit as $\epsilon \to 0$. This limiting process yields $dy/d\tau=0$; that is, y is constant in the fast time-scale. This implies that as $\epsilon \to 0$, the only variations are the deviations of z from its quasi-steady state z_s. Denoting them by $z_f = z - z_s$ and letting $\epsilon = 0$ in (2.2.11), (2.2.12) we obtain

$$dz_f/d\tau = g(y_0, z_s(t_0) + z_f(\tau), t_0), \qquad z_f(0) = z_0 - z_s(t_0). \tag{2.2.13}$$

The fixed instant t' has been chosen to be t_0 and hence the model constants are t_0, y_0, and $z_s(t_0)$. The model (2.2.13) is suitable for the study of fast phenomena occurring near t_0.

While the full order models (2.2.7), (2.2.8) and (2.2.11), (2.2.12) are exact, the separated lower order models (2.2.9), (2.2.10) and (2.2.13) are in error because they assume $\epsilon = 0$, instead of the actual $\epsilon > 0$. This parameter perturbation is called singular, since the dependence of the solutions of (2.2.7), (2.2.8) on ϵ is not continuous. With well-damped fast modes, the state z rapidly reaches its quasi-steady state z_s. When the state z exhibits high frequency oscillations, the state y is still approximated by the slow subsystem (2.2.9), (2.2.10) due to the "averaging" or filtering effect of the slow subsystem. In both cases, we expect the slow state y to be continuous in ϵ, and the discontinuity in z to be corrected by z_f. Thus, using (2.2.9), (2.2.10) as the slow model and (2.2.13) as the fast model, we expect to approximate y and z by

$$y(t) = y_s(t) + O(\epsilon), \tag{2.2.14}$$

$$z(t) = z_s(t) + z_f((t-t_0)/\epsilon) + O(\epsilon), \tag{2.2.15}$$

where z_f is expressed in the t time-scale and $O(\epsilon)$ denotes an "order of ϵ error"[1]. A result which establishes when this approximation is valid is the following theorem due to Tihonov [55], proof and extensions of which can be found in [57,23,33].

Theorem 2.2.1: Let f and g in (2.2.7), (2.2.8) be twice differentiable functions of x, z and t. Assume that:

Assumption 2.2.1: The equilibrium $z_f = 0$ of (2.2.13) is asymptotically stable and $z_f(0)$ belongs to its domain of attraction.

---

[1] A function $f(\epsilon)$ is of the order of ϵ^k, $O(\epsilon^k)$, if there exist positive constants c and ϵ^* such that the norm of f satisfies $|f(\epsilon)| < c\epsilon^k$ for all $0 < \epsilon \leq \epsilon^*$.

Assumption 2.2.2: The eigenvalues of $\partial g/\partial z$ evaluated along $y_s(t)$, $z_s(t)$ for all t in the interval $[t_0, T]$ have real parts strictly smaller than a fixed negative number.

Then the approximation (2.2.14), (2.2.15) holds for all t in $[t_0, T]$.

We point out that (2.2.14), (2.2.15) is a uniform approximation over an interval including the initial constant t_0. To achieve this, the fast part $z_f(\tau)$ is added to $z_s(t)$. In singular perturbation literature $z_f(\tau)$ is called a boundary layer correction and (2.2.13) is a boundary layer system. Because of Assumption 2.2.2, the term

$$z_f(\tau) = z_f((t - t_0)/\epsilon) \qquad (2.2.16)$$

rapidly decays in t-scale. Hence, a corollary of Theorem 2.2.1 is that for ϵ sufficiently small, there exists $t_1 > t_0$ such that the approximation

$$y(t) = y_s(t) + 0(\epsilon), \quad z(t) = z_s(t) + 0(\epsilon) \qquad (2.2.17)$$

holds for all t in $[t_1, T]$. Thus, if we are not interested in the behavior during an initial boundary layer interval $[t_0, t_1)$, we can use Assumptions 2.2.1 and 2.2.2 to justify the classical quasi-steady state approximation (2.2.17).

In general, the quasi-steady state model (2.2.9), (2.2.10) does not yield a unique pair $y_s(t)$, $z_s(t)$. In other words, the boundary layer system may have several equilibrium states, since equation (2.2.10) may have several roots z_s. Our choice of the simplified model then depends on which of the equilibrium states attracts z from its initial value z_0. To illustrate this aspect of the boundary layer analysis, we show that for $\epsilon=0$ the system

$$\dot{y} = y^2 t/z, \qquad t_0 = 0, \ y_0 = 1, \qquad (2.2.18)$$

$$\epsilon\dot{z} = -(z + yt)(z - 2)(z - 4), \qquad (2.2.19)$$

reduces to either

$$\dot{y}_s = -y_s, \quad \text{if } z_0 < 2, \qquad (2.2.20)$$

or

$$\dot{y}_s = (t/4)\,y_s^2, \quad \text{if } z_0 > 2. \qquad (2.2.21)$$

This is the consequence of the fact that

$$0 = -(z_s + y_s t) (z_s - 2) (z_s - 4) \tag{2.2.22}$$

has three roots

$$z_s = -y_s t, \quad z_s = 2, \quad z_s = 4, \tag{2.2.23}$$

and only $z_s = -y_s t$ and $z_s = 4$ satisfy the assumptions of Theorem 2.2.1. When substituted in (2.2.18), these two roots result in (2.2.20) and (2.2.21), respectively. For $y_s(0)=y(0)=1$, the respective slow solutions are

$$y_s(t) = e^{-t}, \quad z_s(t) = -t e^{-t}, \quad \text{for } z_0 < 2 \text{ and} \tag{2.2.24}$$

$$y_s(t) = 8/(8-t^2), \quad z_s(t) = 4, \quad \text{for } z_0 > 2 . \tag{2.2.25}$$

It can be easily checked that Assumption 2.2.2 is satisfied. Furthermore, with (2.2.24) Assumption 2.2.1 is satisfied for $z_0 < 2$ and with (2.2.25) for $z_0 > 2$. In contrast, root $z_s = 2$ violates Assumption 2.2.2 and cannot be used for quasi-steady state approximation. The boundary layer corrections $z_f(\tau)$ for $z_s = y_s t$ and $z_s = 4$ are respectively obtained from

$$dz_f/d\tau = -z_f(z_f - 2) (z_f - 4), \quad z_f(0) = z_0, \tag{2.2.26}$$

$$dz_f/d\tau = -z_f(z_f + 4) (z_f + 2), \quad z_f(0) = z_0 - 4. \tag{2.2.27}$$

Sketches of z_s and $z_s + z_f$ approximations (dotted) with $\epsilon=0.3$ for four different initial conditions are given in Figure 2.2.1 along with sketches (solid) of the exact solutions z. This example also shows that the stability of the reduced solution is not required for (2.2.14), (2.2.15) to hold over an interval $[t_0, T]$. In fact, $y_s(t)$ in (2.2.25) escapes to infinity as $t \to \sqrt{8}$, but the approximation is still valid over $[t_0, T]$, where $T < \sqrt{8}$. However, the boundary layer stability Assumptions 2.2.1 and 2.2.2 are crucial.

An important application of the singular perturbation method is the possibility of a two-time-scale stability analysis. There are several results [25,23,10] using separate stability properties of the slow and fast solutions $y_s(t)$ and $z_f(\tau)$ to guarantee stability properties of the full solution $y(t,\epsilon)$, $z(t,\epsilon)$. Methods for two-time-scale design and optimization of control systems are surveyed in [28].

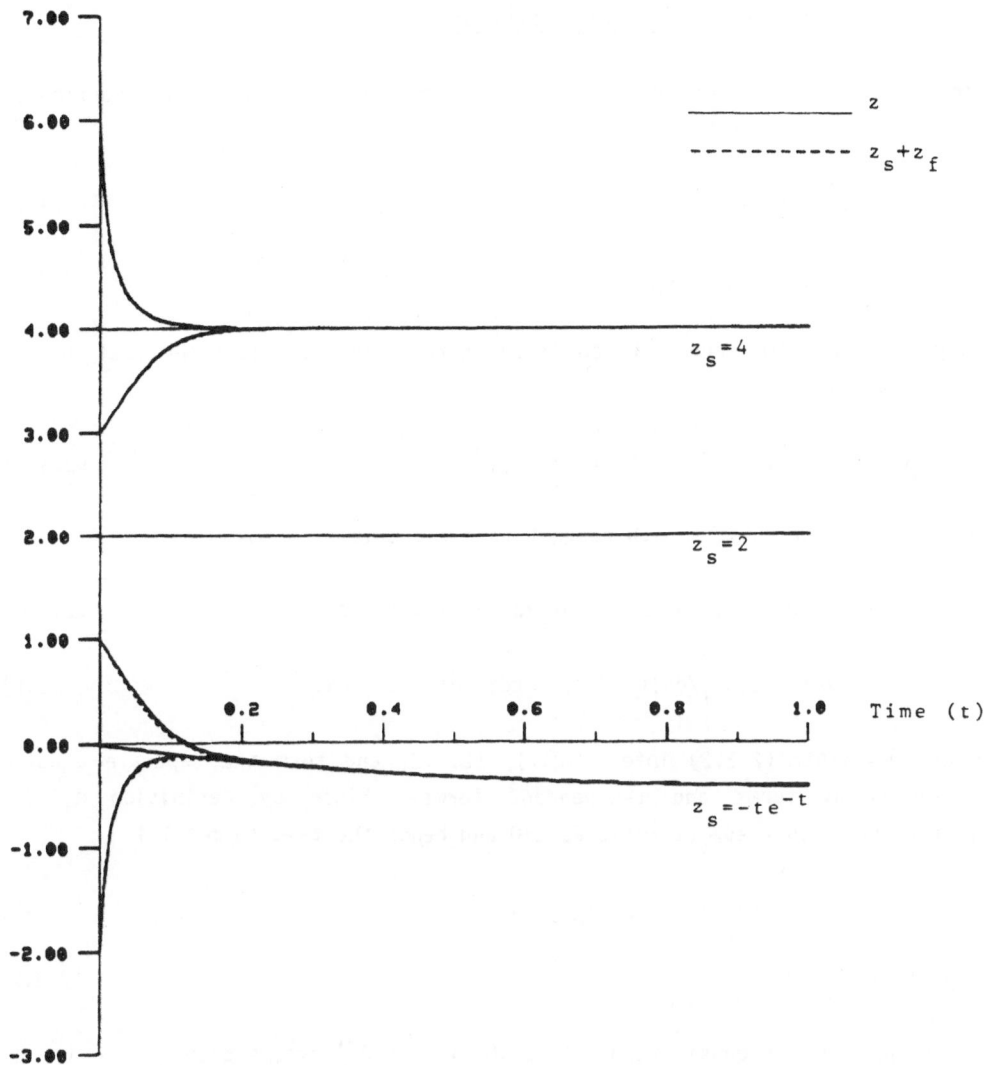

Figure 2.2.1   Approximate and exact solutions of (2.2.18), (2.2.19)
for four different initial conditions. Only the
stable quasi-steady states $z_S=4$ and $z_S=-te^{-t}$
serve as slow approximations of z.

2.3 Time-Scale Decomposition of Linear Systems

The time-scale properties of singularly perturbed systems are particularly clear in linear time-invariant systems

$$dy/dt = Ay + Bz, \quad y(t_0) = y_0, \tag{2.3.1}$$

$$\varepsilon\, dz/dt = Cy + Dz, \quad z(t_0) = z_0, \tag{2.3.2}$$

where y is an r-vector and z is an (n-r)-vector. We introduce the fast and slow parts of y and z as

$$y(t) = y_s(t) + y_f(\tau), \quad z(t) = z_s(t) + z_f(\tau), \tag{2.3.3}$$

and express the derivatives with respect to t and τ as

$$dy/dt = dy_s/dt + (dy_f/d\tau)\,(d\tau/dt) = dy_s/dt + (1/\varepsilon)dy_f/d\tau \tag{2.3.4}$$

$$\varepsilon\, dz/dt = \varepsilon\, dz_s/dt + \varepsilon(dz_f/d\tau)(d\tau/dt) = \varepsilon dz_s/dt + dz_f/d\tau. \tag{2.3.5}$$

Then we substitute (2.3.3) into (2.3.1), (2.3.2) and form the separate equations for τ-dependent terms and t-dependent terms. Since by definition $z_s(t)$ is slow, it follows that $\varepsilon dz_s(t)/dt \to 0$ as $\varepsilon \to 0$ and hence the t-scale model is

$$dy_s(t)/dt = Ay_s(t) + Bz_s(t), \quad y_s(t_0) = y_0, \tag{2.3.6}$$

$$0 = Cy_s(t) + Dz_s(t) \tag{2.3.7}$$

which is the familiar quasi-steady state model. If D^{-1} exists then

$$z_s(t) = -D^{-1}Cy_s(t) \tag{2.3.8}$$

can be substituted into (2.3.6). The result is the slow reduced model

$$dy_s(t)/dt = (A - BD^{-1}C)\, y_s(t), \quad y_s(t_0) = y_0. \tag{2.3.9}$$

For τ-dependent terms after letting ε→0 we obtain

$$dy_f(\tau)/d\tau = 0, \quad y_f(0) = y_0 - y_s(t_0) = 0, \tag{2.3.10}$$

$$dz_f(\tau)/d\tau = Cy_s(\tau) + Dz_f(\tau), \quad z_f(0) = z_0 - z_s(t_0) \; . \tag{2.3.11}$$

Noting from (2.3.10) that the fast part of $y(t)$ is zero, $y_f(\tau)=0$, we conclude that the fast reduced model is

$$dz_f(\tau)/d\tau = Dz_f(\tau), \quad z_f(0) = z_0 + D^{-1}C\, y_0. \tag{2.3.12}$$

Another way to arrive at the same conclusion is to introduce a new variable

$$\eta^* = z + D^{-1}\, C\, y \tag{2.3.13}$$

which can be seen as the difference between z and its quasi-steady state. The substitution of (2.3.13) into (2.3.1), (2.3.2) yields

$$dy/dt = (A - BD^{-1}C)y + B\eta^*, \tag{2.3.14}$$

$$\epsilon d\eta^*/dt = \epsilon D^{-1}C\,(A - BD^{-1}C)\,y + (D + \epsilon D^{-1}CB)\eta^*. \tag{2.3.15}$$

If we now let $\epsilon \to 0$ in the t-scale then $\eta_s^*(t)=0$, that is $y_s(t)$ satisfies (2.3.9). On the other hand, letting $\epsilon \to 0$ in the τ-scale shows that $\eta_f^*(\tau)=z_f(\tau)$. Therefore, the states in (2.3.14), (2.3.15) are already separated into predominantly slow states $y(t)$ and predominantly fast states $\eta^*(t)$. For this reason, we call (2.3.14), (2.3.15) an <u>explicit separated form</u>.

Let us now support the above qualitative considerations by a rigorous analysis. Generalizing (2.3.13), we will find a matrix L such that after the transformation

$$\eta = z - Ly \tag{2.3.16}$$

the slow modes of (2.3.1), (2.3.2) do not appear in η. The substitution of (2.3.16) into (2.3.1), (2.3.2) gives

$$dy/dt = (A + BL)y + B\eta, \tag{2.3.17}$$

$$\epsilon\, d\eta/dt = [C + DL - \epsilon L\,(A + BL)]y - (D - \epsilon LB)\eta \; . \tag{2.3.18}$$

Hence, for all L satisfying the algebraic Riccati equation

$$C + DL - \epsilon L\,(A + BL) = 0 \; , \tag{2.3.19}$$

the η-system

$$\varepsilon \, d\eta/dt = (D - \varepsilon LB)\eta \qquad\qquad (2.3.20)$$

separates from (2.3.17). A further transformation

$$\xi = y + H\eta , \qquad\qquad (2.3.21)$$

where H satisfies the linear equation

$$H (D - \varepsilon LB) - \varepsilon (A + BL) H + \varepsilon B = 0 , \qquad\qquad (2.3.22)$$

transforms (2.3.17) into

$$d\xi/dt = (A + BL)\xi . \qquad\qquad (2.3.23)$$

If such L and H exist, and if (D - εLB) is nonsingular, then (2.3.20) and (2.3.23) are, respectively, the exact fast and slow subsystems of the original system (2.3.1), (2.3.2). This follows from the fact that the transformation defined by (2.3.16) and (2.3.21) is nonsingular. The eigenvalues of (2.3.20) are $O(1/\varepsilon)$, that is, they are the eigenvalues of (2.3.1), (2.3.2) which tend to infinity as $\varepsilon \to 0$.

The existence of L and H and a bound for ε can be established as follows.

Lemma 2.3.1: Suppose that D^{-1} exists and its norm is bounded by

$$\|D^{-1}\| \le \alpha/(1+\alpha) , \ \alpha > 0 . \qquad\qquad (2.3.24)$$

Then for every ε in the interval

$$0 \le \varepsilon \le \varepsilon_1 = \frac{\rho}{\|A - BD^{-1}C\| + (3+2\alpha) \, \|B\|\|D^{-1}C\|} , \ \rho < 1 , \qquad\qquad (2.3.25)$$

there exists an isolated root L of the Riccati equation (2.3.19), which can be approximated by

$$L = -D^{-1}C[I_r + \varepsilon D^{-1}C(A-BD^{-1}C)] + O(\varepsilon^2) . \qquad\qquad (2.3.26)$$

where I_r is the rxr identity matrix. The corresponding root of the linear equation (2.3.22) is approximated by

$$H = -\varepsilon BD^{-1} + O(\varepsilon^2) . \qquad\qquad (2.3.27)$$

Proof: Denoting $A_o = A - BD^{-1}C$ we rewrite (2.3.19) as

$$L = -D^{-1}C + \epsilon D^{-1}L(A_o + BL + BD^{-1}C) = F(L) \tag{2.3.28}$$

and show that F is a contraction mapping. First we note that the implication

$$\|L\| \leq (1+\alpha) \|D^{-1}C\| \rightarrow \|F(L)\| \leq (1+\alpha) \|D^{-1}C\| \tag{2.3.29}$$

in view of (2.3.24) holds for all ϵ in the interval

$$0 \leq \epsilon \leq \epsilon_2 = \frac{1}{\|A_o\| + (2+\alpha) \|B\| \|D^{-1}C\|}. \tag{2.3.30}$$

Next we consider $F(L_1) - F(L_2)$ for any two bounded L_1 and L_2. Using the identity

$$L_1BL_1 - L_2BL_2 = (L_1 - L_2)BL_1 + L_2B(L_1 - L_2) \tag{2.3.31}$$

we obtain

$$F(L_1) - F(L_2) = \epsilon D^{-1}[(L_1 - L_2)(A + BL_1) + L_2B(L_1 - L_2)] \tag{2.3.32}$$

and hence

$$\|F(L_1) - F(L_2)\| \leq \epsilon \|D^{-1}\| \|L_1 - L_2\| (\|A_o\| + \|BL_1\| + \|BD^{-1}C\| + \|L_2B\|) . \tag{2.3.33}$$

Thus, for all L_1 and L_2 satisfying

$$\|L_i\| \leq (1 + \alpha) \|D^{-1}C\| , \qquad i=1,2 , \tag{2.3.34}$$

and all ϵ in the interval $0 \leq \epsilon \leq \epsilon_1$ we have

$$\|F(L_1) - F(L_2)\| \leq \rho \|L_1 - L_2\| . \tag{2.3.35}$$

Since $\epsilon_1 \leq \epsilon_2$, it follows that F(L) satisfies the contraction mapping theorem and iterations

$$L_{k+1} = F(L_k), \quad L_1 = -D^{-1}C , \tag{2.3.36}$$

converge to the solution of the form (2.3.26). After k iterations, the exact solution is approximated to an $O(\epsilon^k)$ error. The proof of (2.3.27) is analogous. □

It should be pointed out that condition (2.3.24), which requires that $\|D^{-1}\| < 1$, can always be satisfied by scaling the actual system matrices D/ϵ and C/ϵ while keeping A, B and $D^{-1}C$ unchanged. A convenient choice is $\alpha = 0.5$, that is $\|D^{-1}\| \leq 1/3$. Condition (2.3.25) then gives a bound on ϵ in terms of the slow subsystem matrix and the matrix representing the interaction between the slow and the fast subsystems.

With the help of Lemma 2.3.1, we now summarize the two-time-scale properties of the linear explicit singular perturbation form (2.3.1), (2.3.2).

<u>Theorem 2.3.1</u>: Under the conditions of Lemma 2.3.1, the system (2.3.1), (2.3.2) has r small eigenvalues

$$\lambda_s = \lambda (A + BL) = \lambda(A - BD^{-1}C) + O(\epsilon) = \lambda(A_0) + O(\epsilon) \qquad (2.3.37)$$

and n-r large eigenvalues

$$\lambda_f = \lambda(D - \epsilon LB)/\epsilon = (\lambda(D) + O(\epsilon))/\epsilon . \qquad (2.3.38)$$

If, in addition, $\lambda(D)$ have negative real parts

$$Re \{\lambda(D)\} \leq -\sigma_0 < 0 \qquad (2.3.39)$$

where σ_0 is a positive scalar independent of ϵ, then for all $t > t_0$

$$y(t) = y_s(t) + O(\epsilon) \qquad (2.3.40)$$

$$z(t) = -D^{-1}C\, y_s(t) + z_f((t - t_0)/\epsilon) + O(\epsilon) \qquad (2.3.41)$$

where $y_s(t)$ and $z_f(\tau)$ are the solutions of (2.3.9) and (2.3.12), respectively.

<u>Proof</u>: This result immediately follows from the nonsingularity of the transformation (2.3.16), (2.3.21),

$$\begin{bmatrix} y \\ z \end{bmatrix} = \begin{bmatrix} I_r & -H \\ L & I_{n-r} - LH \end{bmatrix} \begin{bmatrix} \xi \\ \eta \end{bmatrix} \qquad (2.3.42)$$

whose inverse is

$$\begin{bmatrix} \xi \\ \eta \end{bmatrix} = \begin{bmatrix} I_r - HL & H \\ -L & I_{n-r} \end{bmatrix} \begin{bmatrix} y \\ z \end{bmatrix} \tag{2.3.43}$$

where I_r and I_{n-r} are $r \times r$ and $(n-r) \times (n-r)$ identity matrices, respectively. Transformation (2.3.42) block-diagonalizes the original system (2.3.1), (2.3.2) into the slow and the fast blocks whose eigenvalues are, respectively, λ_s and λ_f. Analogous approximations of the eigenvectors can also be obtained. □

Condition (2.3.39) implies that the fast modes are well damped. This would be the case for first order systems such as RC-circuits. Mechanical and electromechanical systems often have slightly damped modes oscillating at frequencies much higher than the rest of the systems. Well-known examples of these second order systems are mass-springs systems and multi-machine power systems. In linearized models of such systems some eigenvalues have small real parts and large imaginary parts. Typically, they are due to either strong springs, or small masses and inertias, or both.

We model a linear time-invariant system with poorly damped fast modes as

$$dy/dt = A(\epsilon)y + B(\epsilon)z, \quad y(t_0) = y_0,$$
$$\epsilon dz/dt = C(\epsilon)y + D(\epsilon)z, \quad z(t_0) = z_0, \tag{2.3.44}$$

where A, B, C, D are now assumed to be analytic functions of the small parameter ϵ, and D(0) is nonsingular. The assumption establishing that the fast modes are poorly damped is

$$Re\{\lambda(D(0))\} = 0. \tag{2.3.45}$$

To show that system (2.3.44) has two time-scales, we follow the steps used when the modes due to D are well damped (2.3.39). We first solve for L from the Riccati equation (2.3.19) and then for H from the linear equation (2.3.22). With the transformation (2.3.42), system (2.3.44) separates into the slow subsystem

$$d\xi/dt = (A + BL)\xi \tag{2.3.46}$$

and the fast subsystem

$$d\eta/d\tau = (D - \epsilon LB)\eta \tag{2.3.47}$$

which is poorly damped because of (2.3.45). For systems with

$$Re\{\lambda(A_0(0))\} = 0, \tag{2.3.48}$$

that is, the slow subsystem is also oscillatory, the separation in time-scale is in terms of low and high frequencies. The eigenvalue approximations

$$\lambda_s = \lambda(A_0(0)) + O(\varepsilon), \tag{2.3.49}$$

$$\lambda_f = (\lambda(D(0)) + O(\varepsilon))/\varepsilon \tag{2.3.50}$$

of Theorem 2.3.2 still hold. However, the approximation for the fast modes is purely oscillatory because $O(\varepsilon)$ damping has been neglected. To obtain $O(\varepsilon^2)$ approximation for the damping in case when it is important, we retain the first order ε terms in $(D - \varepsilon LB)$.

For poorly damped high frequency modes, the boundary layer stability condition (2.3.39) is not satisfied and the approximation of time responses (2.3.40) and (2.3.41) in Theorem 2.3.1 for well-damped modes no longer holds for all t. The following result is from [8].

Theorem 2.3.2: Under the conditions of Lemma 2.3.1 and condition (2.3.45), there exist ε^* and T such that for all ε in $[0,\varepsilon^*]$ and t in $[0,T]$,

$$y(t) = y_s(t) + O(\varepsilon) \tag{2.3.51}$$

$$z(t) = -D^{-1}Cy_s(t) + z_f(t) + O(\varepsilon), \tag{2.3.52}$$

where y_s and z_f are the slow and fast states of the subsystems (2.3.9) and (2.3.12), respectively.

The proof of (2.3.51) and (2.3.52) is immediate from (2.3.46) and (2.3.47). The approximation (2.3.51), (2.3.52) is valid up a finite T of $O(1)$. After a long time of $O(1/\varepsilon)$ an $O(\varepsilon)$ error in the frequency of oscillations results in an $O(1)$ error in the time response. Special methods have been developed in classical perturbation theory [21] to deal with these secular terms. We do not pursue this topic here for two practical reasons. First, the validity of models we are dealing with is limited to shorter time intervals. An example is the electromechanical power system model which is valid only during a short period before the excitation system actions and power plant transients begin. The second reason is that purely oscillatory modes without any damping seldom appear in the dynamic networks studied here, large space structure such as antennas being a notable exception [5].

2.4 Two-Time-Scale Modeling and Approximations

We now illustrate the modeling discussion of Section 2.2 and the applications of Theorems 2.3.1 and 2.3.2 to analyze the time-scales of the simple systems shown in Figure 2.4.1. For the RC-circuit in Figure 2.4.1a, the two-time-scale behavior is due to the fact that capacitors C_2 and C_3 are much smaller than C_1, while all the resistors are of the same order of magnitude. The electromechanical model of the three machine power system in Figure 2.4.1b, in which the inertias of the machines 2 and 3 are much smaller than that of machine 1, exhibits a similar two-time-scale oscillatory behavior. Its linearized analog is the mass-spring system in Figure 2.4.2c, where masses m_1 and m_2 are much smaller than m_3, and spring constants are of the same order of magnitude.

Using capacitor voltages as the state variables, the RC-circuit model is

$$dx_1/dt_d = -(1/R_1C_1)x_1 + (1/R_1C_1)x_2 \, ,$$

$$dx_2/dt_d = (1/R_1C_2)x_1 - (1/R_1C_2 + 1/R_2C_2)x_2 + (1/R_2C_2)x_3 \, , \qquad (2.4.1)$$

$$dx_3/dt_d = (1/R_2C_3)x_2 - (1/R_2C_3 + 1/R_3C_3)x_3 \, ,$$

where the time variable t_d is arbitrary, that is, it has not been scaled for either slow or fast phenomena. Let us now select R_1C_1 as the unit for the slow dimensionless time t

$$t_d = R_1C_1t \, . \qquad (2.4.2)$$

Then (2.4.1) becomes

$$\frac{dx_1}{dt} = -x_1 + x_2 \, ,$$

$$\frac{dx_2}{dt} = \frac{C_1}{C_2} x_1 - \frac{C_1}{C_2}(1 + \frac{R_1}{R_2})x_2 + \frac{C_1}{C_2} \frac{R_1}{R_2} x_3 \, , \qquad (2.4.3)$$

$$\frac{dx_3}{dt} = \frac{C_1}{C_3} \frac{R_1}{R_2} x_2 - \frac{C_1}{C_3} (\frac{R_1}{R_2} + \frac{R_1}{R_3}) x_3 \, ,$$

where by assumption

$$C_1/C_2 \gg 1 \, , \ C_1/C_3 \gg 1 \, , \ R_1/R_2 = 0(1) \, , \ R_1/R_3 = 0(1) \, . \qquad (2.4.4)$$

For numerical illustration we further assume

$$C_2 = C_3 \, , \quad R_1 = R_2 = R_3 \, . \qquad (2.4.5)$$

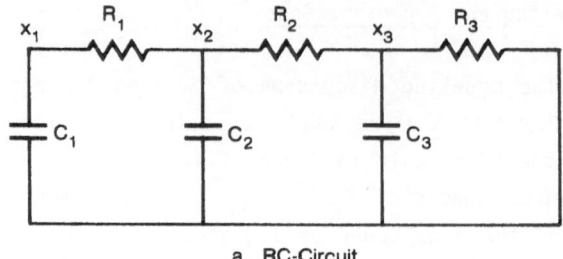

a. RC-Circuit

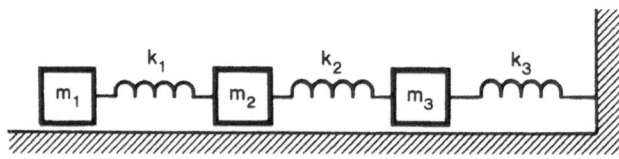

b. Power System

c. Mass-Spring System

Figure 2.4.1   Examples   of   two-time-scale   systems   in   which
time-scales   are   due   to   the   smallness   of C_2/C_1,
C_3/C_1 and m_2/m_1, m_3/m_1.

Comparing (2.4.3) with the model (2.2.1), (2.2.2), we recognize the right hand sides of the x_2 and x_3 equations in (2.4.3) as G because of the large factors C_1/C_2 and C_1/C_3. Hence, the y-variable is x_1 and the z-variables are $z_1 = x_2$ and $z_2 = x_3$. As in (2.2.6), we rescale G to g/ϵ. As the singular perturbation parameter, we take

$$\epsilon = \beta\ C_2/C_1 \qquad (2.4.6)$$

where β is a scaling factor to be chosen. With (2.4.5) and (2.4.6) the model (2.4.3) has the explicit singular perturbation form (2.2.7), (2.2.8) for the linear case

$$dy/dt = -y + [1 \quad 0]\ z\ , \qquad (2.4.7)$$

$$\epsilon dz/dt = \frac{1}{\beta}\begin{bmatrix} 1 \\ 0 \end{bmatrix} y + \frac{1}{\beta}\begin{bmatrix} -2 & 1 \\ 1 & -2 \end{bmatrix} z\ , \qquad (2.4.8)$$

where, as in (2.3.1), (2.3.2), we define

$$A = -1\ , \qquad B = [1 \quad 0]\ ,$$
$$C = \frac{1}{\beta}\begin{bmatrix} 1 \\ 0 \end{bmatrix}, \qquad D = \frac{1}{\beta}\begin{bmatrix} -2 & 1 \\ 1 & -2 \end{bmatrix}. \qquad (2.4.9)$$

The time unit for the fast time-scale τ is $R_1\beta C_2$, that is

$$\tau = t/\epsilon = t_d/(\epsilon R_1 C_1) = t_d/(R_1\beta C_2)\ . \qquad (2.4.10)$$

The choice $\beta = 3$ yields $\|D^{-1}\| \le 1/3$ and the eigenvalues of D are then

$$\lambda(D) = -\ 1/3\ ,\ -1\ . \qquad (2.4.11)$$

With this choice all the conditions of Theorem 2.3.1 are met. Hence, the eigenvalue approximations (2.3.37), (2.3.38) and the time domain approximations (2.3.40), (2.3.41) are valid. For a numerical experiment we let $\epsilon = 0.3$ which corresponds to $C_2/C_1 = 0.1$ and also satisfies Lemma 2.3.1. The slow and the fast eigenvalues for $\epsilon = 0.3$ are

$$\lambda(A-BD^{-1}C) = -0.33\ ,\quad \lambda(D/\epsilon) = -10\ ,\ -30\ , \qquad (2.4.12)$$

and represent excellent approximations of the exact eigenvalues

$$\lambda_1 = -0.32\ ,\ \lambda_2 = -10.5\ ,\ \lambda_3 = -30.2\ . \qquad (2.4.13)$$

Exact and approximate time responses of y and z_2 in (2.4.7), (2.4.8) for the initial condition

$y(0) = 2$, $z_1(0) = 1$, $z_2(0) = 1.5$ at $t_o = 0$ (2.4.14)

are shown in Figure 2.4.2. The "boundary layer" phenomenon, clearly noticeable on $z_2(t)$, is absent from $z_{2s}(t)$ (Figure 2.4.2b). Addition of the last term $z_{2f}(\tau)$ corrects this initial error (Figure 2.4.2c).

Let us now consider the mass-spring system in Figure 2.4.1c. Neglecting friction, letting $m_2 = m_3$, $k_1 = k_2 = k_3$ and

$$t_d = \sqrt{(m_1/k_1)} \; t \; , \quad \varepsilon = \beta m_2/m_1 \; ,$$ (2.4.15)

we obtain the second order analog of (2.4.7), (2.4.8)

$$d^2 y/dt^2 = Ay + Bz,$$
$$\varepsilon d^2 z/dt^2 = Cy + Dz,$$ (2.4.16)

where A, B, C, D are as in (2.4.9) and y, z_1 and z_2 are the displacements of m_1, m_2 and m_3, respectively. We note that the eigenvalues of this system are purely imaginary

$$\pm \, j\sqrt{-\lambda_1} \; , \quad \pm \, j\sqrt{-\lambda_2} \; , \quad \pm \, j\sqrt{-\lambda_3} \; ,$$ (2.4.17)

where λ_1, λ_2, λ_3 are the eigenvalues of the RC-circuit (2.4.7), (2.4.8) and for $\beta = 3$ and $\varepsilon = 0.3$ are given by (2.4.13). Clearly the eigenvalue approximation (2.3.37), (2.3.38) of Theorem 2.3.1 holds with the modification that instead of $O(\varepsilon)$, the error is now $O(\sqrt{\varepsilon})$.

To illustrate the time response approximation of Theorem 2.3.2, we show in Figure 2.4.3 the exact and approximate time responses of the mass-spring system (2.4.16) for the initial condition as in (2.4.14) and with

$$dy/dt = dz_1/dt = dz_2/dt = 0 \quad \text{at } t_o = 0 \; .$$ (2.4.18)

The approximation of the slow state y in Figure 2.4.3a is good, but, as expected, deteriorates with time. The slow component z_{1s} of the fast state z_1 appears in Figure 2.4.3b as an average value of the exact response. With fast oscillations z_{1f} superimposed (Figure 2.4.3c), the approximation is satisfactory.

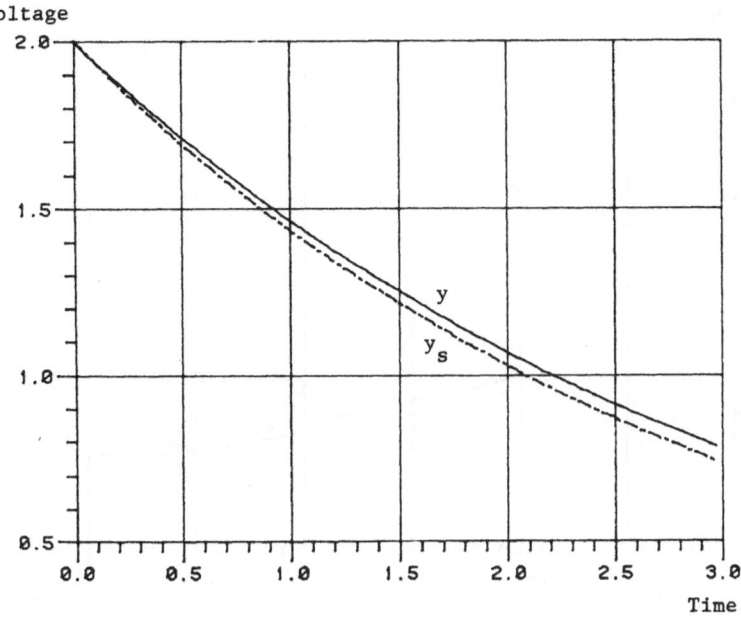

a

Figure 2.4.2   Time response approximation of RC-circuit (2.4.7),
(2.4.8).   The boundary layer error in z_{2s} (b) is
corrected by z_{2f} (c).

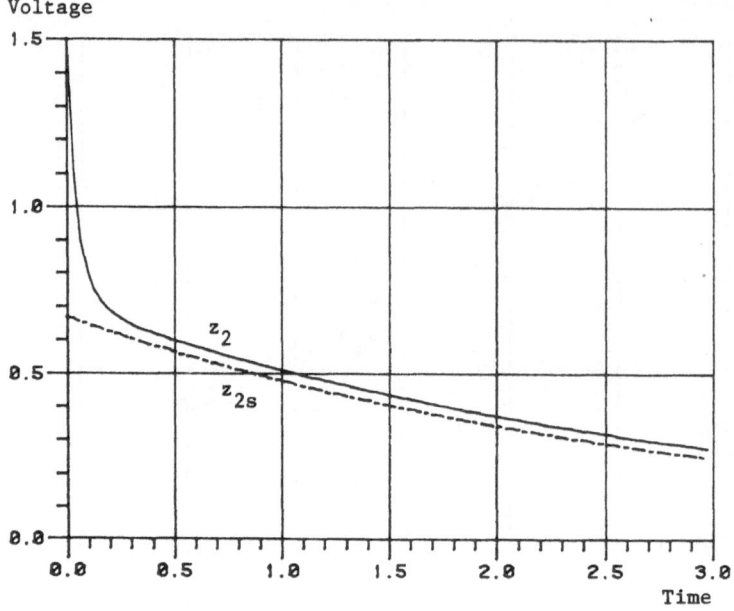

b

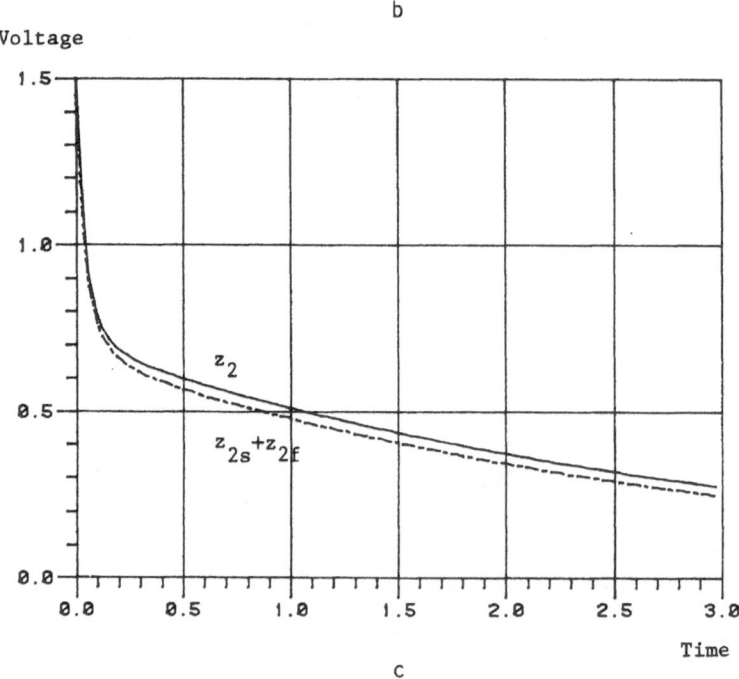

c

Figure 2.4.2   Time response approximation of RC-circuit (2.4.7),
(2.4.8).   The boundary layer error in z_{2s} (b) is
corrected by z_{2f} (c).

Displacement

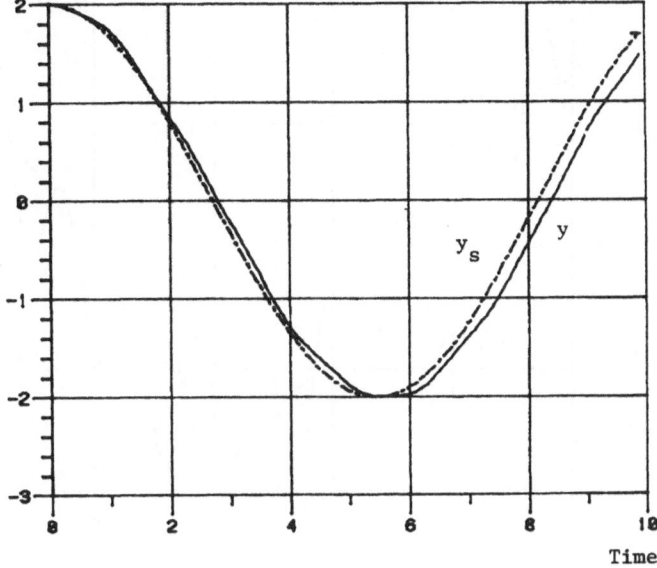

a

Figure 2.4.3   Time response approximation of mass-spring system (2.4.16). The slow part of z is well approximated by z_s (b). The two-time-scale approximation is good up to t=6 (c). Due to $O(\varepsilon)$ error, the approximation of the fast oscillation deteriorates for larger t.

Displacement

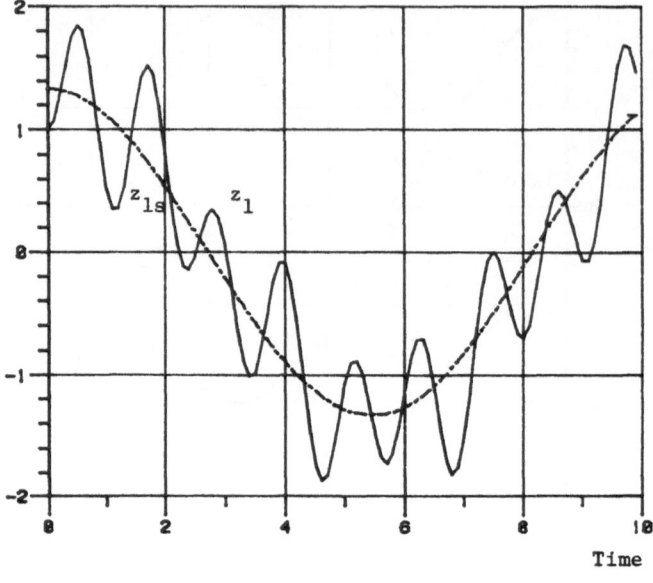

b

Displacement

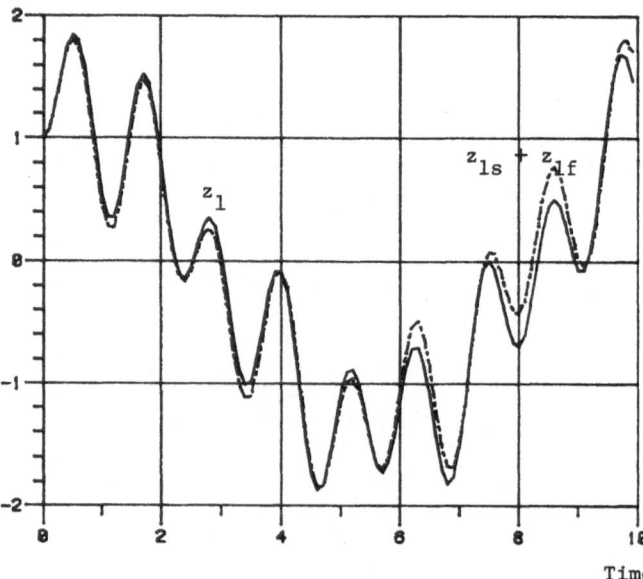

c

Figure 2.4.3   Time response approximation of mass-spring system
(2.4.16). The slow part of z is well approximated by
z_s (b). The two-time-scale approximation is good up
to t=6 (c). Due to $O(\varepsilon)$ error, the approximation of
the fast oscillation deteriorates for larger t.

We conclude this section with a discussion on the so-called "equivalents." High frequency and low frequency "equivalent" schemes or networks have been among the most practical tools of electrical engineers. Our time-scale analysis represents a systematic approach to the development and use of such tools. In Figure 2.4.4 we give physical representation of the slow and fast equivalents of the systems in Figure 2.4.1.

Letting C_2 and C_3 go to zero, that is $\epsilon = 0$ in (2.4.6), we reduce (2.4.1) to

$$C_1 dy_s/dt_d = -y_s/R_1 + z_{1s}/R_1, \qquad (2.4.19)$$

$$0 = y_s/R_1 - (1/R_1 + 1/R_2)z_{1s} + z_{2s}/R_2, \qquad (2.4.20)$$

$$0 = z_{1s}/R_2 - (1/R_2 + 1/R_3)z_{2s}. \qquad (2.4.21)$$

We use t_d instead of the slow time t because the RC-parameters of the equivalent circuits remain explicit. The slow parts z_{1s} and z_{2s} are solved for from (2.4.20) and (2.4.21) as

$$z_{1s} = (R_2 + R_3)y_s/(R_1 + R_2 + R_3), \qquad (2.4.22)$$

$$z_{2s} = R_3 y_s/(R_1 + R_2 + R_3), \qquad (2.4.23)$$

and hence the slow subsystem is

$$C_1 dy_s/dt_d = -y_s/(R_1 + R_2 + R_3). \qquad (2.4.24)$$

The meaning of this slow model is that the capacitor C_1 discharges slowly through the series connection of the resistors R_1, R_2 and R_3, and z_{1s} and z_{2s} are voltage dividers in the series connection. The equivalent RC-circuit (2.4.24) is shown in Figure 2.4.4a. This equivalent is obtainable from the original circuit by opening the small capacitors C_2 and C_3, which is a meaningful approximation for small capacitors in the slow time-scale.

In the fast time-scale, (2.4.1) becomes

$$C_2 dz_{1f}/dt_d = -(1/R_1 + 1/R_2)z_{1f} + (1/R_2)z_{2f}, \qquad (2.4.25)$$

$$C_3 dz_{2f}/dt_d = (1/R_2)z_{1f} - (1/R_2 + 1/R_3)z_{2f}. \qquad (2.4.26)$$

30

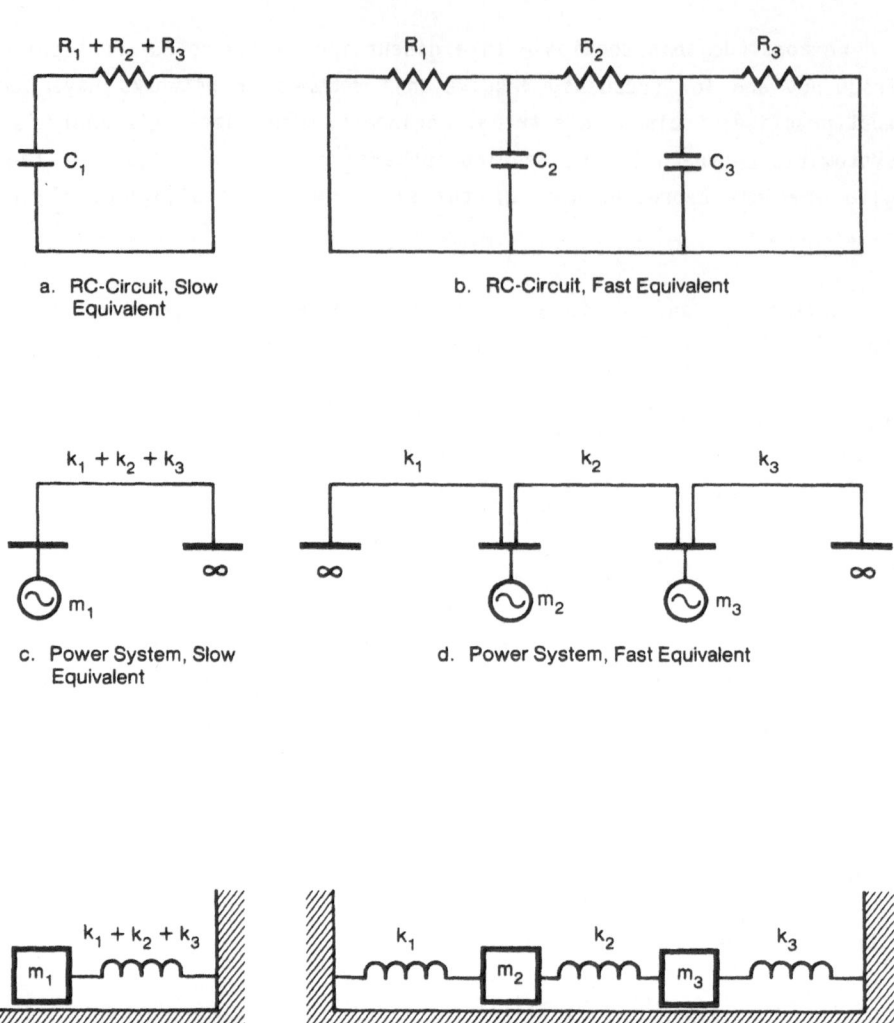

a. RC-Circuit, Slow
   Equivalent

b. RC-Circuit, Fast Equivalent

c. Power System, Slow
   Equivalent

d. Power System, Fast Equivalent

e. Mass-Spring System,
   Slow Equivalent

f. Mass-Spring System, Fast
   Equivalent

Figure 2.4.4   Equivalents for two-time-scale systems in Figure
                2.4.1. In the fast equivalents, large capacitor is
                shorted, large machine replaced by infinite bus, large
                mass represented by a fixed point. In the slow
                equivalents, small storage elements are neglected.

This fast equivalent RC-circuit is shown in Figure 2.4.4b. It can be obtained directly from the original circuit by shorting the large capacitor C_1, which is a meaningful approximation for large capacitors in the fast time-scale.

Similarly, in the fast "equivalent" of the power system the large machine 1 is replaced by an infinite bus, Figure 2.4.4d. Analogously, the large mass m_1 in the fast "equivalent" of the mass-spring system is replaced by a fixed point, Figure 2.4.4f. The slow "equivalents" of the latter two systems, Figures 2.4.4c and 2.4.4e, represent the behavior of the large machine and large mass alone.

2.5 Conclusions

This chapter has introduced the so-called explicit singular perturbation form of two-time-scale systems. This form is natural for systems whose two-time-scale behavior is due to the presence of small and large storage elements, such as capacitors, masses, etc. The singular perturbation parameter represents the ratio of the time constant of a representative small storage element versus the time constant of a representative large storage element.

Other less obvious causes of two-time-scale behavior may lead to some "hidden" rather than the explicit singular perturbation forms. The next chapter deals with some of these forms.

CHAPTER 3

MODELING OF TWO-TIME-SCALE SYSTEMS

3.1 Introduction

When the model of a two-time-scale system is expressed in terms of physical variables, it often fails to be in the explicit form (2.2.7), (2.2.8). A requirement in (2.2.7), (2.2.8) is that $\partial g/\partial z$ be nonsingular along $y_s(t)$, $z_s(t)$. When this condition is violated, the analysis in Chapter 2 has to be modified. Nonexplicit models have been called by some researchers as "singular-singularly perturbed" systems [58,34,7] and are related to descriptor systems [11,59]. In this chapter, we use a manifold approach in [18] for coordinate-free characterizations of two-time-scale systems, that is, characterizations that are independent of the state variables used to model the systems. From this analysis, we can pinpoint the physical phenomena leading to two-time-scales and, at the same time, obtain the slow and fast variables.

We examine time-scales in nonexplicit models in terms of two properties. In the fast time-scale, the slow motions of a two-time-scale system remain constant while the fast motions are restricted to a "dynamic" manifold. We interpret the constancy of the slow motions to be an equilibrium property and the restriction of the fast motions to be a conservation property. For a different set of state variables, the description of the properties in terms of manifolds changes. However, the slow motions remain constant and the fast motions are still conserved. From the manifolds, a transformation to separate the slow and fast variables can be constructed. The equilibrium and conservation properties are suitable for characterizing time-scales in both linear and nonlinear systems. This chapter is for linear time-invariant systems. Extensions to nonlinear systems are postponed until Chapter 7.

In Section 3.2 we change the parameters of the physical systems in Chapter 2 to motivate the discussion and illustrate the relationship between time-scales, equilibrium and conservation properties. In Section 3.3 this relationship is established for linear time-invariant systems and a transformation is constructed such that with the new state variables, a two-time-scale system will be in the explicit singular perturbation form. In Section 3.4, we use the technique to demonstrate how weak connections can give rise to time-scales in the example systems discussed in Chapter 2, and how small leakage can also result in time-scales for a nonideal transformer. Section 3.5 applies the transformation to two-time-scale systems which are already partially structured and serves as a preparation for the study of dynamic networks with weak connections in Chapter 6.

3.2 Equilibrium and Conservation Properties

Let us begin by showing how the same RC-circuit discussed in Chapter 2 can give rise to a nonexplicit singular perturbation form. Recall that in Figure 2.4.1a, with $C_2 = C_3 = \epsilon C_1$ ($\beta = 1$), the z variables, which are the voltages of capacitors 2 and 3, are fast and the model (2.4.7), (2.4.8) is in explicit form.

In the same circuit we now let the capacitors be of the same order of magnitude, but the resistors be of different orders of magnitude. For example, let

$$C_1 = C_2 = C_3 = C, \tag{3.2.1}$$

$$R_1 = R_2 = r \quad , \quad R_3 = R \quad , \quad r/R = \epsilon, \tag{3.2.2}$$

where ϵ is a small positive parameter; that is, R_1 and R_2 are small and R_3 is large (Figure 3.2.1a). For this choice of parameters, we select RC and rC as the units for the slow and fast dimensionless times,

$$t = t_d/RC \quad , \quad \tau = t_d/rC \quad , \quad t/\tau = \epsilon. \tag{3.2.3}$$

Then the circuit (2.4.1) becomes

$$\epsilon(dx/dt) = dx/d\tau = \begin{bmatrix} -1 & 1 & 0 \\ 1 & -2 & 1 \\ 0 & 1 & -1-\epsilon \end{bmatrix} x = A(\epsilon)\, x. \tag{3.2.4}$$

Note that ϵ multiplies the time derivatives of all the states in the slow time-scale t. Thus it seems that there are no slow dynamics in this system. If $\partial g/\partial z$ at $\epsilon = 0$, that is $A(0)$, were nonsingular, no slow phenomenon would exist in (3.2.4) and the system would not have two time-scales. However, rank $A(0) = 2$ and $A(0)$ is singular. If $x(0) = [1 \ 1 \ 1]^T$ in (3.2.4), then at t = 0,

$$\epsilon dx/dt = \begin{bmatrix} 0 \\ 0 \\ -\epsilon \end{bmatrix} , \tag{3.2.5}$$

that is, the slow-time derivatives dx/dt remain finite when $\epsilon \to 0$, suggesting that (3.2.4) is a two-time-scale system. Physically the slow phenomenon is the "leakage" of the capacitor charges through the large resistor R_3. Neglecting this leakage, the slow phenomenon becomes infinitely slow, that is, constant. This corresponds to setting $\epsilon = 0$ in the fast-time model of (3.2.4)

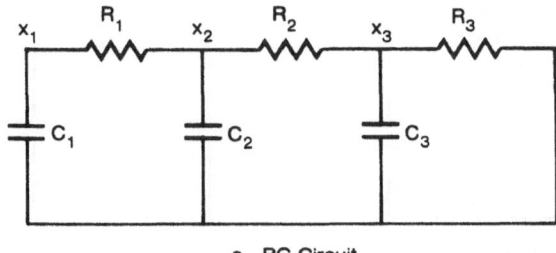

a. RC-Circuit

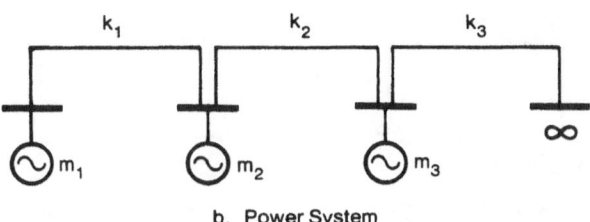

b. Power System

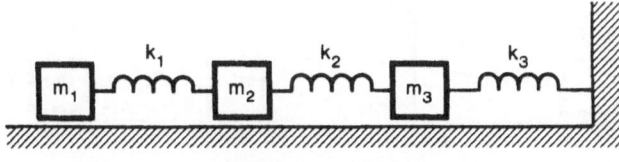

c. Mass-Spring System

Figure 3.2.1   Examples of nonexplicit two-time-scale systems. The time-scales are due to the smallness of R_3/R_1, R_2/R_1 and k_3/k_1, k_2/k_1.

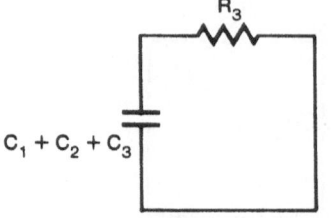

a. RC-Circuit, Slow
   Equivalent

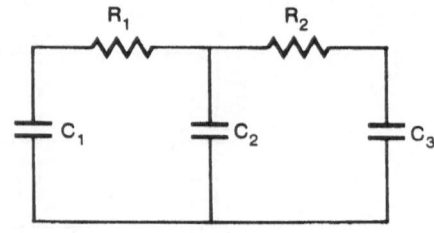

b. RC-Circuit, Fast Equivalent

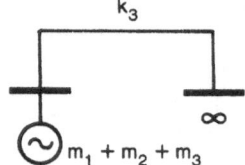

c. Power System, Slow
   Equivalent

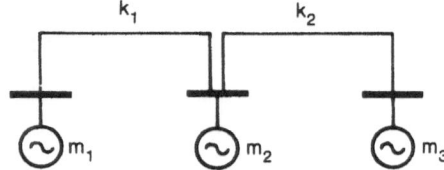

d. Power System, Fast Equivalent

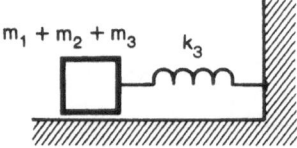

e. Mass-Spring System,
   Slow Equivalent

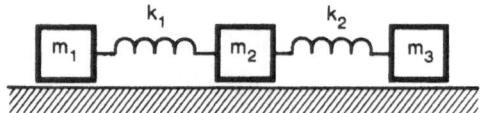

f. Mass-Spring System, Fast
   Equivalent

Figure 3.2.2   Equivalents for nonexplicit models of Figure 3.2.1.
               Fast equivalents b, d, and f have continuous equilbria
               expressing the conservation property.

$$dx/d\tau = \begin{bmatrix} -1 & 1 & 0 \\ 1 & -2 & 1 \\ 0 & 1 & -1 \end{bmatrix} x = A(0)x .$$

(3.2.6)

The RC-circuit model of (3.2.6) is given in Figure 3.2.2b. Since $A(0)$ is singular, the linear equation

$$A(0) x = 0$$

(3.2.7)

has an infinite number of solutions of the form

$$x = \alpha \begin{bmatrix} 1 \\ 1 \\ 1 \end{bmatrix}$$

(3.2.8)

where α is any real number, that is, (3.2.6) has a continuum of equilibrium points. This can be seen from the circuit of Figure 3.2.2b, where voltages x are an equilibrium whenever

$$x_1 - x_2 = 0 \quad , \quad x_3 - x_2 = 0 .$$

(3.2.9)

The line defined by (3.2.9) is denoted by S, and system (3.2.6) is said to have an equilibrium property. Note that the line S is in the null space of $A(0)$.

To examine the fast dynamics, we apply Kirchhoff's current law to the ground node of Figure 3.2.2b to obtain

$$C_1 dx_1/d\tau + C_2 dx_2/d\tau + C_3 dx_3/d\tau = 0.$$

(3.2.10)

Integration of (3.2.10) reveals that the total charge q_0 is conserved for all τ,

$$C_1 x_1(\tau) + C_2 x_2(\tau) + C_3 x_3(\tau) = C_1 x_1(0) + C_2 x_2(0) + C_3 x_3(0) = q_0.$$

(3.2.11)

This property is called the conservation property.

Every trajectory $x(\tau)$ of (3.2.6) is confined to a plane F defined by (3.2.11) which is orthogonal to the vector $[C_1 \ C_2 \ C_3]^T$ and passing through the initial point $x(0)$. The quantity in (3.2.11) is constant when $\varepsilon = 0$, but becomes slowly varying when $\varepsilon > 0$, that is, when the leakage resistor R_3 is not infinite. A circuit describing this slow phenomenon is given in Figure 3.2.2a and will be derived in the next section.

From the equilibrium and conservation properties of systems (3.2.6) and (3.2.16), we conclude that the trajectories x(t) of the original systems (3.2.4) consist of two distinct parts, as sketched in Figure 3.2.3. For system (3.2.4), the state x(t) moves rapidly in a boundary layer near the plane F, and if the motion is stable, approaches the line S. Then, from a neighborhood of the intersection of plane F with line S, x(t) slowly slides along line S. The motion on F conserves the total charge, while the motion on S is moving slowly since the capacitors are discharging slowly through R_3. Note that the behavior of x(t) is similar to the fast state z of the explicit model (2.3.1), (2.3.2), that is, a fast transient is followed by a slow motion close to a line of quasi-equilibria S. The basic difference is that in the explicit model (2.3.1), (2.3.2) the plane F close to which the boundary layer occurs is orthogonal to the y axis (Figure 3.2.4). Figures 3.2.3 and 3.2.4 indicate that in nonexplicit models fast dynamics should be present in all the states, whereas in explicit models their presence in the y variables is $O(\epsilon)$.

The models of the three machine system in Figure 3.2.1b and its mass-spring analog in Figure 3.2.1c are also nonexplicit if the masses are equal

$$m_1 = m_2 = m_3 = m \qquad (3.2.12)$$

but the spring constants

$$k_1 = k_2 = k \qquad (3.2.13)$$

are much larger than k_3, that is, $k_3 = \epsilon k$. Letting the slow and fast times be

$$t = t_d/\sqrt{(m/k)}, \quad \tau = t_d/\sqrt{(m/\epsilon k)}, \qquad (3.2.14)$$

the model using the displacements of the masses as the states x becomes

$$\epsilon(d^2x/dt^2) = d^2x/d\tau^2 = A(\epsilon)x \qquad (3.2.15)$$

where $A(\epsilon)$ is the same as in (3.2.4).

Since $A(0)$ is singular, there are two time-scales in the mass-spring system. The slow phenomenon is the motion of the three masses as a unit. When the soft spring is neglected, $k_3=0$, this is a constant velocity motion with the springs k_1 and k_2 relaxed. In the (x_1, x_2, x_3)-space, this motion is along the line S defined by

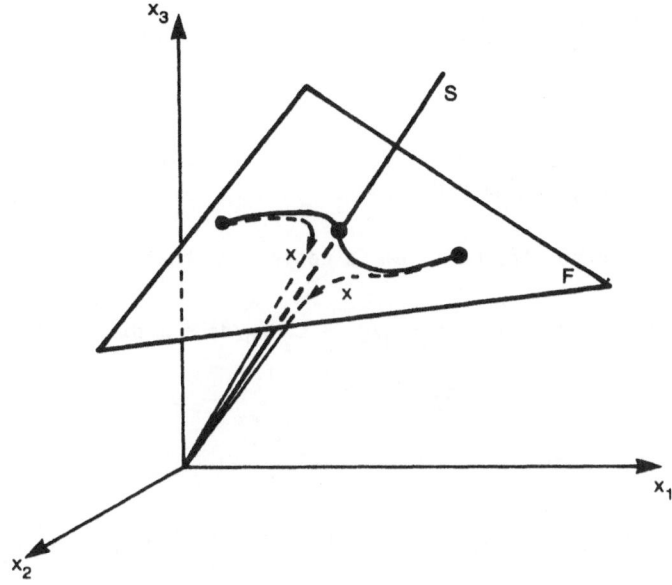

Figure 3.2.3   Trajectories of the auxiliary system (3.2.6) lie on
F.   Trajectories of the actual system (3.2.4) are
denoted by x.

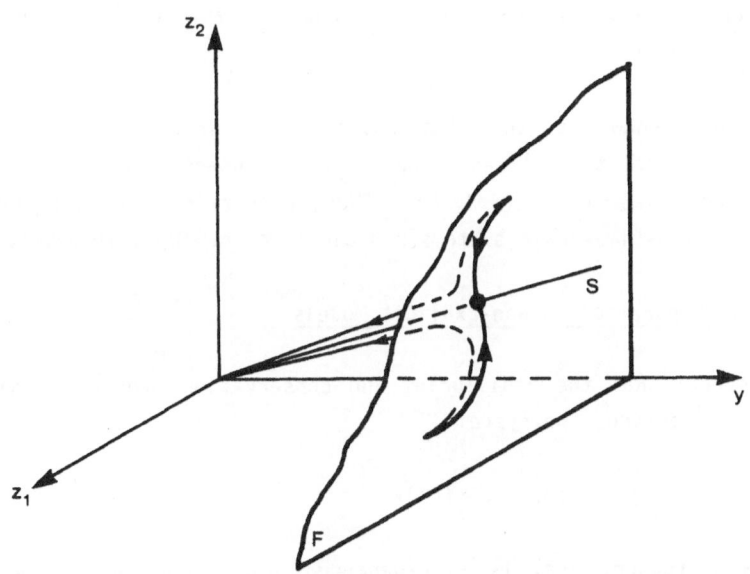

Figure 3.2.4   F for explicit model is orthogonal to the y-axis.

$$x_1 - x_2 = 0, \; x_3 - x_2 = 0. \qquad\qquad (3.2.16)$$

Noting that

$$[m_1 \; m_2 \; m_3] \, d^2x/d\tau^2 = [m_1 \; m_2 \; m_3] \, A(0)x = 0, \qquad\qquad (3.2.17)$$

we conclude that for $k_3=0$, the momentum is conserved, that is,

$$m_1 dx_1/d\tau + m_2 dx_2/d\tau + m_3 dx_3/d\tau = (m_1 dx_1/d\tau + m_2 dx_2/d\tau + m_3 dx_3/d\tau)|_{\tau=0} \qquad (3.2.18)$$

$$= c_0.$$

Integrating (3.2.18) we obtain

$$m_1 x_1 + m_2 x_2 + m_3 x_3 = c_0\tau + (m_1 x_1(0) + m_2 x_2(0) + m_3 x_3(0)) = c_0\tau + c_1 . \qquad (3.2.19)$$

Equation (3.2.19) defines a moving plane F. When $k_3=0$, the fast motion is confined to the plane F defined by (3.2.19). When the initial momentum c_0 is small, the plane F slowly drifts remaining orthogonal to the vector $[m_1 \; m_2 \; m_3]^T$. With the weak connection k_3 included, the plane F, instead of drifting with constant speed, oscillates slowly about the origin while maintaining orthogonality to the vector $[m_1 \; m_2 \; m_3]^T$. The fact that the mass-spring system has three oscillatory modes, one slow and two fast, will be made explicit in the following sections.

These examples show that the time-scales of the original systems (3.2.4) and (3.2.15) are related to the equilibrium and conservation properties of the auxiliary systems (3.2.6) and (3.2.16). These properties are coordinate-free and characterize all two-time-scale systems reducible to the explicit model.

3.3 Time-Scale Separation in Non-Explicit Models

To demonstrate that the equilibrium and conservation properties always induce times-scales, we consider the system

$$\varepsilon \, dx/dt = dx/d\tau = A(\varepsilon) \, x = (A_0 + \varepsilon A_1(\varepsilon))x \qquad\qquad (3.3.1)$$

where x is an n-vector, $A(\varepsilon)$ is an ε-dependent time-invariant nxn matrix, t and τ are the slow and fast time variables, respectively, $A_1(\varepsilon)$ is bounded at $\varepsilon = 0$, and $A(0) = A_0$.

<u>Assumption 3.3.1</u>: A_0 satisfies

$$R(A_0) \oplus N(A_0) = R^n, \; \rho + \nu = n, \tag{3.3.2}$$

where $N(A_0)$ is the null space of A_0 with

$$dim(N(A_0)) = \nu \geq 1, \tag{3.3.3}$$

$R(A_0)$ is the range space of A_0 with

$$dim(R(A_0)) = \rho \geq 1, \tag{3.3.4}$$

and $\oplus$ denotes the direct sum of two subspaces [53].

Assumption 3.3.1 is equivalent to requiring A_0 to have a complete set of eigenvectors corresponding to its zero eigenvalues, which is also equivalent to the following: $R(A_0)$ is the invariant subspace (eigenspace) of A_0 corresponding to the non-zero eigenvalues, and $N(A_0)$ is the invariant subspace (eigenspace) corresponding to the zero eigenvalues.

To study the time-scale behavior of (3.3.1) we obtain the <u>auxiliary system</u>

$$dx/d\tau = A_0 x \tag{3.3.5}$$

by setting $\epsilon = 0$ in (3.3.1). By Assumption 3.3.1, (3.3.5) has a ν-dimensional <u>equilibrium subspace</u> or <u>manifold</u>

$$S = \{x : A_0 x = 0\} , \tag{3.3.6}$$

that is, $S = N(A_0)$. Therefore, (3.3.5) has the equilibrium property since S is a continuum of equilibria. If the rows of a $\rho \times n$ matrix Q span the row space of A_0, then $A_0 x = 0$ can be reduced to

$$Qx = 0, \text{ for all } x \text{ in } S . \tag{3.3.7}$$

To see the conservation property of (3.3.5), we note that if the rows of a $\nu \times n$ matrix P span the left null space of A_0, that is, $PA_0 = 0$, then

$$P(dx/d\tau) = PA_0 x = 0 \tag{3.3.8}$$

for all τ and all $x(0)$ in R^n. Thus, the ν-vector Px is constant along the trajectories of (3.3.5),

$Px(\tau) = Px(0)$, for all $x(0)$ in R^n.   (3.3.9)

This means that for each value of $x(0)$ the trajectory of (3.3.5) is confined to a translation of a ν-dimensional subspace, that is, a linear manifold, defined by (3.3.9). Thus, system (3.3.5) has the conservation property. The linear manifold, which we called the <u>dynamic manifold</u> $F_{x(0)}$, is orthogonal to the rows of P and contains the initial point $x(0)$:

$$F_{x(0)} = \{x : Px = Px(0)\}.$$ (3.3.10)

We will frequently drop the subscript $x(0)$ and use F to denote a dynamic manifold with the understanding that F depends on $x(0)$. Since the rows of P span the left $N(A_0)$, F is parallel to $R(A_0)$.

   Equations (3.3.7) and (3.3.9) are our algebraic characterization of equilibrium and conservation properties (3.2.9) and (3.2.11) found in the RC-circuit of the previous section. The behavior of the trajectories governed by (3.3.7) and (3.3.9) is still the one depicted in Figure 3.2.3 with S and F defined by (3.3.7) and (3.3.9), respectively. We are now ready to define a new set of coordinates in which the time-scales are explicit.

<u>Theorem 3.3.1</u>: Under Assumptions 3.3.1, the change of coordinates

$$y = Px \quad , \quad z = Qx$$ (3.3.11)

transforms (3.3.1) into the explicit model (2.3.1), (2.3.2) with $z_s(t) = 0$.

<u>Proof</u>: Since the rows of P,Q form bases for the left null and row spaces of A_0, respectively, the transformation matrix

$$T = \begin{bmatrix} P \\ Q \end{bmatrix}$$ (3.3.12)

defined by (3.3.11) has as its inverse

$$T^{-1} = [V \quad W]$$ (3.3.13)

where the columns of V and W form bases for $N(A_0)$ and $R(A_0)$, respectively. Hence

$$T((A_0/\varepsilon) + A_1(\varepsilon))T^{-1} = \frac{1}{\varepsilon} \begin{bmatrix} PA_0V & PA_0W \\ QA_0V & QA_0W \end{bmatrix} + \begin{bmatrix} PA_1(\varepsilon)V & PA_1(\varepsilon)W \\ QA_1(\varepsilon)V & QA_1(\varepsilon)W \end{bmatrix}$$

$$= \begin{bmatrix} PA_1(\varepsilon)V & PA_1(\varepsilon)W \\ QA_1(\varepsilon)V & QA_0W/\varepsilon + QA_1(\varepsilon)W \end{bmatrix}, \tag{3.3.14}$$

that is,

$$dy/dt = A_s(\varepsilon) \, y + A_{sf}(\varepsilon) \, z \; ,$$

$$\varepsilon \, dz/dt = \varepsilon \, A_{fs}(\varepsilon) \, y + A_f(\varepsilon) \, z \; , \tag{3.3.15}$$

where

$$A_s(\varepsilon) = PA_1(\varepsilon)V \; ,$$

$$A_{sf}(\varepsilon) = PA_1(\varepsilon)W \; ,$$

$$A_{fs}(\varepsilon) = QA_1(\varepsilon)V \; ,$$

$$A_f(\varepsilon) = QA_0W + \varepsilon QA_1(\varepsilon)W \; . \tag{3.3.16}$$

To show that (3.3.15) is an explicit model, we need to show that $A_f(0)$ is nonsingular. Since $R(A_0)$ is the eigenspace of the non-zero eigenvalues of A_0, that is, there exists a $\rho \times \rho$ nonsingular matrix G whose eigenvalues are the non-zero eigenvalues of A_0 such that

$$A_0W = W \, G \; , \tag{3.3.17}$$

which implies that

$$A_f(0) = QA_0W = QWG = G \tag{3.3.18}$$

is nonsingular. Since A_{fs} is multiplied by ε, $z_s(t) = 0$ is obtained from (3.3.15) by setting $\varepsilon = 0$. $\square$

As seen from

$$x = T^{-1} \begin{bmatrix} y \\ z \end{bmatrix} = Vy + Wz \; , \tag{3.3.19}$$

y and z are the representations of x with respect to the bases V and W of $N(A_0)$

and $R(A_0)$, respectively. In other words, Vy is the projection of x on $N(A_0)$ along $R(A_0)$ and hence, y is the representation of this projection with respect to the basis P. A similar interpretation holds for Wz and z.

The model (3.3.15) is in the explicit separated singular perturbation form where y is predominantly slow and z is predominantly fast (see (2.3.14), (2.3.15)). To decompose (3.3.15) into slow and fast subsystems, we follow the transformation approach of (2.3.16) and (2.3.21).

Introduce the variable

$$\eta = z - Ly \qquad (3.3.20)$$

where L satisfies the Riccati equation

$$\epsilon A_{fs} + A_f L - \epsilon L(A_s + A_{sf}L) = 0. \qquad (3.3.21)$$

The solution to (3.3.21) in the form

$$L = -\epsilon(A_f(0))^{-1} A_{fs}(0) + O(\epsilon^2) = \epsilon L_\epsilon + O(\epsilon^2) \qquad (3.3.22)$$

guarantees that η is purely fast and the resulting fast subsystem is

$$d\eta/d\tau = (A_f - \epsilon L A_{sf})\eta, \quad \eta(0) = z(0) - Ly(0). \qquad (3.3.23)$$

Then introduce the purely slow variable

$$\xi = y + H\eta \qquad (3.3.24)$$

where H satisfies the linear equation

$$H(A_f - \epsilon L A_{sf}) - \epsilon(A_s + A_{sf}L)H + \epsilon A_{sf} = 0. \qquad (3.3.25)$$

The solution to (3.3.25) is in the form

$$H = -\epsilon A_{sf}(0)(A_f(0))^{-1} + O(\epsilon^2) = \epsilon H_\epsilon + O(\epsilon^2), \qquad (3.3.26)$$

and the resulting slow subsystem is

$$d\xi/dt = (A_s + A_{sf}L)\xi, \quad \xi(0) = (I_r - HL)y(0) + Hz(0). \qquad (3.3.27)$$

Neglecting the ϵ dependent terms in (3.2.27) and (3.3.23), we obtain the decoupled subsystems

$$dy_s/dt = A_s(0)y_s, \quad y_s(0) = y(0), \tag{3.3.28}$$

$$dz_f/d\tau = A_f(0)z_f, \quad z_f(0) = z(0). \tag{3.3.29}$$

The following result is obvious.

<u>Corollary 3.3.1</u>: The subsystems (3.3.28) and (3.3.29) approximate the slow modes λ_s of (3.3.15) to $0(\epsilon)$ and fast modes λ_f of (3.3.15) to $0(1)$, that is,

$$\lambda_s = \lambda(A_s(0)) + 0(\epsilon),$$
$$\lambda_f = \lambda(A_f(0))/\epsilon + 0(1). \tag{3.3.30}$$

Furthermore, if $Re\{\lambda(A_f(0))\} \leq -\rho_0 < 0$, where ρ_0 is a positive scalar independent of ϵ,

$$y(t) = y_s(t) + 0(\epsilon),$$
$$z(t) = z_f(t) + 0(\epsilon). \tag{3.3.31}$$

Corollary 3.3.1 qualifies (3.3.15) as a separated form where y is predominantly slow and z predominantly fast. Note that (3.3.28) and (3.3.29) can be directly obtained from (3.3.15) by setting $\epsilon = 0$ on the right-hand side of the equations (3.3.15) and neglecting the fast contribution $A_{sf}z$ in the slow state y.

The computation of the first order ϵ terms L_ϵ and H_ϵ in (3.3.22) and (3.3.26) is straightforward. They can be readily incorporated if corrections to the subsystems (3.3.28) and (3.3.29) are needed, for example, in recovering the damping of high frequency modes. Retaining the first order ϵ terms, we obtain the separated subsystems

$$dy_{s\epsilon}/dt = (A_s - \epsilon A_{sf}A_f^{-1}A_{fs})y_{s\epsilon}, \ y_{s\epsilon}(0) = y(0) - \epsilon A_{sf}A_f^{-1}z(0), \tag{3.3.32}$$

$$dz_{f\epsilon}/d\tau = A_f z_{f\epsilon}, \ z_{s\epsilon}(0) = z(0) - \epsilon A_f^{-1}A_{fs}y(0), \tag{3.3.33}$$

where terms of order higher than ϵ in $A_s - \epsilon A_{sf}A_f^{-1}A_{fs}$ and A_f are neglected.

<u>Corollary 3.3.2</u>: The subsystems (3.3.32) and (3.3.33) approximate the slow modes λ_s of (3.3.15) to $0(\epsilon^2)$ and the fast modes λ_f of (3.3.15) to $0(\epsilon)$, that is,

$$\lambda_s = \lambda(A_s - \epsilon A_{sf}A_f^{-1}A_{fs}) + O(\epsilon^2),$$

$$\lambda_f = \lambda(A_f)/\epsilon + O(\epsilon).$$

(3.3.34)

Furthermore, if $Re\{\lambda(A_f)\} \leq -\rho_0 < 0$, then for all t,

$$y(t) = y_{s\epsilon}(t) + \epsilon A_{sf}A_f^{-1}z_{f\epsilon}(t) + O(\epsilon^2),$$

$$z(t) = -\epsilon A_f^{-1}A_{fs}y_{s\epsilon}(t) + z_{f\epsilon}(t) + O(\epsilon^2).$$

(3.3.35)

Note that by not setting $\epsilon = 0$ in A_f, we obtain an $O(\epsilon)$ approximation of the fast modes λ_f. For high frequency oscillatory modes, this means that damping comes only from the interaction between the fast states. The interaction between the fast and slow states contributes negligible damping. Consequently, we will use $A_f(\epsilon)$ in place of $A_f(0)$ in (3.3.29) when we deal with high frequency oscillatory system.

The manifold approach can also be used to investigate time-scales in oscillatory systems written as second order differential equations

$$\epsilon d^2x/dt^2 = d^2x/d\tau^2 = A(\epsilon)x = (A_0 + \epsilon A_1(\epsilon))x$$

(3.3.36)

where x is an n-vector and A_0 satisfies Assumption 3.3.1. We follow the steps in (3.3.5) to (3.3.10) and set $\epsilon = 0$ in (3.3.36) to obtain the auxiliary system

$$d^2x/d\tau^2 = A_0x.$$

(3.3.37)

By Assumption 3.3.1, (3.3.37) has a ν-dimensional equilibrium manifold

$$S = \{x : A_0x = 0\},$$

(3.3.38)

that is, (3.3.37) has the equilibrium property. If the $\nu \times n$ matrix P spans the left null space of A_0, then

$$P(d^2x/d\tau^2) = PA_0x = 0$$

(3.3.39)

for all τ and all $x(0)$ in R^n. Thus, the ν-vector $P(dx/d\tau)$ is constant along the trajectories of (3.3.37),

$$P(dx/d\tau) = P(dx/d\tau)|_{\tau=0},$$

(3.3.40)

which is the conservation property analogous to a conservation of momentum. The dynamic manifold is then defined as:

$$F = \{x : P(dx/d\tau) = P(dx/d\tau)|_{\tau=0}\}. \tag{3.3.41}$$

The time-scale separation result of Theorem 3.3.1 that $y = Px$ are the slow states and $z = Qx$ are the fast states holds for (3.3.36), and the y-, z-variable formulation of (3.3.36) is the separated form. Subsystems similar to (3.3.38), (3.3.29) and (3.3.32), (3.3.33) can be obtained for (3.3.36) to separately approximate the slow and fast oscillations. Results similar to Corollaries 3.3.1 and 3.3.2 are valid when ε are replaced by $\sqrt{\varepsilon}$, but the time approximation is only valid up to a finite time T.

3.4 Examples

We continue the investigation of the time-scales of the examples discussed in Section 3.2 by applying the results in the last section to obtain equivalent models. An example of a transformer with small leakage is also included.

We begin with the RC-circuit of Figure 2.3.1a in which the time-scales are due to large and small resistors as in (3.2.2). The auxiliary system is given in (3.2.6) and the equilibrium and dynamic manifolds are defined by (3.2.9) and (3.2.11), respectively. Accordingly, a choice of coordinates is

$$y = (C_1 x_1 + C_2 x_2 + C_3 x_3)/C_a , \tag{3.4.1}$$

$$z_1 = x_1 - x_2 \quad , \quad z_2 = x_3 - x_2 , \tag{3.4.2}$$

where the division by

$$C_a = C_1 + C_2 + C_3 \tag{3.4.3}$$

is introduced in (3.4.1) to retain the physical meaning of y as a voltage variable. In the new coordinates the circuit with parameters (3.4.1) and (3.4.2) is described by

$$dy/dt = -y/3 + 2z_1/9 - 2z_2/9 \tag{3.4.4}$$

$$\varepsilon(dz_1/dt) = -2z_1 - z_2 \tag{3.4.5}$$

$$\varepsilon(dz_2/dt) = -\varepsilon y - (1 - 2\varepsilon/3)z_1 - (2 + 2\varepsilon/3)z_2. \tag{3.4.6}$$

In the limit as $\epsilon \to 0$, (3.4.5) and (3.4.6) yield $z_s(t) = 0$. The slow model

$$dy_s/dt = -y_s/3 \tag{3.4.7}$$

is obtained by neglecting the fast states in (3.4.4) and is represented by the circuit in Figure 3.2.2a. The fast model

$$dz_{1f}/d\tau = -2z_{1f} - z_{2f}$$
$$dz_{2f}/d\tau = -z_{1f} - 2z_{2f} \tag{3.4.8}$$

is obtained by neglecting the ϵ terms on the right-hand side of (3.4.5) and (3.4.6) and is represented by the circuit in Figure 3.2.2b where the voltages with respect to the reference node 2 are used as states. With $\epsilon = 0.1$, the eigenvalues of (3.4.7) and (3.4.8) with respect to the t-scale are -0.33, -10.0 and -30.0 which approximate the eigenvalues -0.32, -10.5 and -30.2 of (3.4.4), (3.4.5) and (3.4.6) to $O(\epsilon)$.

For the power system in Figure 3.2.1b and the mass-spring system in Figure 3.2.1c with parameters (3.2.12) and (3.2.13), we use the transformation

$$y = (m_1 x_1 + m_2 x_2 + m_3 x_3)/m_a, \quad m_a = m_1 + m_2 + m_3, \tag{3.4.9}$$

$$z_1 = x_1 - x_2, \quad z_2 = x_3 - x_2. \tag{3.4.10}$$

Following the earlier derivation, in the limit as $\epsilon \to 0$, the slow model is

$$d^2 y_s/dt^2 = -y_s/3 \tag{3.4.11}$$

and is represented by the systems in Figures 3.2.2c and 3.2.2e. The fast model is

$$d^2 z_{1f}/d\tau^2 = -2z_{1f} - z_{2f}$$
$$d^2 z_{2f}/d\tau^2 = -z_{1f} - 2z_{2f} \tag{3.4.12}$$

and is represented by the systems in Figures 3.2.2d and 3.2.2f where the displacements of machine 2 and mass 2 are used as references. With $\epsilon = 0.1$, the eigenvalues $\pm j0.58$, $\pm j3.16$ and $\pm j5.48$ of (3.4.11) and (3.4.12) with respect to the t-scale approximate the eigenvalues $\pm j0.56$, ± 3.24 and $\pm j5.50$ of the full second order system to $O(\sqrt{\epsilon})$.

As another example, consider the transformer in Figure 3.3.1 where L_1, L_2 are the self-inductance of the coils, M is the mutual inductance, i_1, i_2 are the currents through the coils and v is a slowly varying voltage. Using $x_1 = i_1$, $x_2 = i_2$ as the states, the equations of the system are

$$dx_1/dt = -(R_1L_2/(L_1L_2 - M^2))x_1 - (MR_2/(L_1L_2 - M^2))x_2 + (L_2/(L_1L_2 - M^2))v,$$

$$(3.4.13)$$

$$dx_2/dt = -(MR_1/(L_1L_2 - M^2))x_1 - (R_2L_1/(L_1L_2 - M^2))x_2 + (M/(L_1L_2 - M^2))v.$$

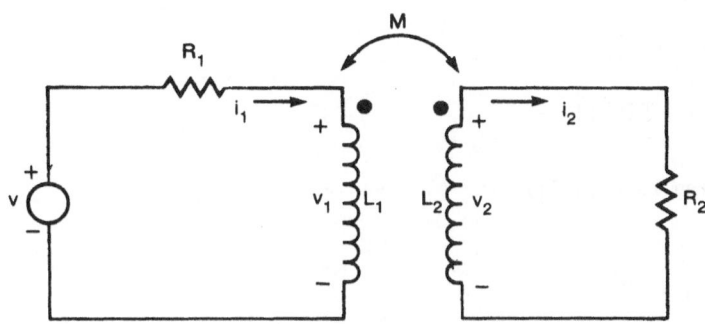

Figure 3.4.1 A non-ideal transformer with small leakage $(L_1L_2 - M_2)/(L_1L_2) = \epsilon$ where ϵ is a small positive parameter.

In the case of an ideal transformer, $L_1L_2 - M^2 = 0$. For non-ideal transformer with small leakage,

$$(L_1L_2 - M^2)/(L_1L_2) = \epsilon \qquad (3.4.14)$$

where ϵ is a small positive parameter. In the notation (3.4.14), the system matrix of (3.4.13) becomes

$$A(\epsilon) = (1/\epsilon) \begin{bmatrix} -R_1/L_1 & -\sqrt{1-\epsilon}\ R_2/\sqrt{L_1 L_2} \\ -\sqrt{1-\epsilon}\ R_1/\sqrt{L_1 L_2} & -R_2/L_2 \end{bmatrix} \qquad (3.4.15)$$

which, with the approximation $\sqrt{1-\epsilon} \simeq 1 - \epsilon/2$, can be rewritten as

$$A(\epsilon) = (1/\epsilon)\ (A_0 + \epsilon A_1)\ , \qquad (3.4.16)$$

where

$$A_0 = \begin{bmatrix} -R_1/L_1 & R_2/\sqrt{L_1 L_2} \\ R_1/\sqrt{L_1 L_2} & -R_2/L_2 \end{bmatrix}. \qquad (3.4.17)$$

The left null space of A_0

$$P = [L_1 \quad -\sqrt{L_1 L_2}] \qquad (3.4.18)$$

and the row space of A_0

$$Q = [(R_1/L_1)\ (R_2/\sqrt{L_1 L_2})] \qquad (3.4.19)$$

define, according to (3.3.11), the slow variable

$$y = L_1 x_1 - \sqrt{L_1 L_2}\ x_2 \qquad (3.4.20)$$

and the fast variable

$$z = R_1 x_1 + R_2 \sqrt{L_1/L_2}\ x_2\ . \qquad (3.4.21)$$

The slow variable y has the interpretation of a flux linkage and the fast variable z has the interpretation of a voltage.

In the new coordinates y,z the state equation (3.4.13) becomes

$$dy/dt = -[1/(T_1 + T_2)]y + [(T_1 - T_2)/2(T_1 + T_2)]z + v/2\ ,$$
$$\epsilon(dz/dt) = \epsilon\ [(1/T_2 - 1/T_1)/2(T_1 + T_2)]y - [1/T_1 + 1/T_2 - \epsilon/(T_1 + T_2)]z \qquad (3.4.22)$$
$$+ (1/T_1 + 1/T_2)\ v,$$

where $T_1 = L_1/R_1$ and $T_2 = L_2/R_2$ are the time constants of the primary and secondary RL-circuits. Because of the $O(1)$ presence of v, z contains a slow as well as a fast part. The slow model

$$dy_s/dt = [-1/(T_1 + T_2)]y_s + [T_1/(T_1 + T_2)]v \tag{3.4.23}$$

is obtained by setting $\varepsilon = 0$ in the second equation of (3.4.22) and substituting the quasi-steady state

$$z_s = v \tag{3.4.24}$$

into the first equation. The fast model

$$dz_f/d\tau = -(1/T_1 + 1/T_2)z_f \tag{3.4.25}$$

is obtained by writing the second equation of (3.4.22) in the fast time-scale and setting $\varepsilon = 0$.

It is interesting to note the physical interpretation of the new variables y,z. By writing

$$y = L_1x_1 - \sqrt{L_1L_2}\, x_2 = L_1x_1 + Mx_2 + O(\varepsilon) = \phi_{11} + \phi_{12} + O(\varepsilon) \tag{3.4.26}$$

we see that y is, to $O(\varepsilon)$, the total flux linage $\phi_{11} + \phi_{12}$ in coil 1 where ϕ_{11} is due to x_1 and ϕ_{12} is due to x_2. This total flux linkage is an aggregate quantity and is slowly varying. In the transformation (3.4.21) we decompose z into z_s and z_f to obtain

$$z_s + z_f = v + z_f = R_1x_1 + R_2 \sqrt{L_1/L_2}\, x_2. \tag{3.4.27}$$

Rearranging (3.4.27) we obtain

$$v_2 = R_2x_2 = \sqrt{L_2/L_1} \,(v - R_1x_1 + z_f)$$
$$= (N_2/N_1)(v_1 + z_f) , \tag{3.4.28}$$

where N_1 and N_2 are the number of turns in coils 1 and 2. After z_f, due to initial conditions, has decayed, $v_2 = (N_2/N_1)v_1$, which is the voltage relationship of an ideal transformer.

3.5 Other Singular Perturbation Forms

The results of Theorem 3.3.1 are broad enough to encompass several practically important singular perturbation forms. The first form is the explicit singularly perturbed model (2.3.1), (2.3.2) discussed in Chapter 2. Recall that in (2.3.1), (2.3.2), the state y is predominantly slow and the state z is mixed, that is, it contains both slow and fast components. To put this in the separated form, we only need to obtain a purely fast state $\eta = z + D^{-1}Cy$ (2.3.13), which is the second part of the transformation (3.3.11). Thus, we also refer to the explicit singular perturbation form as the slow separated form. We will examine in this section two other forms, namely, the fast separated form and the weak connection form.

The fast separated singular perturbation form is

$$\varepsilon \begin{bmatrix} dx_1/dt \\ dx_2/dt \end{bmatrix} = \begin{bmatrix} dx_1/d\tau \\ dx_2/d\tau \end{bmatrix} = \begin{bmatrix} \varepsilon A_{11} & A_{12} \\ \varepsilon A_{21} & A_{22} \end{bmatrix} \begin{bmatrix} x_1 \\ x_2 \end{bmatrix} \tag{3.5.1}$$

where x_1 is a ν-vector, x_2 is a ρ-vector, A_{11}, A_{12}, A_{21}, A_{22} are matrices of appropriate dimensions and A_{22} is nonsingular. We separate A into

$$A = \begin{bmatrix} \varepsilon A_{11} & A_{12} \\ \varepsilon A_{21} & A_{22} \end{bmatrix} = \begin{bmatrix} 0 & A_{12} \\ 0 & A_{22} \end{bmatrix} + \varepsilon \begin{bmatrix} A_{11} & 0 \\ A_{21} & 0 \end{bmatrix}$$

$$= A_0 + \varepsilon A_1 . \tag{3.5.2}$$

Since A_{22} is nonsingular, the range and row spaces of A_0 have dimension ρ, whereas the left and right null spaces of A_0 have dimension ν. Therefore, A_0 satisfies Assumption 3.3.1. Furthermore, it can be verified that

$$P = [I_\nu \quad -A_{12}A_{22}^{-1}] \tag{3.5.3}$$

and

$$Q = [0 \quad I_\rho] \tag{3.5.4}$$

span the left null and row spaces of A_0, respectively, and that

$$V = \begin{bmatrix} I_\nu \\ 0 \end{bmatrix} \tag{3.5.5}$$

and

$$W = \begin{bmatrix} A_{12}A_{22}^{-1} \\ I_\rho \end{bmatrix} \tag{3.5.6}$$

span the right null and range spaces of A_0, respectively. Moreover,

$$\begin{bmatrix} P \\ Q \end{bmatrix} [V \quad W] = TT^{-1} = I_n . \tag{3.5.7}$$

Corollary 3.5.1: If A_{22} is nonsingular, then

(i)   the change of coordinates

$$y = x_1 - A_{12}A_{22}^{-1}x_2 \quad , \quad z = x_2 \tag{3.5.8}$$

transforms (3.5.1) into the explicit model (3.3.15) with $z_s(t) = 0$;

(ii) y is predominantly slow and z is predominantly fast, and they are approximated by

$$y(t) = y_s(t) + 0(\epsilon) ,$$
$$z(t) = z_f(t) + 0(\epsilon) , \tag{3.5.9}$$

where the slow model is

$$dy_s/dt = (A_{11} - A_{12}A_{22}^{-1}A_{21})y_s, \quad y_s(0) = y(0), \tag{3.5.10}$$

and the fast model is

$$dz_f/d\tau = A_{22} z_f , \quad z_f(0) = z(0); \tag{3.5.11}$$

(iii)   the state x_2 of (3.5.1) is predominantly fast, whereas x_1 is mixed.

Proof: Since (3.5.8) is equivalent to (3.5.3) and (3.5.4), (i) follows directly from Theorem 3.3.1; (ii) follows from Corollary 3.3.1; and (iii) follows by inverting (3.5.8)

$$x_1 = y + A_{12}A_{22}^{-1}z \quad , \quad x_2 = z . \ \square \qquad (3.5.12)$$

Note that x_2 can be used as the state in the fast model (3.5.11), justifying the name "fast separated."

As an example of the fast separated form, we consider the systems in Figure 2.4.1 used to illustrate the slow separated form. For the RC-circuit, instead of using voltages v across the capacitors as the state variables, we now use the charges stored in the capacitors as the state variables q and obtain the equations as

$$\frac{dq_1}{dt} = -q_1 + \frac{C_1}{C_2} q_2 \quad ,$$

$$\frac{dq_2}{dt} = q_1 - \frac{C_1}{C_2} (1 + \frac{R_1}{R_2}) q_2 + \frac{C_1}{C_3} \frac{R_1}{R_2} q_3 \quad , \qquad (3.5.13)$$

$$\frac{dq_3}{dt} = \frac{C_1}{C_2} \frac{R_1}{R_2} q_2 - \frac{C_1}{C_3} (\frac{R_1}{R_2} + \frac{R_1}{R_3}) q_3.$$

Comparing with (2.4.3), we note that some of the locations of the coefficients C_1/C_2 and C_1/C_3 have changed due to the scaling q = Cv. Using the parameters

$$\epsilon C_1 = C_2 = C_3, \ R_1 = R_2 = R_3 \qquad (3.5.14)$$

as in (2.4.5) and (2.4.6) where $\beta = 1$, we obtain

$$\epsilon dx_1/dt = \epsilon A_{11}x_1 + A_{12}x_2 \quad ,$$

$$\epsilon dx_2/dt = \epsilon A_{21}x_1 + A_{22}x_2 \quad , \qquad (3.5.15)$$

where

$$x_1 = q_1, \qquad x_2 = [q_2 \ q_3]^T,$$

$$A_{11} = [-1], \qquad A_{12} = [1 \ 0],$$

$$A_{21} = \begin{bmatrix} 1 \\ 0 \end{bmatrix}, \qquad A_{22} = \begin{bmatrix} -2 & 1 \\ 1 & -2 \end{bmatrix}, \qquad (3.5.16)$$

which is in the form (3.5.1). It is interesting to note that in (3.5.13), the charge of the large capacitor 1 consists of both slow and fast components while in

(2.4.3) the voltage of capacitor is predominantly slow. This is due to the fact that the fast charge component becomes negligible when it is scaled by C_1 to form the fast voltage component. On the other hand, the slow components of the charges of capacitors 2 and 3 become important when they are scaled by C_1 to form the slow voltage components.

Fast separated forms can be obtained for the power system and the mass-spring system in Figure 2.4.1 if the angular momenta of the machines and the linear momenta of the masses are used. The derivations are similar to that of the RC-circuit and will not be repeated here.

Another structured form is the weak connection form arising frequently in dynamic networks. This is a principal subject of the remainder of the monograph. A system is said to be in the weak connection form if its dynamics are described by

$$\epsilon \begin{bmatrix} dx_1/dt \\ dx_2/dt \end{bmatrix} = \begin{bmatrix} dx_1/d\tau \\ dx_2/d\tau \end{bmatrix} = \begin{bmatrix} A_{11} + \epsilon A_{11}' & \epsilon A_{12} \\ \epsilon A_{21} & A_{22} + \epsilon A_{22}' \end{bmatrix} \begin{bmatrix} x_1 \\ x_2 \end{bmatrix} , \qquad (3.5.17)$$

where x_1 and x_2 are n_1- and n_2-vectors, A_{11}, A_{11}', A_{12}, A_{21}, A_{22}, A_{22}' are matrices of appropriate dimensions, and A_{11}, A_{22} are singular matrices satisfying Assumption 3.3.1, that is,

$$R(A_{11}) \oplus N(A_{11}) = R^{n_1} , \qquad R(A_{22}) \oplus N(A_{22}) = R^{n_2} , \qquad (3.5.18)$$

with

$$\dim R(A_{11}) = \rho_1 \geq 1 , \qquad \dim N(A_{11}) = \nu_1 \geq 1 , \qquad \rho_1 + \nu_1 = n_1 , \qquad (3.5.19)$$

$$\dim R(A_{22}) = \rho_2 \geq 1 , \qquad \dim N(A_{22}) = \nu_2 \geq 1 , \qquad \rho_2 + \nu_2 = n_2 . \qquad (3.5.20)$$

For convenience we deal with only two subsystems, but the ideas are directly applicable to any number of subsystems. With ϵ multiplying the interaction terms between x_1 and x_2, it seems that the dynamics of the two subsystems are weakly coupled. We now show that this statement is only partially true.

Writing

$$\begin{bmatrix} A_{11} + \epsilon A_{11}' & \epsilon A_{12} \\ \epsilon A_{21} & A_{22} + \epsilon A_{22}' \end{bmatrix} = \begin{bmatrix} A_{11} & 0 \\ 0 & A_{22} \end{bmatrix} + \epsilon \begin{bmatrix} A_{11}' & A_{12} \\ A_{21} & A_{22}' \end{bmatrix} , \qquad (3.5.21)$$

we obtain

$$A_0 = \begin{bmatrix} A_{11} & 0 \\ 0 & A_{22} \end{bmatrix}$$
(3.5.22)

which, because of (3.5.18), satisfies Assumption 3.3.1 with $\rho \geq 2$ and $\nu \geq 2$. Let P_i and Q_i span the left null and row spaces of A_{ii}, respectively, and V_i and W_i span the right null and range spaces, respectively, $i = 1,2$, such that

$$P_i V_i = I_{\nu_i} \quad , \quad Q_i W_i = I_{\rho_i} \quad , \quad i = 1,2 \quad .$$
(3.5.23)

<u>Corollary 3.5.2</u>: If A_{11} and A_{22} satisfy (3.5.18), (3.5.19) and (3.5.20), then

(i)   the change of coordinates

$$\begin{bmatrix} y_1 \\ y_2 \end{bmatrix} = \begin{bmatrix} P_1 x_1 \\ P_2 x_2 \end{bmatrix} \quad , \quad \begin{bmatrix} z_1 \\ z_2 \end{bmatrix} = \begin{bmatrix} Q_1 x_1 \\ Q_2 x_2 \end{bmatrix}$$
(3.5.24)

transforms (3.5.17) into the explicit model (3.3.15) with $z_s(t) = 0$;

(ii) y_1, y_2 are predominantly slow and z_1, z_2 are predominantly fast, and they are approximated by

$$y_1(t) = y_{1s}(t) + 0(\varepsilon), \quad y_2(t) = y_{2s}(t) + 0(\varepsilon),$$
$$z_1(t) = z_{1f}(t) + 0(\varepsilon), \quad z_2(t) = z_{2f}(t) + 0(\varepsilon),$$
(3.5.25)

where the slow model is

$$(d/dt) \begin{bmatrix} y_{1s} \\ y_{2s} \end{bmatrix} = \begin{bmatrix} P_1 A_{11}' V_1 & P_1 A_{12} V_2 \\ P_2 A_{21} V_1 & P_2 A_{22}' V_2 \end{bmatrix} \begin{bmatrix} y_{1s} \\ y_{2s} \end{bmatrix}$$
(3.5.26)

and the fast model is

$$(d/d\tau) \begin{bmatrix} z_{1f} \\ z_{2f} \end{bmatrix} = \begin{bmatrix} Q_1 A_{11} W_1 + \varepsilon Q_1 A_{11}' W_1 & \varepsilon Q_1 A_{12} W_2 \\ \varepsilon Q_2 A_{21} W_1 & Q_2 A_{22} W_2 + \varepsilon Q_2 A_{22}' W_2 \end{bmatrix} \begin{bmatrix} z_{1f} \\ z_{2f} \end{bmatrix} .$$
(3.5.27)

<u>Proof:</u> The proof of (i) and (ii) follows immediately from noting that

$$
P = \begin{bmatrix} P_1 & 0 \\ 0 & P_2 \end{bmatrix} \quad , \quad Q = \begin{bmatrix} Q_1 & 0 \\ 0 & Q_2 \end{bmatrix} \tag{3.5.28}
$$

span the left null and row spaces of A_0, and $z_s(t) = 0$. □

Corollary 3.5.2 reveals some interesting properties of the weak connection form (3.5.17). First, from (3.5.24) each subsystem has its own slow and fast variables. For example, the slow state y_1 and the fast state z_1 are defined in terms of x_1 only. Second, from (3.5.27) the fast variables z_{1f}, z_{2f} are only weakly coupled to each other and, since $Q_i A_{ii} W_i$, $i = 1,2$, are nonsingular, the coupling can be neglected for an $O(\varepsilon)$ approximation. Hence, for each subsystem there is a local fast model z_{if} connected with $O(\varepsilon)$ coupling to other local fast models. The states y_{is} from each subsystem are strongly coupled and form a "slow core" describing the aggregate dynamics of (3.5.17). This two level decomposition plays an important role in this monograph and will be dealt with in more detail in Chapters 6, 7 and 8. We shall postpone the illustration of the weak connection form to after we have discussed dynamic networks and aggregations.

3.6 Conclusions

We have used a manifold approach to investigate the time-scale characteristics of nonexplicit singularly perturbed models. These models include systems whose storage elements are interconnected with weak and strong springs, admittances, etc. The characteristics are coordinate free - the constancy of the slow motions is an equilibrium property and the restriction of the fast motion is a conservation property. From these physical phenonmena, we can readily construct a transformation to put the model into a separated form whose states are either predominantly slow or predominantly fast.

The coordinate-free characterizations are also applicable to nonexplicit models which are nonlinear. This aspect will be covered in Chapter 7. The weak connection form will be used in Chapter 6 to model dynamic networks whose areas are weakly connected. The technique presented in this chapter is the main analytical tool to analyze time-scale in these dynamic networks as well as to obtain reduced equivalents.

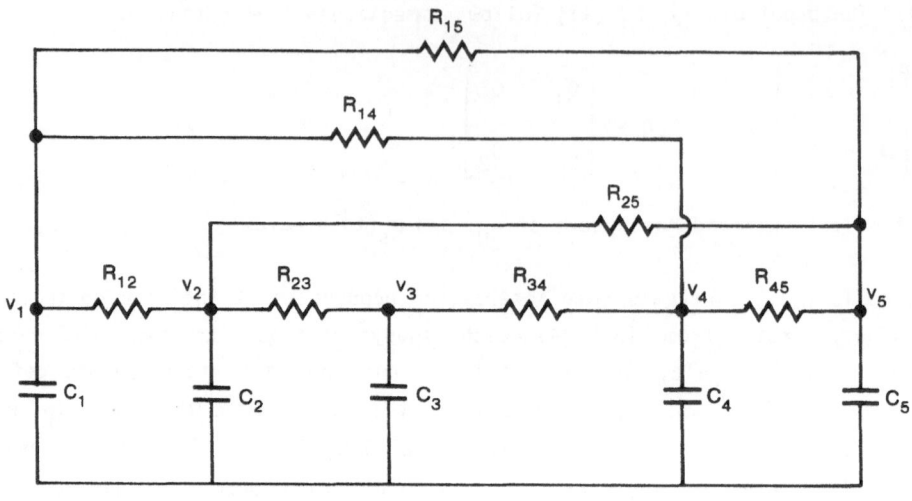

Figure 4.2.1   A five capacitor circuit in the configuration of a dynamic network

CHAPTER 4

DYNAMIC NETWORKS AND AREA AGGREGATION

4.1 Introduction

Aggregation is commonly used to obtain reduced models for large scale interconnected systems. For example, in power systems, aggregate machines are used to represent the dynamics of groups of machines [51, 41]. In economic systems, aggregate consumption and investment are used to describe the dynamic behavior of an industry [50]. In this chapter, we develop an aggregation method for a class of dynamic networks which includes electromechanical models of power systems, electrical circuits, mass-spring systems, and torsional systems. We also derive structural conditions under which groups of states of a dynamic network are aggregable.

We start by formulating the properties of dynamic networks which consist of interconnected storage elements. For the same dynamic network, two choices of state models are considered: the storage form in which the state variables are the stored quantities and the potential form in which the state variables are the potentials across the storage elements. To simplify the derivation of the aggregation results, we introduce the notion of areas and classify the connections between the state variables into two types: internal for connections between the states in the same areas and external for connections between the states in different areas.

Using the areas, we construct a matrix C_a which aggregates the state variables in each area into the area "center of inertia" variable. We obtain an eigenspace condition for a dynamic network to be aggregable with respect to the new variables. This aggregability condition involves only the external connections. As shown in the next chapter, a dynamic implication of the condition is that the states in the same areas be coherent with respect to the aggregate modes. The aggregation, which is equivalent to lumping the inertias and external connections, results in an aggregate dynamic network. It is of practical importance that the aggregate model preserves the network structure and leads to construction of lower order equivalents. For real dynamic networks which seldom exactly satisfy the structural conditions, we pursue a perturbation analysis and show when they are near-aggregable. The area aggregation procedure is illustrated by RC-circuits and power systems.

In Section 4.2 we introduce the notion of dynamic networks and illustrate their properties using an RC-circuit. In Section 4.3, we show how electromechanical models of power systems are obtained as dynamic networks. Section 4.4 introduces the notion of area partition, and internal and external connections. Section 4.5 discusses the area aggregation process for first order dynamic networks and presents the main results on the eigenspace characterization and the structural conditions of aggregability. These results are extended to second order dynamic networks in Section 4.6. A perturbation analysis is performed in Section 4.7 to deal with systems which satisfy the aggregability condition only approximately.

In this and the next chapter, we use t_d as an arbitrary time variable since the results are not dependent on time-scales. For brevity, we use the dot to denote the derivative with respect to time t_d.

4.2 Dynamic Networks

We consider a class of large scale systems which can be modeled as dynamic networks. For our purpose, a dynamic network consists of non-storage branches connecting n storage nodes. The flow from node i to node j is denoted by f_{ij}. The dynamic behavior is governed by the condition that the rate of change of the storage variable ξ_i at node i equals the algebraic sum of the flows f_{ij} in the branches connected to this node

$$\dot{\xi}_i = \sum_{\substack{j=1 \\ j \neq i}}^{n} f_{ij}, \quad i = 1, 2, \ldots, n \ . \tag{4.2.1}$$

If there is no branch connecting nodes i and j, then $f_{ij} = 0$. Furthermore, the flow f_{ij} is a function of the difference of the potential variables x_i and x_j at the nodes i and j. We first assume that the branch characteristics are linear, that is,

$$f_{ij} = k_{ij} (x_i - x_j) \ , \tag{4.2.2}$$

where k_{ij} is a branch constant. In Chapter 7 we will investigate dynamic networks with nonlinear branch characteristics.

In RC-circuits such as the one in Figure 4.2.1, we consider as storage variables the capacitor charges and as flows the currents in resistors. In mass-spring systems, we consider masses as the only storage elements, and hence the storage variables are momenta and the flows are spring forces.

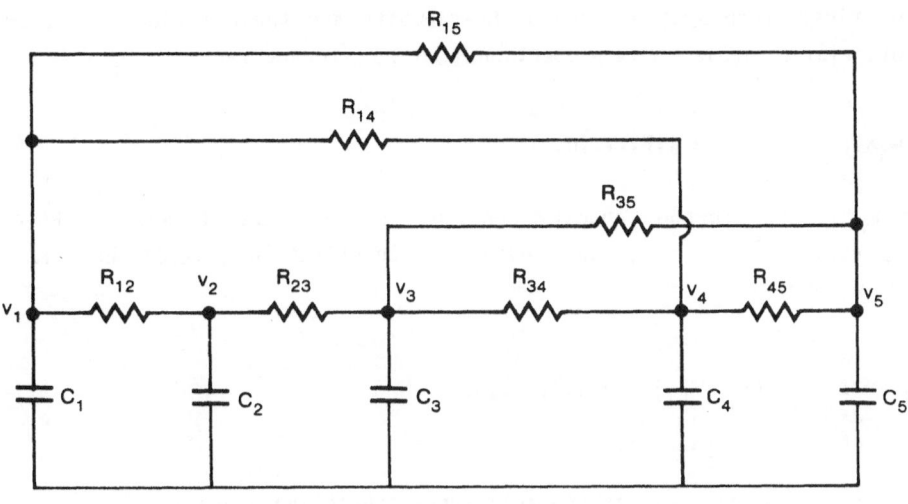

Figure 4.2.1   A five capacitor circuit in the configuration
of a dynamic network

For first order systems such as RC-circuits and their analogs, we assume that the potential variable x_i is proportional to the storage variable ξ_i

$$\xi_i = m_i x_i, \quad m_i > 0, \quad i = 1,2,\ldots,n, \tag{4.2.3}$$

where m_i is the storage capacity constant such as capacitance. In RC-circuits, the x_i variables are capacitor voltages. Substituting (4.2.2) and (4.2.3) into (4.2.1) we obtain

$$m_i \, \dot{x}_i = \sum_{\substack{j=1 \\ j \neq i}}^{n} k_{ij} (x_j - x_i) \; , \quad i=1,2,\ldots,n, \tag{4.2.4}$$

where for RC-circuits, k_{ij} is the admittance connecting nodes i and j.

For second order systems, the storage variable is proportional to the time derivative of the potential variable

$$\xi_i = m_i \dot{x}_i, \quad m_i > 0, \quad i = 1,2,\ldots,n. \tag{4.2.5}$$

This is the case with mass-spring systems where ξ_i is the momentum and x_i the displacement of the i-th mass. Substituting (4.2.2) and (4.2.5) into (4.2.1) we obtain

$$m_i \ddot{x}_i = \sum_{\substack{j=1 \\ j \neq 1}}^{n} k_{ij} (x_j - x_i), \quad i=1,2,\ldots,n, \tag{4.2.6}$$

where for mass-spring systems, k_{ij} is the spring constant connecting masses i and j. In spite of this difference, the study of aggregation of first and second order systems remains the same because all the fundamental properties are determined by the network and n storage constants.

The model (4.2.6) is a purely oscillatory system which is an approximation of real systems with damping neglected. When damping d_i is included, the storage and potential variable relationship (4.2.5) becomes

$$\xi_i = m_i \dot{x}_i + d_i x_i, \quad i = 1,2,\ldots,n. \tag{4.2.7}$$

Consequently, (4.2.1) becomes

$$m_i \ddot{x}_i = d_i \dot{x}_i + \sum_{\substack{j=1 \\ j \neq 1}}^{n} k_{ij} (x_j - x_i), \quad i = 1,2,\ldots,n. \qquad (4.2.8)$$

For stability, damping is important. Basic aggregability theory is first developed for the form (4.2.6) and then extended to the form (4.2.8).

Let us rewrite (4.2.4) as

$$m_i \dot{x}_i = - \sum_{\substack{j=1 \\ j \neq i}}^{n} k_{ij} x_i + \sum_{\substack{j=1 \\ j \neq i}}^{n} k_{ij} x_j. \qquad (4.2.9)$$

We denote by K the connection matrix, whose (i,j)-th entry is k_{ij}, $i \neq j$, and whose (i,i)-th entry is

$$k_{ii} = - \sum_{\substack{j=1 \\ j \neq i}}^{n} k_{ij}. \qquad (4.2.10)$$

Then (4.2.9) can be expressed in matrix form as

$$M\dot{x} = Kx, \qquad (4.2.11)$$

where

$$x = [x_1, x_2, \ldots, x_n]^T, \qquad (4.2.12)$$

$$M = \text{diag}(m_1, m_2, \ldots, m_n) \qquad (4.2.13)$$

are the potential vector and the inertia matrix, respectively.

There are two crucial properties of system (4.2.11). The first property is that since there is no storage in the branches,

$$f_{ij} = k_{ij}(x_i - x_j) = -k_{ji}(x_j - x_i) = -f_{ji} \qquad (4.2.14)$$

implying

$$k_{ij} = k_{ji}, \qquad (4.2.15)$$

that is, K is symmetric. The second property is that because of (4.2.10), the entries in any row of K sum to zero, that is,

Ku = 0   (4.2.16)

where

$u = [1 \ 1 \ldots 1]^T.$ (4.2.17)

We call (4.2.11) a <u>first order dynamic network</u> in the <u>potential form</u> if it has properties (4.2.15) and (4.2.16). Similarly, the second order system (4.2.6) expressed as

$M \ddot{x} = Kx$ (4.2.18)

is called a <u>second order dynamic network</u> in the <u>potential form</u> since it has propertries (4.2.15) and (4.2.16).

To illustrate a first order dynamic network, consider the RC-circuit example in Figure 4.2.1. The state equation of this circuit is given by (4.2.11) with

$x = [v_1, v_2, v_3, v_4, v_5]^T ,$ (4.2.19)

$M = \text{diag} (C_1, C_2, C_3, C_4, C_5) ,$ (4.2.20)

and

$$K = \begin{bmatrix} -(k_{12}+k_{14}+k_{15}) & k_{12} & 0 & k_{14} & k_{15} \\ k_{12} & -(k_{12}+k_{23}+k_{25}) & k_{23} & 0 & k_{25} \\ 0 & k_{23} & -(k_{23}+k_{34}) & k_{34} & 0 \\ k_{14} & 0 & k_{34} & -(k_{14}+k_{34}+k_{45}) & k_{45} \\ k_{15} & k_{25} & 0 & k_{45} & -(k_{15}+k_{25}+k_{45}) \end{bmatrix} ,$$

           (4.2.21)

where $k_{ij} = k_{ji} = 1/R_{ij}$. Note that K has both properties (4.2.15) and (4.2.16).

An example of a second order dynamic network will be given in the next section where we show how a linearized electromechanical model of power systems is put in the form (4.2.18).

Property (4.2.16) implies that K has a zero eigenvalue with eigenvector u. Hence, A also has a zero eigenvalue with eigenvector u since

$$M^{-1}Ku = 0. \qquad\qquad (4.2.22)$$

This zero mode is frequently called the system mode or reference mode. For first order dynamic networks, (4.2.22) means that any x satisfying

$$x_i - x_j = 0, \text{ for all } i,j = 1,2,\ldots,n, \qquad\qquad (4.2.23)$$

is an equilibrium. Relation (4.2.23) represents a continuum of equilibrium points. In RC-circuits, (4.2.23) corresponds to all the capacitors having the same voltage. Thus, property (4.2.16) rules out RC-circuits with either ungrounded capacitors or grounded resistors or both. For second order dynamic networks, (4.2.22) means that if (4.2.23) and the relation

$$\dot{x}_i - \dot{x}_j = 0, \text{ for all } i,j = 1,2,\ldots,n, \qquad\qquad (4.2.24)$$

are satisfied at any t_d, then (4.2.23) and (4.2.24) hold for all t_d even though the system may not be in equilibrium.

Property (4.2.15) guarantees that K has real eigenvalues and a full set of eigenvectors. Thus, the eigenvalues of A are also real because A is similar to the matrix $M^{-1/2}KM^{-1/2}$. The symmetry of K is important for establishing the aggregability results.

At this point it is helpful to make a remark on stability conditions. The zero eigenvalue of A is often eliminated by letting one of the states be the reference state and rewriting (4.2.11) and (4.2.18) in terms of the difference of the other states with respect to this reference state [43,54]. Consequently, (4.2.11) and (4.2.18) are said to be in the absolute reference frame, while the models obtained by eliminating the zero eigenvalue are said to be in the relative reference frame. For our purpose, we shall retain the zero mode and eliminate it only when we study local subsystems in Chapters 6 to 8. In the relative reference frame, system (4.2.11) is said to be asymptotically stable if its (n-1) eigenvalues are negative, while in the absolute refrence frame, it is stable. This requirement is satisfied if $k_{ij} \geq 0$ for all $i \neq j$, in which case K is negative semi-definite. An example is the RC-circuit in Figure 4.2.1.

If λ_i is an eigenvalue of A, then $\pm\sqrt{\lambda_i}$ are the eigenvalues of (4.2.18). Thus, if A has (n-1) negative eigenvalues, system (4.2.18) has (n-1) oscillatory modes with frequencies $\sqrt{|\lambda_i|}$, and 2 zero eigenvalues. The effect of damping on (4.2.18) can be determined by computing the eigenvalues of the matrix

$$\begin{bmatrix} 0 & I_n \\ M^{-1}K & M^{-1}D \end{bmatrix},$$

(4.2.25)

where I_n is the nxn identity matrix and D is a diagonal matrix with entries d_i. We apply the transformation matrix diag(T,T) where $TM^{-1}KT^{-1}$ is a diagonal matrix, to (4.2.25) to obtain the characteristic polynomial

$$\det (s^2 I_n - sTM^{-1}DT^{-1} - TM^{-1}KT^{-1}) = 0.$$

(4.2.26)

When D is small, the off-diagonal entries of $TM^{-1}DT^{-1}$ can be neglected and the determinant in (4.2.24) is approximated by the product of n quadratic terms [8]

$$\prod_{i=1}^{n} (s^2 - \overline{d}_i s - \lambda_i),$$

(4.2.27)

where $\overline{d}_i$ is the i-th diagonal entry of $TM^{-1}DT^{-1}$. Thus, the eigenvalues of (4.2.25) are approximately

$$\overline{d}_i/2 \pm j\sqrt{|\lambda_i|}, \text{ for } \lambda_i \neq 0$$

(4.2.28)

and

$$0, \overline{d}_i \quad , \text{ for } \lambda_i = 0.$$

(4.2.29)

When the damping is uniform system-wide, that is,

$$d_1/m_1 = d_2/m_2 = \dots = d_n/m_n = c,$$

(4.2.30)

(4.2.28) and (4.2.29) are the exact eigenvalues of A since $M^{-1}D$ and hence $TM^{-1}DT^{-1}$ are diagonal matrices with all their entries equal to c. In this case,

$$\overline{d}_i = c, i = 1,2,\dots,n.$$

(4.2.31)

We conclude our introduction of dynamic networks by observing that they can also be modeled with the storage variables as

$$\dot{\xi}_i = \sum_{\substack{j=1 \\ j \neq i}}^{n} k_{ij} \left(\xi_j / m_j - \xi_i / m_i \right) \qquad (4.2.32)$$

for first order systems, and

$$\ddot{\xi}_i = \sum_{\substack{j=1 \\ j \neq i}}^{n} k_{ij} \left(\xi_j / m_j - \xi_i / m_i \right) \qquad (4.2.33)$$

for second order systems. In matrix form, they are

$$\dot{\xi} = KM^{-1} \xi \qquad (4.2.34)$$

and

$$\ddot{\xi} = KM^{-1} \xi . \qquad (4.2.35)$$

These models are called the <u>storage form</u>. In this monograph, we mainly deal with the potential form since coherency behavior is more easily identified via the potential variables. This reasoning will become clear in the next chapter. The results developed for the potential form will be equally applicable to the storage form through an appropriate scaling with respect to the masses.

In Sections 4.4 to 4.5, we will perform aggregation on first order dynamic networks in the potential form (4.2.11). In Section 4.6, these results, which are stated in terms of $M^{-1}K$, are extended to second order dynamic networks (4.2.18). The results will also be translated to systems in the storage forms (4.2.34) and (4.2.35). The RC-circuit example in Figure 4.2.1 will be used for illustration throughout this chapter.

4.3 Electromechanical Model of Power Systems

As an illustration of second order dynamic networks, we consider the nonlinear electromechanical model of multi-machine power systems, which is the simplest model for the study of transient stability [1]. For an n machine power system, the electromechanical model is

$$\dot{\delta}_i = \Omega(\omega_i - 1), \qquad (4.3.1)$$

$$2H_i \dot{\omega}_i = -d_i(\omega_i - 1) + (P_{mi} - P_{ei}), \qquad (4.3.2)$$

where

i	=	1,2,...,n,
δ_i	=	rotor angle of machine i (radians),
ω_i	=	speed of machine i (per unit),
P_{mi}	=	mechanical input power of machine i (per unit),
P_{ei}	=	electrical output power of machine i (per unit),
H_i	=	inertia constant of machine i (seconds),
d_i	=	damping constant of machine i (per unit),
Ω	=	base frequency (radians per second).

In this model, the mechanical input power P_{mi} is assumed to be constant. The electrical output power is

$$P_{ei} = \sum_{\substack{j=1 \\ j \neq i}}^{n} v_i v_j [B_{ij}\sin(\delta_i-\delta_j) + G_{ij}\cos(\delta_i-\delta_j)] + v_i G_{ii}^{2},$$

$$i = 1,2,...,n, \tag{4.3.3}$$

where the per unit voltage v_i behind transient reactance is assumed to be constant and saliency is neglected. Loads are represented by passive impedances, and G_{ij} and B_{ij} are the (i,j)-th real and imaginary entries of the admittance matrix $Y=G+jB$ reduced to the internal machine nodes.

Linearizing the model (4.3.1), (4.3.2) about an equilibrium operating condition δ_i^e and $\omega_i^e = 1.0$, we obtain

$$\Delta\dot{\delta}_i = \Omega\Delta\omega_i, \tag{4.3.4}$$

$$2H_i\Delta\dot{\omega}_i = -d_i\Delta\omega_i + \sum_{j=1}^{n} \overline{k}_{ij}\Delta\delta_j, \tag{4.3.5}$$

where

$$\Delta\delta_i = \delta_i - \delta_i^e, \tag{4.3.6}$$

$$\Delta\omega_i = \omega_i - 1, \tag{4.3.7}$$

$$\overline{k}_{ij} = v_i v_j ((B_{ij}\cos(\delta_i-\delta_j)-G_{ij}\sin(\delta_i-\delta_j)))|_{\delta^e} , \quad j \neq i, \tag{4.3.8}$$

$$\overline{k}_{ii} = -\sum_{\substack{j=1 \\ j \neq i}}^{n} \overline{k}_{ij}. \tag{4.3.9}$$

The coefficients $\overline{k}_{ij}$ are functions of the operating point as well as the admittances.

Neglecting the damping constants d_i which do not significantly affect the frequencies, and the G_{ij} terms which are generally small compared with the B_{ij} terms, we reduce system (4.3.4), (4.3.5) to

$$\ddot{x} = M^{-1} K x = Ax, \tag{4.3.10}$$

where

$$x_i = \Delta\delta_i$$

$$m_i = 2 H_i/\Omega$$

$$M = \text{diag} (m_1, m_2, \ldots, m_n) \tag{4.3.11}$$

$$k_{ij} = v_i v_j B_{ij} \cos(\delta_i - \delta_j)$$

$$k_{ii} = -\sum_{\substack{j=1 \\ j \neq 1}}^{n} k_{ij} .$$

and K is a matrix of entries k_{ij}. From (4.3.8) and (4.3.9) K is symmetric if B is symmetric which is true for transmission networks without phase shifters. Therefore, (4.3.10) has properties (4.2.15) and (4.2.16) and is a dynamic network. In general, B_{ij} are positive and $(\delta_i-\delta_j)$ are small, implying that K is a negative semidefinite matrix and the eigenvalues of A are nonpositive.

Let us illustrate the above procedure of approximating an electromechanical model as a linear dynamic network with the three machine power system in Figure 4.3.1 [47] and examine the approximation of neglecting damping and G_{ij} terms. The system parameters and operating conditions are given in the figure. With the assumption of constant impedance loads, the load buses in the system are eliminated using the Ward reduction procedure [60] to obtain the admittance matrix Y of the internal machine nodes.

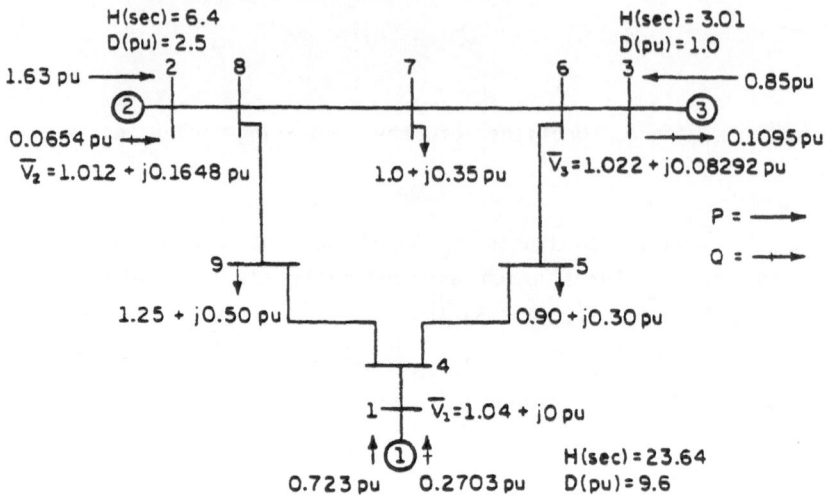

Line Parameters

Line	From	To	Resistance (pu)	Reactance (pu)	Charging/2 (pu)
1	1	4	0.	0.0576	0.
2	4	5	0.017	0.092	0.079
3	5	6	0.039	0.170	0.179
4	3	6	0.	0.0586	0.
5	6	7	0.0119	0.1008	0.1045
6	7	8	0.0085	0.072	0.0745
7	8	2	0.	0.0625	0.
8	8	9	0.032	0.161	0.153
9	9	4	0.01	0.085	0.088

Machine Parameters

Generator	Transient Reactance (pu)
1	0.0608
2	0.1198
3	0.1813

Figure 4.3.1   A three machine system as an
example of a dynamic network.

The inertia matrix is

$$M = \text{diag } (0.125, 0.0340, 0.0160),$$

(4.3.12)

the damping constants are

$$d_1 = 0.0255, \quad d_2 = 0.00663, \quad d_3 = 0.00265,$$

(4.3.13)

and the connection matrix is

$$\bar{K} = K + K_G,$$

(4.3.14)

where

$$K = \begin{bmatrix} -2.896 & 1.602 & 1.294 \\ 1.602 & -2.756 & 1.154 \\ 1.294 & 1.154 & -2.448 \end{bmatrix},$$

(4.3.15)

is due to the B_{ij} terms only and

$$K_G = \begin{bmatrix} 0.139 & -0.096 & -0.043 \\ 0.096 & -0.122 & 0.026 \\ 0.043 & -0.026 & -0.017 \end{bmatrix}$$

(4.3.16)

is due to the G_{ij} terms only. Note that the K_G entries are much smaller than the K entries.

The eigenvalues of the second order system (4.3.4), (4.3.5) including damping and G_{ij} terms, are

$$0, \quad -0.199, \quad -0.0975 \pm j8.699 \quad \text{and} \quad -0.0858 \pm j13.361.$$

Neglecting the K_G term, the eigenvalues of

$$\ddot{x} = M^{-1}D\dot{x} + M^{-1}Kx$$

(4.3.17)

are

$$0, \quad -0.198, \quad -0.0972 \pm j8.804, \quad \text{and} \quad -0.0858 \pm j13.403.$$

If both damping and K_G are neglected, then the eigenvalues of

$$\ddot{x} = M^{-1}Kx = \begin{bmatrix} -23.161 & 12.812 & 10.349 \\ 47.084 & -81.023 & 33.939 \\ 80.850 & 72.150 & -153.000 \end{bmatrix} x \qquad (4.3.18)$$

are

0, 0, $\pm j8.805$ and $\pm j13.404$.

Thus, (4.3.18) achieves excellent eigenvalue approximation of (4.3.4), (4.3.5). This three machine example will be used for illustrations of aggregation and coherency.

4.4 Areas, Internal and External Connections

For dynamic networks, an intuitively appealing reduction technique is to aggregate storage elements such that a subset of the dynamics is described by a small number of storage elements. To prepare for the aggregation discussion, we introduce the notion of areas, and internal and external connections. The aggregation result will be formulated in terms of these notions.

Definition 4.4.1: A partition of a dynamic network into r areas is the partition of the states of x into r sets such that every state x_i is assigned to one and only one set. The set containing the indices of the states in area α is denoted by J_α.

From this definition, the union of all the areas is the whole system while the intersection of any two areas is empty. An area can have only one state. Following this definition, a permissible two area partition of the RC-circuit example in Figure 4.2.1 is

$$\text{area 1} = \{x_1, x_2, x_3\}, \text{ area 2} = \{x_4, x_5\}, \qquad (4.4.1)$$

that is,

$$J_1 = \{1,2,3\} \quad , \quad J_2 = \{4,5\} . \qquad (4.4.2)$$

For each area partition, we construct an nxr partition matrix U whose rows represent the states and whose columns represent the areas as follows: the (i,α)-th entry of U is 1 if state x_i is in area α, and it is 0 otherwise. Thus, there is only one non-zero entry in each row of U. This entry is equal to 1. The number of non-zero entries in column α of U is equal to the number of states in area α. For the RC-circuit example, the partition (4.4.1) yields

$$U = \begin{bmatrix} 1 & 0 \\ 1 & 0 \\ 1 & 0 \\ 0 & 1 \\ 0 & 1 \end{bmatrix}, \tag{4.4.3}$$

whose 1 entries appear consecutively.

For convenience we put the states in area α into a vector x^α where the first state in x^α, x_1^α, is the <u>reference state</u> of the area. We also introduce the <u>sequential ordering</u> of $x = x_{seq}$ where

$$x_{seq} = \begin{bmatrix} x^1 \\ x^2 \\ \cdot \\ \cdot \\ \cdot \\ x^r \end{bmatrix}. \tag{4.4.4}$$

The U corresponding to x_{seq} is in the form

$$U_{seq} = \begin{bmatrix} u_1 & & & \\ & u_2 & & 0 \\ & & \cdot & \\ & & & \cdot \\ 0 & & & \cdot \\ & & & u_r \end{bmatrix} = \text{diag}(u_1, u_2, \ldots, u_r) \tag{4.4.5}$$

where the n_α-vector u_α is $[1\ 1\ \ldots\ 1]^T$. We have used the diagonal matrix notation in (4.4.5) to denote the zero and nonzero entries in U_{seq}. It does not require that u_i be square matrices. Accordingly, we denote

$$M = \text{diag}(M_1, M_2, \ldots, M_r) \tag{4.4.6}$$

where M_α is the inertia matrix of area α.

If x_1 and x_4 are the reference states of areas 1 and 2, respectively, in (4.4.1), then the sequential ordering is

$$x = x_{seq} = \begin{bmatrix} x^1 \\ x^2 \end{bmatrix} , \qquad (4.4.7)$$

where

$$x^1 = \begin{bmatrix} x_1 \\ x_2 \\ x_3 \end{bmatrix} ,$$

$$\qquad (4.4.8)$$

$$x^2 = \begin{bmatrix} x_4 \\ x_5 \end{bmatrix} .$$

and U of (4.4.3) is U_{seq}.

For an alternative notation, we use the reference states as the first r state variables x_r^1 and let the other states in each area appear consecutively in the last $(n-r)$ variables x_r^2. In other words,

$$x_r^1 = [x_1^1 , x_1^2 , \ldots , x_1^r]^T \qquad (4.4.9)$$

and x_r^2 consists of, in sequence, x^1, x^2, $\ldots$, x^r without the reference states. We call this form of expressing the state variables the reference ordering $x = x_{ref}$ and denote the corresponding U by U_{ref}. The inertia matrix is denoted by

$$M = diag(M_r^1, M_r^2) . \qquad (4.4.10)$$

For the partition (4.4.1) with x_1 and x_4 as the references, the reference ordering is

$$x_{ref} = \begin{bmatrix} x_r^1 \\ x_r^2 \end{bmatrix} \qquad (4.4.11)$$

where

$$x_r^1 = \begin{bmatrix} x_1 \\ x_4 \end{bmatrix} ,$$

$$\qquad (4.4.12)$$

$$x_r^2 = \begin{bmatrix} x_2 \\ x_3 \\ x_5 \end{bmatrix} ,$$

resulting in

$$U_{ref} = \begin{bmatrix} 1 & 0 \\ 0 & 1 \\ 1 & 0 \\ 1 & 0 \\ 0 & 1 \end{bmatrix} . \qquad (4.4.13)$$

Note that the first 2x2 submatrix of U_{ref} is an identity matrix. In general, using x_{ref}, U becomes

$$U_{ref} = \begin{bmatrix} I_r \\ \\ L_g \end{bmatrix} \qquad (4.4.14)$$

where I_r is an rxr identity matrix. L_g is called the <u>grouping matrix</u> and is given by

$$L_g = \begin{bmatrix} u_1' & & & \\ & u_2' & & 0 \\ & & \cdot & \\ & 0 & & \cdot & \\ & & & & u_r' \end{bmatrix} = \text{diag} (u_1', u_2', \ldots, u_r'), \qquad (4.4.15)$$

where the $(n_\alpha - 1)$ vector u_α' is $[1 \ 1 \ \ldots \ 1]^T$. When the reference states of the areas are given, L_g can be used to assign the other states to the areas. When $n_\alpha = 1$, that is, area α has only one state, u_α' is omitted in L_g, resulting in the α-th column being identically zero.

Some of the aggregation results are more easily shown with the x_{seq} ordering while others with the x_{ref} ordering. We will point out the notation used whenever a particular choice is preferred.

For an area partition, we classify the connections of a dynamic network into two types: internal connections which connect the states within the same area and external connections which connect the states from two different areas. That is, the connection with branch constant k_{ij} between the states x_i and x_j is called an internal connection if x_i and x_j are in the same area, and an external connection if x_i and x_j are in two different areas. The internal connections determine the flow between states in the same areas, while the external connections determine the flow between states in different areas. If x_i is in area α, then (4.2.1) for x_i can be rewritten as

$$m_i \dot{x}_i = \sum_{j,j \neq i}^{\alpha} k_{ij}(x_j - x_i) + \sum_{\substack{\beta=1 \\ \beta \neq \alpha}}^{r} \sum_j {}^{\beta} k_{ij}(x_j - x_i) , \tag{4.4.16}$$

where

$$\sum_j^{\alpha} = \text{summation over all } j \text{ in } J_\alpha. \tag{4.4.17}$$

Note that

$$\sum_{\substack{\beta=1 \\ \beta \neq \alpha}}^{r} \sum_j {}^{\beta} \tag{4.4.18}$$

is a double summation which sums all j in all area β not equal to α. In vector form, (4.4.16) becomes

$$M\dot{x} = K^I x + K^E x \tag{4.4.19}$$

where the internal connection matrix K^I is composed of internal k_{ij}'s, and the external connection matrix K^E is composed of external k_{ij}'s.

For the RC-circuit example with partition (4.4.1),

$$K^I = \begin{bmatrix} -k_{12} & k_{12} & 0 & 0 & 0 \\ k_{12} & -(k_{12}+k_{23}) & k_{23} & 0 & 0 \\ 0 & k_{23} & -k_{23} & 0 & 0 \\ 0 & 0 & 0 & -k_{45} & k_{45} \\ 0 & 0 & 0 & k_{45} & -k_{45} \end{bmatrix}, \tag{4.4.20}$$

$$
K^E = \begin{bmatrix}
-(k_{14}+k_{15}) & 0 & 0 & k_{14} & k_{15} \\
0 & -k_{25} & 0 & 0 & k_{25} \\
0 & 0 & -k_{34} & k_{34} & 0 \\
k_{14} & 0 & k_{34} & -(k_{14}+k_{34}) & 0 \\
k_{15} & k_{25} & 0 & 0 & -(k_{15}+k_{25})
\end{bmatrix} .
\qquad (4.4.21)
$$

By construction, it follows that

$$
K^I + K^E = K. \qquad (4.4.22)
$$

With x_{seq} as the state variables, K^I is block diagonal (see for example (4.4.20)). Furthermore, each of the α-th diagonal blocks K_α^I of K^I has property (4.2.16) with $u=u_\alpha$, that is

$$
K_\alpha^I u_\alpha = 0, \qquad \alpha = 1,2,\ldots,n. \qquad (4.4.23)
$$

Therefore, the rank of K^I is $(n-r)$ where r is the number of areas. Combining (4.4.23) for all α we obtain the following.

<u>Lemma 4.4.1</u>: The columns of the participation matrix U span the null space of K^I, that is,

$$
K^I U = 0. \qquad (4.4.24)
$$

<u>Proof</u>: Writing (4.4.23) in matrix form, we obtain

$$
K^I U_{seq} = 0. \qquad (4.4.25)
$$

The result (4.4.24) for any state ordering is obtained by performing an appropriate permutation. $\square$

The rank of K^E is at most $(n-1)$ as $K^E u=0$. Since K is symmetric, K^I and K^E are also symmetric. Thus both K^I and K^E have properties (4.2.15) and (4.2.16).

As will be shown in the next section, the separation of K into K^I and K^E simplifies the aggregability conditions and aids in their interpretation.

4.5 Area Aggregation

Once the areas of a dynamic network have been determined by a geographic, economic or dynamic criterion, the next task is the aggregation, that is, the representation of each area by a single aggregate variable. A physical aggregation of this type is to sum up the storage quantities ξ_i in the same area as

$$\zeta_\alpha = \sum_i^\alpha \xi_i \; . \tag{4.5.1}$$

These aggregate quantities are assumed to be stored in aggregate elements whose inertias are defined to be

$$m_{a\alpha} = \sum_i^\alpha m_i \; . \tag{4.5.2}$$

Letting y_α be the potential across the α-th aggregate element, we obtain for first order dynamic networks

$$y_\alpha = \zeta_\alpha/m_{a\alpha} = \sum_i^\alpha \xi_i / \sum_i^\alpha m_i = \sum_i^\alpha m_i x_i / \sum_i^\alpha m_i . \tag{4.5.3}$$

The y_α variables are commonly known as the center of inertia variables.

We now investigate conditions under which the aggregate variables decouple and form a subsystem by themselves. Using the partition matrix U, the aggregations (4.5.1) and (4.5.3) can be written in vector form as

$$\zeta = U^T \xi \; , \tag{4.5.4}$$

$$y = C_a x \; , \tag{4.5.5}$$

where

$$C_a = M_a^{-1} U^T M, \; M_a = U^T M U \; , \tag{4.5.6}$$

and the superscript T denotes matrix transposition. Note that the matrix M_a is a diagonal matrix whose (α,α)-th entry is the sum of the inertias in area α. Furthermore

$$C_a U = I_r \tag{4.5.7}$$

where I_r is the rxr identity matrix.

In the RC-circuit example with partition (4.4.1), we aggregate the charges in capacitors 1, 2 and 3 and capacitors 4 and 5 as

$$q_{a1} = q_1 + q_2 + q_3, \ q_{a2} = q_4 + q_5 , \tag{4.5.8}$$

and let the capacitances of the aggregate capacitors be

$$C_{a1} = C_1 + C_2 + C_3, \ C_{a2} = C_4 + C_5 , \tag{4.5.9}$$

such that

$$M_a = \text{diag} \ (C_{a1}, C_{a2}) . \tag{4.5.10}$$

Thus, the transformation (4.5.5) is defined by

$$C_a = \begin{bmatrix} C_1/C_{a1} & C_2/C_{a1} & C_3/C_{a1} & 0 & 0 \\ 0 & 0 & 0 & C_4/C_{a2} & C_5/C_{a2} \end{bmatrix}, \tag{4.5.11}$$

where the y variables are the averages of the capacitor voltages in each area weighted according to the capacitances.

From (4.5.5), we obtain

$$\dot{y} = C_a \dot{x} = C_a M^{-1} Kx . \tag{4.5.12}$$

For the aggregate variables y to be decoupled from the other variables, that is,

$$\dot{y} = Fy = F C_a x, \tag{4.5.13}$$

we require F to satisfy

$$F C_a = C_a M^{-1} K. \tag{4.5.14}$$

Equation (4.5.14) is the aggregation condition stated in [2]. If F satisfies (4.5.14), then the eigenvalues of F are the observable eigenvalues of the pair $(M^{-1}K, \ C_a)$, and the row space of C_a is the left eigenspace of $M^{-1}K$ corresponding to those eigenvalues which are also the eigenvalues of F.

In (4.5.14), the aggregation condition is formulated in terms of the left eigenspace of A. For dynamic networks, the same condition can be formulated in terms of the right eigenspace of A due to the symmetry of K.

Theorem 4.5.1: A first order dynamic network $\dot{x}=M^{-1}Kx$ is aggregable with respect to $y = C_a x$ if and only if the columns of U span an r-dimensional eigenspace of $M^{-1}K$. The resulting aggregate model is

$$\dot{y} = M_a^{-1}K_a y = A_a y, \qquad (4.5.15)$$

where

$$K_a = U^T K^E U . \qquad (4.5.16)$$

Proof: Substituting (4.5.6) into (4.5.14) we obtain

$$FM_a^{-1}U^T M = M_a^{-1}U^T MM^{-1}K \qquad (4.5.17)$$

which can be transposed into

$$MUM_a^{-1}F^T = KUM_a^{-1} \qquad (4.5.18)$$

because K is symmetric. Pre-multiplying (4.5.18) with M^{-1} and post-multiplying it with M_a, we obtain

$$U(M_a^{-1}F^T M_a) = M^{-1}KU , \qquad (4.5.19)$$

that is, the columns of U span the eigenspace of $M^{-1}K$ corresponding to the eigenvalues of $M_a^{-1}F^T M_a$. To show (4.5.12), we post-multiply (4.5.17) by U, which yields

$$F = M_a^{-1}U^T KU = M_a^{-1} U^T K^E U = M_a^{-1} K_a = A_a \qquad (4.5.20)$$

because $K^I U = 0$. □

Consider the RC-circuit example with partition (4.4.1). Let $C_i = c$, $k_{34} = k_{25} = 2p$ and $k_{15} = k_{14} = p$, that is,

$$M = \text{diag} (c,c,c,c,c) , \qquad (4.5.21)$$

$$K^E = \begin{bmatrix} -2p & 0 & 0 & p & p \\ 0 & -2p & 0 & 0 & 2p \\ 0 & 0 & -2p & 2p & 0 \\ p & 0 & 2p & -3p & 0 \\ p & 2p & 0 & 0 & -3p \end{bmatrix} . \qquad (4.5.22)$$

Note that we do not have to specify the internal connections. For these parameters, U from (4.4.2) is an eigenbasis matrix of the eigenvalues 0 and $-5p/c$ since

$$M^{-1}KU = (K^E/c) \begin{bmatrix} 1 & 0 \\ 1 & 0 \\ 1 & 0 \\ 0 & 1 \\ 0 & 1 \end{bmatrix} = (1/c) \begin{bmatrix} -2p & 2p \\ -2p & 2p \\ -2p & 2p \\ 3p & -3p \\ 3p & -3p \end{bmatrix} = U \begin{bmatrix} -2p/c & 2p/c \\ 3p/c & -3p/c \end{bmatrix} = UA_a . \qquad (4.5.23)$$

Therefore, the RC-circuit example is aggregable with respect to

$$y = C_a x = \begin{bmatrix} 1/3 & 1/3 & 1/3 & 0 & 0 \\ 0 & 0 & 0 & 1/2 & 1/2 \end{bmatrix} x , \qquad (4.5.24)$$

and

$$\dot{y} = A_a y = M_a^{-1} K_a y \qquad (4.5.25)$$

where M_a is given in (4.5.10) and

$$K_a = U^T K^E U = \begin{bmatrix} -6p & 6p \\ 6p & -6p \end{bmatrix} . \qquad (4.5.26)$$

The interpretations of the subspace result in Theorem 4.5.1 are given in the following corollaries.

Corollary 4.5.1: A first-order dynamic network $\dot{x} = M^{-1}Kx$ is aggregable with respect to $y = C_a x$ if and only if the external connections satisfy

$$M^{-1}K^E U = UM_a^{-1}K_a . \qquad (4.5.27)$$

The proof of (4.5.27) follows from the substitution of (4.5.20) into (4.5.19). The aggregability condition (4.5.27) depends on the external connections only.

Thus, changing the internal connections does not affect aggregability. In the RC-circuit example, the aggregability condition is satisfied by (4.5.23).

Corollary 4.5.2: The aggregate model (4.5.15) is a dynamic network of r nodes with the inertia matrix M_a and the connection matrix K_a.

Proof: M_a is diagonal and positive definite. The symmetry of K_a follows directly from (4.5.16) and hence K_a has property (4.2.15). The (α,β)-th entry of K_a is the summation of all the (i,j)-th entries of K^E where i is in J_α and j is in J_β. Furthermore,

$$K_a u_r = U^T K^E U u_r = U^T K^E u = 0 \qquad\qquad (4.5.28)$$

for an r-vector $u_r = [1\ 1\ \ldots\ 1]^T$. Therefore, K_a has property (4.2.16) and hence (4.5.15) is a dynamic network. □

Corollary 4.5.2 states that the aggregate model (4.5.15) has the same structure as the original dynamic network. The inertias of the aggregate model are the sum of the inertias in each area. The connection between y_α and y_β is the sum of all the connections between the states in the areas α and β, and the matrix K_a has an interpretation of an aggregate connection matrix. Furthermore, K_a always contains the zero eigenvalue. The aggregate model of the RC-circuit is shown in Figure 4.5.1 where the aggregate capacitors are now of capacitances $C_{a1} = 3c$ and $C_{a2} = 2c$ and are connected through an admittance of $1/R_a = 6p$ which is the sum of all the external admittances.

In the remainder of this section, we give further interpretation of the aggregation result (4.5.27).

Let us denote $(s_i)_\alpha$ as the sum of external connections of the state x_i in area β with all the states in area α. Corollary 4.5.1 is restated as follows.

Corollary 4.5.3: A dynamic network is aggregable with respect to $y = C_a x$ if and only if the external connections and the inertias satisfy

$$(s_i)_\alpha/m_i = (s_j)_\alpha/m_j \qquad\qquad (4.5.29)$$

for all areas α, and x_i and x_j in area β, $\beta \neq \alpha$.

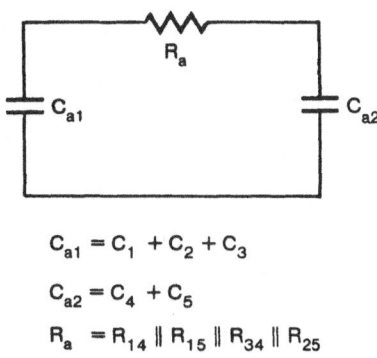

$$C_{a1} = C_1 + C_2 + C_3$$

$$C_{a2} = C_4 + C_5$$

$$R_a = R_{14} \parallel R_{15} \parallel R_{34} \parallel R_{25}$$

Figure 4.5.1 Aggregate RC-circuit of Figure 4.2.1. C_{a1} is formed by aggregating C_1, C_2 and C_3, and C_{a2} is formed by C_4 and C_5. R_a is the parallel combination of R_{14}, R_{15}, R_{34} and R_{35}.

The result (4.5.29) follows immediately by writing (4.5.27) in scalar form. It is satisfied by the RC-circuit example (4.5.4), (4.5.5) as

$$(s_1)_2/m_1 = (s_2)_2/m_2 = (s_3)_2/m_3 = (s_4)_1/m_4 = (s_5)_1/m_5 = 2p/c \ . \tag{4.5.30}$$

This condition has physical meaning in dynamic networks. In RC-circuits with capacitance m_i and admittance $(s_i)_\alpha$, (4.5.29) implies that with respect to the aggregate modes, the voltage of the capacitors in the same area will change at the same rate for any change in another area. In mass-spring systems with mass m_i and spring constant $(s_i)_\alpha$, (4.5.29) implies that masses in the same area have the same acceleration with respect to the aggregate modes for any change in another area.

Corollary 4.5.3 can be derived using an alternative approach. Using the reference ordering of state variables $x = x_{ref}$, we rewrite (4.5.5) as

$$y = M_a^{-1} U^T M x$$

$$= M_a^{-1} \ [I_r \ \ L_g^T] \begin{bmatrix} M_r^1 & 0 \\ 0 & M_r^2 \end{bmatrix} \begin{bmatrix} x_r^1 \\ x_r^2 \end{bmatrix}, \tag{4.5.31}$$

and introduce the transformation

$$
\begin{bmatrix} y \\ x_r^2 \end{bmatrix} = \begin{bmatrix} M_a^{-1}M_r^1 & M_a^{-1}L_g^TM_r^2 \\ 0 & I_{n-r} \end{bmatrix} \begin{bmatrix} x_r^1 \\ x_r^2 \end{bmatrix}.
$$

(4.5.32)

The inverse transformation of (4.5.32) is

$$
\begin{bmatrix} x_r^1 \\ x_r^2 \end{bmatrix} = \begin{bmatrix} (M_r^1)^{-1} & (M_r^1)^{-1}L_g^TM_r^2 \\ 0 & I_{n-r} \end{bmatrix} \begin{bmatrix} y \\ x_r^2 \end{bmatrix}.
$$

(4.5.33)

For the y variables to decouple from x_r^2 when (4.5.32) is applied to the first order dynamic network (4.2.10), we require that

$$
M_a^{-1}[I_r \; L_g^T] M \quad M^{-1}(K^I + K^E) \begin{bmatrix} -(M_r^1)^{-1}L_g^TM_r^2 \\ I_{n-r} \end{bmatrix} = 0.
$$

(4.5.34)

Because K^I is symmetric, $[I_r \; L_g^T]K^I = 0$. Thus the term K^I in (4.5.34) is eliminated. We now partition K^E into

$$
K^E = \begin{bmatrix} K_{11}^E & K_{12}^E \\ K_{21}^E & K_{22}^E \end{bmatrix}
$$

(4.5.35)

such that K_{11}^E and K_{22}^E are square matrices of dimensions $r \times r$ and $(n-r) \times (n-r)$, respectively. Then (4.5.34) pre-multiplied by M_a and post-multiplied by $(M_r^2)^{-1}$ becomes

$$
-K_{11}^E(M_r^1)^{-1}L_g^T - L_g^TK_{21}^E(M_r^1)^{-1}L_g^T + K_{12}^E(M_r^2)^{-1} + L_g^TK_{22}^E (M_r^2)^{-1} = 0
$$

(4.5.36)

which is a Riccati equation for L_g similar to that of (2.3.19). The results of Corollary 4.5.3 is obtained by writing (4.5.36) in scalar form.

We conclude this section by deriving the aggregation condition for a first order dynamic network expressed in the storage form. We first observe that

$$
(K^I \; M^{-1})(MU) = 0
$$

(4.5.37)

that is, the null space of K^IM^{-1} is the subspace spanned by the columns of MU. The matrix MU has the same zero entries as U, but the 1 entries in U are replaced by appropriate inertias. For example, using the capacitor charges as the states for the RC-circuit example, the partition (4.4.1) yields

$$
MU = \begin{bmatrix} m_1 & 0 \\ m_2 & 0 \\ m_3 & 0 \\ 0 & m_4 \\ 0 & m_5 \end{bmatrix} . \tag{4.5.38}
$$

__Corollary 4.5.4:__ A dynamic network in the storage form $\dot{\xi}=KM^{-1}\xi$ is aggregable with respect to $\zeta = U^T\xi$ if and only if it is aggregable with respect to $y = C_a x$. The aggregate model is

$$
\dot{\zeta} = K_a M_a^{-1} \zeta \quad , \tag{4.5.39}
$$

where K_a and M_a are given by (4.5.16) and (4.5.6).

__Proof:__ Since $\zeta = M_a y$, and U is an eigenbasis matrix of $M^{-1}K$ if and only if MU is an eigenbasis matrix of KM^{-1}, the result of Corollary 4.5.4 follows from Theorem 4.5.1. □

In the storage form, we aggregate the storage quantities to form ζ. Returning to the RC-circuit example, the aggregate model in storage form (4.5.39) is identical to the model in Figure 4.5.1 derived from the potential form. However, the aggregate model is obtained by summing the charges in capacitors in each area. The structural conditions for aggregation are the same using either approach.

4.6 Second Order Dynamic Networks

The aggregation results of Theorem 4.5.1 and Corollaries 4.5.1 to 4.5.4 are also applicable to second order dynamic networks (4.2.19) without damping

$$
\ddot{x} = M^{-1}Kx . \tag{4.6.1}
$$

For second order dynamic networks, the aggregation of the stored quantities $\xi_i = m_i \dot{x}_i$ into

$$\zeta_\alpha = \sum_i^\alpha \xi_i = \sum_i^\alpha m_i \dot{x}_i \qquad (4.6.2)$$

and the inertias m_i into

$$m_{a\alpha} = \sum_i^\alpha m_i \qquad (4.6.3)$$

defines the potential variable y_α across the α-th aggregate element to be

$$\dot{y}_\alpha = \zeta_\alpha / m_{a\alpha} = \sum_i^\alpha \xi_i / m_{a\alpha} = \sum_i^\alpha m_i \dot{x}_i / m_{a\alpha} , \qquad (4.6.4)$$

which yields

$$y_\alpha = \sum_i^\alpha m_i x_i / m_{a\alpha} \quad . \qquad (4.6.5)$$

The aggregation result for (4.6.1) follows directly from re-deriving the proof of Theorem 4.5.1 and Corollary 4.5.1 for

$$y = C_a x = (U^T M U)^{-1} U^T M x . \qquad (4.6.6)$$

<u>Corollary 4.6.1</u>: The second order dynamic network (4.6.1) is aggregable with respect to $y = C_a x$ if and only if the aggregability condition (4.5.27)

$$M^{-1} K^E U = U M_a^{-1} K_a \qquad (4.6.7)$$

is satisfied. The aggregate model is

$$\ddot{y} = M_a^{-1} K_a y \qquad (4.6.8)$$

where $M_a = U^T M U$ and $K_a = U^T K^E U$ are given by (4.5.6) and (4.5.16), respectively.

The aggregability condition (4.5.27) is likewise extendable to second order dynamic networks with damping

$$M\ddot{x} = -D\dot{x} + Kx , \qquad (4.6.9)$$

where D is the diagonal matrix of damping coefficients

$$D = \text{diag}(d_1, d_2, \ldots, d_n) \; . \tag{4.6.10}$$

For (4.6.9) we assume the following.

<u>Assumption 4.6.1</u>: The damping within each area is uniform; that is,

$$d_i/m_i = d_j/m_j, \quad \text{for all } i, j \text{ in } J_\alpha, \; \alpha = 1,2,\ldots,r \; . \tag{4.6.11}$$

Under this assumption, if we define the aggregate damping coefficient for area α to be

$$d_{a\alpha} = \sum_i^\alpha d_i \; , \quad \alpha = 1,2,\ldots,r \; , \tag{4.6.12}$$

then

$$d_{a\alpha}/m_{a\alpha} = d_i/m_i, \quad \text{for all } i \text{ in } J_\alpha, \tag{4.6.13}$$

holds in each area $\alpha = 1,2,\ldots,r$.

<u>Theorem 4.6.1</u>: Let the second order dynamic network (4.6.9) satisfy Assumption 4.6.1. Then (4.6.9) is aggregable with respect to $y = C_a x$ if and only if the aggregability condition (4.6.7) is satisfied. The aggregate model is

$$M_a \ddot{y} = -D_a \dot{y} + K_a y \; , \tag{4.6.14}$$

where

$$D_a = \text{diag}(d_{a1}, d_{a2}, \ldots, d_{ar}) \; . \tag{4.6.15}$$

<u>Proof</u>: In the aggregate variable, (4.6.9) becomes

$$\ddot{y} = C_a \ddot{x} = -C_a M^{-1} D \dot{x} + C_a M^{-1} K x \tag{4.6.16}$$

which simplifies to

$$\ddot{y} = -C_a M^{-1} D \dot{x} + M_a^{-1} K_a y \tag{4.6.17}$$

if and only if the aggregability condition (4.6.7) is satisfied. In the sequential ordering of state x,

$$C_a = \text{diag}(C_{a1}, C_{a2}, \ldots, C_{ar}) \tag{4.6.18}$$

and

$$M^{-1}D = \text{diag}(M_1^{-1}D_1,\ M_2^{-1}D_2,\ \ldots,\ M_r^{-1}D_r) \tag{4.6.19}$$

where $M_\alpha^{-1}D_\alpha$ is an $n_\alpha \times n_\alpha$ identity matrix multiplied by $d_{a\alpha}$, resulting in

$$C_a M^{-1}D = M_a^{-1}D_a C_a \ . \tag{4.6.20}$$

The substitution of (4.6.20) into (4.6.17) proves (4.6.14). □

To formulate an aggregability condition in terms of an eigenspace, like the result in Theorem 4.5.1 for first order dynamic networks, we let

$$x_1' = x \ , \quad x_2' = \dot{x}$$

and write (4.6.9) as

$$\begin{bmatrix} \dot{x}_1' \\ \dot{x}_2' \end{bmatrix} = \begin{bmatrix} 0 & I_n \\ -M^{-1}K & -M^{-1}D \end{bmatrix} \begin{bmatrix} x_1' \\ x_2' \end{bmatrix} \ . \tag{4.6.21}$$

Then

$$\begin{bmatrix} 0 & I_n \\ -M^{-1}K & -M^{-1}D \end{bmatrix} \begin{bmatrix} U & 0 \\ 0 & U \end{bmatrix} = \begin{bmatrix} 0 & U \\ M^{-1}KU & -M^{-1}DU \end{bmatrix}$$

$$= \begin{bmatrix} 0 & U \\ UM_a^{-1}K_a & -UM_a^{-1}D_a \end{bmatrix} = \begin{bmatrix} U & 0 \\ 0 & U \end{bmatrix} \begin{bmatrix} 0 & I_r \\ M_a^{-1}K_a & -M_a^{-1}D_a \end{bmatrix} \tag{4.6.22}$$

where

$$M^{-1}KU = UM_a^{-1}K_a \tag{4.6.23}$$

is due to the aggregability condition (4.6.7) and

$$M^{-1}DU = UM_a^{-1}D_a \tag{4.6.24}$$

is due to Assumption 4.6.1. Thus, diag(U,U) is an eigenbasis matrix of (4.6.21) corresponding to the aggregate modes of (4.6.14). This result is consistent with the area aggregation concept since if x_i and x_j are in the same area, $\dot{x}_i$ and $\dot{x}_j$ are also in the same area.

The term D_a has the interpretation of an aggregate damping matrix for the areas and is crucial in the study of the stability of the aggregate model. When D is zero, Theorem 4.6.1 reduces to the aggregability condition of Corollary 4.6.1. Models in which Assumptions 4.6.1 is not exactly satisfied are treated by perturbation analysis in the next section. A particular case is when D is small, as illustrated in by the three machine example in Figure 4.3.1.

It should be noted that our notion of area-uniformity is less restrictive than the commonly made assumption of system-wide uniformity of damping,

$$d_i/m_i = d_j/m_j , \quad \text{for all } i, j ,$$ (4.6.25)

which implies that

$$d_{a\alpha}/m_{a\alpha} = d_{a\beta}/m_{a\beta} , \quad \text{for all } \alpha, \beta .$$ (4.6.26)

Theorem 4.6.1, of course, encompasses this special case.

4.7 Perturbation Analysis

Dynamic network models for real systems are often obtained through approximations. For example, in electromechanical models of power systems, the damping and conductance terms are neglected to achieve the symmetry of K. Furthermore, real systems seldom satisfy the aggregability condition exactly. This section examines aggregation when the connection matrix has a nonsymmetric part and its symmetric part approximately satisfies the aggregability condition. The three machine system in Section 4.3 will be used as an example.

We separate the connection matrix K into three parts

$$K = K^I + K^E + \epsilon K_\epsilon$$ (4.7.1)

such that K^I and K^E are the symmetrical internal and external connection matrices, K^E satisfies the aggregability condition (4.5.27), and ϵ is a small parameter. The term ϵK_ϵ consists of the nonsymmetric portions of the internal and external connections, and the external connections that do not satisfy the aggregability condition (4.5.27). We assume that the perturbed matrix K has property (6.2.16). Hence, K_ϵ also has property (6.2.16), that is $K_\epsilon u=0$.

Since $K = K^I + K^E$ is symmetric, $M^{-1}K$ has a full set of eigenvectors. It is well known [61, 52] that an $O(\epsilon)$ perturbation in $M^{-1}K$ will result in an

$O(\epsilon)$ perturbation in the eigenvalues and eigenvectors of $M^{-1}K$. That is, there exists

$$U_\epsilon = U + O(\epsilon) \qquad (4.7.2)$$

$$F_\epsilon = M_a^{-1}K_a + O(\epsilon) \qquad (4.7.3)$$

such that

$$M^{-1}K U_\epsilon = U_\epsilon F_\epsilon . \qquad (4.7.4)$$

Then following the steps in the proof of Theorem 4.5.1, we can show that a first order or second order dynamic network with K of (4.7.1) is aggregable with respect to

$$y_\epsilon = C_{a\epsilon}x \qquad (4.7.5)$$

where

$$C_{a\epsilon} = (U_\epsilon^T M U_\epsilon)^{-1} U_\epsilon^T M . \qquad (4.7.6)$$

Because of (4.7.2), $C_{a\epsilon}$ can be expressed as

$$C_{a\epsilon} = C_a + O(\epsilon). \qquad (4.7.7)$$

The approximation (4.7.7) implies that we can aggregate a dynamic network satisfying (4.7.1) with respect to $y = C_a x$ while only incurring an $O(\epsilon)$ error. For first order dynamic network,

$$\dot{y} = C_a\dot{x} = C_a M^{-1}(K^I + K^E + \epsilon K_\epsilon)x$$

$$= M_a^{-1}U^T K^E x + \epsilon C_a M^{-1}K_\epsilon x. \qquad (4.7.8)$$

Using the relation (4.5.27)

$$U^T K^E = K_a M_a^{-1} U^T M = K_a C_a, \qquad (4.7.9)$$

we obtain

$$\dot{y} = M_a^{-1} K_a \, y + \epsilon C_a M^{-1} K_\epsilon x \ .$$

(4.7.10)

<u>Theorem 4.7.1</u>: If the eigenvalues of K are nonpositive, then the system

$$\dot{y}' = M_a^{-1} K_a \, y', \ y'(0) = y(0)$$

(4.7.11)

approximates (4.7.10) to $0(\epsilon)$, that is,

$$y'(t_d) = y(t_d) + 0(\epsilon)$$

(4.7.12)

for all $t_d \geq 0$.

<u>Proof</u>: Letting $e = y' - y$, we obtain

$$\dot{e} = M_a^{-1} K_a \, e - \epsilon C_a M^{-1} K_\epsilon x, \ e(0) = 0 \quad .$$

(4.7.13)

For the theorem to hold, it is sufficient that $|C_a M^{-1} K_\epsilon x| \leq c_1 e^{-c_2 t_d}$ where c_1 and c_2 are positive constants. This is satisfied because the part of $x(t_d)$ which is not exponentially decaying is in the null space of $C_a M^{-1} K_\epsilon$ in view of (4.7.1) and (4.2.16). $\square$

For second order dynamic networks with poorly damped oscillatory modes, we express the small damping as ϵD and obtain the aggregate damping $\epsilon d_{a\alpha}$ for each area. Then we separate D into

$$D = \overline{D} + \tilde{D}$$

(4.7.14)

where

$$\overline{D} = \text{diag}\{\overline{d}_1, \ \overline{d}_2, \ \ldots, \ \overline{d}_n\} \ ,$$

(4.7.15)

$$\overline{d}_i = m_i (d_{a\alpha}/m_{a\alpha}) \ , \quad i \text{ in } J_\alpha \ .$$

(4.7.16)

Thus, $\overline{D}$ satisfies Assumption 4.6.1, and without $\tilde{D}$, the area damping is uniform.

In the aggregate variables $y = C_a x$, the second order dynamic network

$$M\ddot{x} = - \epsilon(\overline{D} + \tilde{D})\dot{x} + (K^I + K^E + \epsilon K_\epsilon)x$$

(4.7.17)

becomes

$$M_a \ddot{y} = - \epsilon D_a \dot{y} + K_a y - \epsilon C_a M^{-1} \tilde{D} x + \epsilon C_a M^{-1} K_\epsilon x. \tag{4.7.18}$$

Neglecting the x terms whose contributions are of $O(\epsilon)$ in (4.7.18) we obtain

$$M_a \ddot{y}' = - \epsilon D_a \dot{y}' + K_a y' \quad , \quad y'(0) = y(0) . \tag{4.7.19}$$

The states $y'(t_d)$ approximate $y(t_d)$ to $O(\epsilon)$ only for t_d less than a finite T since (4.7.18) is poorly damped.

Theorem 4.6.1 and (4.7.18) imply that when a dynamic network satisfies the aggregability condition approximately, the aggregate model (4.7.11) or (4.7.19) can still be used to represent the motions between the areas.

To illustrate the perturbation results, we partition the three machine system in Figure 4.3.1 into area $1 = \{x_1\}$ and area $2 = \{x_2, x_3\}$. We separate the external connection matrix into

$$\begin{bmatrix} -2.896 & 1.602 & 1.294 \\ 1.602 & -1.602 & 0 \\ 1.294 & 0 & -2.448 \end{bmatrix}$$

$$= \begin{bmatrix} -2.896 & 1.970 & 0.926 \\ 1.970 & -1.970 & 0 \\ 0.926 & 0 & -0.926 \end{bmatrix} + \begin{bmatrix} 0 & -0.368 & 0.368 \\ -0.368 & 0.368 & 0 \\ 0.368 & 0 & -0.368 \end{bmatrix}$$

$$= K^E + \epsilon K_\epsilon , \tag{4.7.20}$$

such that K^E satisfy the aggregability condition (4.5.27). The aggregate model using K^E is

$$\ddot{x} = M_a^{-1} K_a x$$

$$= \begin{bmatrix} 0.125 & 0 \\ 0 & 0.050 \end{bmatrix}^{-1} \begin{bmatrix} -2.896 & 2.896 \\ 2.896 & -2.896 \end{bmatrix} x \tag{4.7.21}$$

whose eigenvalues are

0, 0 and $\pm j9.005$,

which approximate well the eigenvalues

0, 0 and $\pm j8.805$

of (4.3.18) when the G_{ij} terms are neglected.

To account for the damping, we compute the aggregate damping coefficients

$$d_{a1} = d_1 = 0.0255$$

$$d_{a2} = d_2 + d_3 = 0.00928 \; .$$

(4.7.22)

Incorporating this damping into (4.7.21) we obtain the eigenvalues as

0, -0.199 and $-0.0956 \pm j9.004$,

which approximate well the eigenvalues

0, -0.198, $-0.0972 \pm j8.804$

of (4.3.17). The result is not surprising since the damping in area 2 is almost uniform:

$$d_2/m_2 = 0.195 \quad , \quad d_3/m_3 = 0.166 \quad , \quad d_{a2}/m_{a2} = 0.186 \; .$$

(4.7.23)

4.8 Conclusions

We have used the center of inertia variables to develop an aggregation method for both first and second order dynamic networks. The spirit of the method follows the concept of Simon and Ando [50] that aggregation be based on physical phenomena, and thus is different from the analytical approaches in [2, 56]. The method leads directly to a set of structural conditions under which a dynamic network will be aggregable. A coherency interpretation of the aggregability condition will be given in the next chapter.

The payoff of the aggregation method will be more apparent in Chapter 6 when it is used to separate time-scales and in Chapter 7 when it is applied to nonlinear dynamic networks.

CHAPTER 5

COHERENCY AND AREA IDENTIFICATION

5.1 Introduction

The first step toward aggregating a dynamic network is to find its areas. One method is to use the structural condition on the external connections and inertias given in Corollary 4.5.3. This method would require a combinatorial search on all the connections and inertias in a dynamic network. Instead, this chapter develops a coherency approach for finding the areas which does not use a combinatorial search. We give an unobservable subspace characterization of coherency, which when combined with the results in Chapter 4 forms an analytical framework for coherency-based aggregation. This characterization also leads to the development of an area identification algorithm suitable for large scale dynamic networks.

An area aggregation criterion, called coherency, has emerged from power system practice. It has been observed that in multimachine transients after a disturbance some synchronous machines have the tendency to "swing together" [51,41]. Such coherent machines are grouped into "coherent areas" which are then represented by "equivalent machines." Considerable research effort is being devoted to analytical formulation of coherency and coherency-based aggregation. It is characterized by two main approaches, one in which disturbance is considered explicitly [17,30,36,41,45,65], and the other which focuses on coherency properties independent of disturbances [3,4,6,27,44,64]. In this chapter, we follow the approach in [4,27,64] which requires the states to be coherent with respect to a selected set of modes σ_a of the system. This approach allows coherency to be examined in terms of the rows of an eigenbasis matrix V which can be used to find coherent groups of states. Based on V, we examine the conditions that local dynamics in coherent groups can be decoupled. For dynamic networks, the total number of coherent groups and non-coherent states is equal to the number of modes in σ_a if and only if the areas formed by the coherent groups are aggregable. Such results analytically justify and make systematic the empirical coherency-based aggregation procedure used in power system model simplications. They also extend the procedure to first and second order dynamic networks where coherent groups can be used as areas for aggregation.

In real dynamic networks where the states are seldom exactly coherent, we identify near-coherent states using a coherency grouping algorithm [3]. To display clearly the coherent groups, we examine the rows of an eigenbasis matrix V. The selection of the reference states and the groupings is posed as a minimization problem. The coherency grouping algorithm is illustrated by two realistic power system models of the northeastern and western portions of the United States.

The organization of this chapter is as follows. Section 5.2 provides characterizations of the proposed coherency criterion in terms of time response, unobservability, eigenspace and controllability conditions. In Section 5.3, the conditions on V for localizability and decomposability are established. Section 5.4 proceeds with the use of coherent groups as areas for aggregation in dynamic networks. Section 5.5 examines the identification of near-coherent states and Section 5.6 develops the grouping algorithm. The area identification of the two power systems is in Section 5.7.

As in Chapter 4, we use t_d as an arbitrary time variable since the results in this chapter do not depend on time-scales.

5.2 Coherency

Most coherency criteria [17,20,30,31,41,45,65] result in coherent states that are disturbance dependent because they simultaneously treat the following two tasks:
  a.   select the modes which are excited by a given disturbance or a set of disturbances,
  b.   find the states with the same content of disturbed modes.

Our approach addresses only the second task; that is, how to find coherent states for a given set of r modes, and how to characterize analytical properties of systems possessing coherency. The selection of the r slowest modes which results in structurally robust coherent groups will be addressed in Chapter 6.

For the case when disturbances are modeled as initial conditions, we obtain coherency results for linear systems in the form

$$\dot{x} = Ax \quad , \quad x(0) = x_0, \tag{5.2.1}$$

where the state x is an n-vector. Let

$$\sigma_a = \{\lambda_1, \lambda_2, \ldots, \lambda_r\} \, , \tag{5.2.2}$$

where λ_i is an eigenvalue of A, denote a set of r modes of A, and σ_a^c denote the set of (n-r) modes of A other than σ_a. We assume that A has a full set of eigenvectors corresponding to σ_a. The coherency results are directly applicable to oscillatory systems modeled as second order linear systems in the form

$$\ddot{x} = Ax \quad , \quad x(0) = x_0, \tag{5.2.3}$$

if we define

$$\sigma_a = \{\pm\sqrt{\lambda_1}, \ \pm\sqrt{\lambda_2}, \ \ldots, \ \pm\sqrt{\lambda_r}\} \quad . \tag{5.2.4}$$

Our definition of coherency is as follows [4,27,64].

Definition 5.2.1: The states x_i and x_j of (5.2.1) are coherent with respect to σ_a if and only if x_0 being in the σ_a-eigenspace implies

$$z_k(t_d) = x_j(t_d) - x_i(t_d) = g_k x(t_d) = 0 \tag{5.2.5}$$

for all t_d, where the only non-zero entries of the row vector g_k are its i-th entry -1 and its j-th entry 1.

A common situation where Definition 5.2.1 is useful is when σ_a are the dominant modes and σ_a^c are high frequency and well-damped modes which are neglected in long term studies. Thus, if we neglect the response due to the σ_a^c-modes which are not dominant, then z_k is zero. Concentrating on the σ_a-modes allows us to study coherency independent of the location of the disturbance.

We point out that by this definition, the coherency is dependent on the scales of the state variables. A less restrictive definition would be to allow in equation (5.2.5) weighted differences $\alpha_j x_j(t_d) - \alpha_i x_i(t_d)$ for some α_i, α_j, and hence eliminate the dependence on the scales of the states. For dynamic networks expressed in the potential form, (5.2.5) is preferable because the states are already appropriately scaled. For dynamic networks expressed in the storage form, scaling will be required. This will be discussed in Section 5.4.

A direct consequence of the coherency definition is

Lemma 5.2.1: The states x_i and x_j of system (5.2.1) are coherent with respect to σ_a if and only if the σ_a-modes are unobservable from z_k.

Letting V be an nxr basis matrix of the σ_a-eigenspace, a second consequence of the coherency definition is

Lemma 5.2.2: The states x_i and x_j of (5.2.1) are coherent with respect to σ_a if and only if the i-th and j-th rows of V are equal.

<u>Proof</u>: According to (5.2.5), the σ_a-modes are unobservable from z_k if and only if

$$g_k V = 0, \tag{5.2.6}$$

which, denoting w_k to be the k-th row of V, reduces to

$$w_i = w_j, \tag{5.2.7}$$

which proves the lemma. □

Lemma 5.2.2 can also be shown by observing that each row w_k of V weights the contribution of the σ_a-modes in the states x_k, k=1,2,...,n. The result of Lemma 5.2.2 will be used later in this chapter to find coherent states. To illustrate Lemma 5.2.2, let V of a 5-state system (5.2.1) corresponding to σ_a = $\{\lambda_1, \lambda_2, \lambda_3\}$ be

$$V = \begin{bmatrix} a & b & c \\ a & b & c \\ a & b & c \\ \star & \star & \star \\ \star & \star & \star \end{bmatrix} \tag{5.2.8}$$

where $\star$ denotes entries of V which make V a full rank matrix but are not important for this discussion. It can easily be checked that any pair of states from $\{x_1, x_2, x_3\}$ are coherent with respect to σ_a.

A simplification of Lemma 5.2.2 is possible for second order systems (5.2.3). Using

$$x_1' = x, \ x_2' = \dot{x}, \tag{5.2.9}$$

we rewrite (5.2.3) as

$$\begin{bmatrix} \dot{x}_1' \\ \dot{x}_2' \end{bmatrix} = \begin{bmatrix} 0 & I_n \\ A & 0 \end{bmatrix} \begin{bmatrix} x_1' \\ x_2' \end{bmatrix}. \tag{5.2.10}$$

Let V be a σ_a-eigenbasis matrix of A, σ_a given by (5.2.2), and

$$\Lambda = \text{diag} (\lambda_1, \lambda_2, \ldots, \lambda_r). \tag{5.2.11}$$

Then

$$\begin{bmatrix} V & 0 \\ 0 & V \end{bmatrix} \tag{5.2.12}$$

is a σ_a-eigenbasis matrix of

$$\begin{bmatrix} 0 & I_n \\ A & 0 \end{bmatrix}, \tag{5.2.13}$$

σ_a given by (5.2.4), since

$$\begin{bmatrix} 0 & I_n \\ A & 0 \end{bmatrix} \begin{bmatrix} V & 0 \\ 0 & V \end{bmatrix} = \begin{bmatrix} 0 & V \\ AV & 0 \end{bmatrix} = \begin{bmatrix} V & 0 \\ 0 & V \end{bmatrix} \begin{bmatrix} 0 & I_r \\ \Lambda & 0 \end{bmatrix}. \tag{5.2.14}$$

From Lemma 5.2.2, x_i and x_j are coherent if and only if the i-th and j-th rows of V are identical. This implies that to examine the coherency of second order systems (5.2.3), we only have to compute V from A.

A dual approach to obtain coherency results is via controllability by modeling disturbances as an m-dimensional input vector v to

$$\dot{x} = Ax + Bv \quad , \quad x(0) = 0, \tag{5.2.15}$$

or

$$\ddot{x} = Ax + Bv \quad , \quad x(0) = 0. \tag{5.2.16}$$

The two disturbance representations can be made equivalent by choosing B such that x_o is in the span of its column. For each x_o in the span of the columns of B, there exists a v_o such that

$$Bv_o = x_o . \tag{5.2.17}$$

The effect of x_o on (5.2.1) or (5.2.3) is the same as that of

$$v = v_o \delta(t_d) \tag{5.2.18}$$

on (5.2.15) or (5.2.16), where $\delta(t_d)$ is a delta function.

For system (5.2.15), a coherency definition equivalent to Definition 5.2.1 is given as follows.

<u>Definition 5.2.2</u>: The states x_i and x_j of (5.2.15) are coherent with respect to σ_a if and only if the σ_a^c-modes being uncontrollable implies that

$$z_k(t_d) = x_j(t_d) - x_i(t_d) = g_k x(t_d) = 0 \qquad\qquad (5.2.19)$$

for all t_d.

To show that the Definitions 5.2.1 and 5.2.2 are equivalent, we make the following observation.

<u>Lemma 5.2.3</u>: The states x_i and x_j of (5.2.15) are coherent with respect to σ_a if and only if σ_a^c being the uncontrollable modes of (5.2.19) implies that g_k is in the left σ_a^c-eigenspace.

<u>Proof</u>: If the σ_a^c-modes are uncontrollable and if g_k is in the left σ_a^c-eigenspace, then (5.2.19) holds for all v. This implies that x_i and x_j are coherent. On the other hand, if (5.2.19) holds for all v and the σ_a^c-modes are uncontrollable, then $g_k x = 0$ for any x in the controllable subspace implies that g_k is in the left σ_a^c-eigenspace. □

In other words, since the σ_a^c-modes of (5.2.15) are uncontrollable, B is in an invariant subspace of A; that is, the columns of B are spanned by a σ_a-eigenbasis matrix. If g_k is in the left σ_a^c-eigenspace, then the i-th and j-th rows of B are identical, since $g_k B = 0$.

Among the different equivalent characterizations of coherencies, the unobservable subspace condition in Lemma 5.2.2 is most convenient for our purpose, because the coherent states can be identified by inspection from the V matrix. For systems with coherent states, the unobservability condition suggests a possibility of reducing the order of the systems by eliminating the unobservable modes. To carry out the analysis, we introduce a few notions.

We define the states that are coherent with each other to be a <u>coherent group</u>. For example, if x_i is coherent with x_j and x_k only, then x_i, x_j and x_k form a coherent group. In example (5.2.8), x_1, x_2 and x_3 form a coherent group. A state which is not coherent with any other states is called a <u>non-coherent state</u>. Consider a system with ρ_1 coherent groups and ρ_2 non-coherent states. Since rank V is r,

$$\rho = \rho_1 + \rho_2 \geq r, \qquad\qquad (5.2.20)$$

that is, the smallest number of coherent groups and non-coherent states is also r. Hence, in example (5.2.8), x_4 and x_5 must be non-coherent states.

For each group, we designate one state as the reference state. The states of system (5.2.1) are ordered in the reference notation (4.4.11)

$$x = x_{ref} = \begin{bmatrix} x_r^1 \\ x_r^2 \end{bmatrix} \qquad (5.2.21)$$

introduced in Chapter 4, such that the ρ-vector x_r^1 consists of the reference states from ρ_1 coherent groups and ρ_2 non-coherent states, and the $(n-\rho)$-vector x_r^2 consists of the $(n-\rho)$ non-reference states. The reference states from ρ_1 coherent groups appear first in x_r^1. In addition, the non-reference states in each coherent group appear consecutively in x_r^2 and the coherent groups appear in x_r^2 in the same sequence as the reference states in x_r^1. In this notation, the $(n-\rho)$ differences z_k in (5.2.5) can be written in vector form

$$z = G\, x_{ref} = [-L_g \ \ I_{n-\rho}] \begin{bmatrix} x_r^1 \\ x_r^2 \end{bmatrix} , \qquad (5.2.22)$$

where $I_{n-\rho}$ is the $(n-\rho) \times (n-\rho)$ identity matrix and the $(n-\rho) \times \rho$ matrix L_g is the grouping matrix given in (4.4.15):

$$L_g = \begin{bmatrix} u_1' & & & 0 & | \\ & u_2' & & & | \\ & & \cdot & & | & 0 \\ & & & \cdot & | \\ 0 & & & u_{\rho_1}' & | \end{bmatrix} = \begin{bmatrix} L_{g1} \\ L_{g2} \\ \cdot \\ \cdot \\ \cdot \\ L_{g\rho_1} \end{bmatrix} , \qquad (5.2.23)$$

where the $(n_\alpha-1)$ vector u_α' is $[1 \ \ 1 \ \ \ldots \ \ 1]^T$ and n_α is the number of states in the α-th coherent group. There are only two non-zero entries per row of G: a 1 entry due to a non-reference state and a -1 entry due to the reference state of the same coherent group.

We call z the <u>local variables</u> since they describe the local behavior within coherent groups. The z variables are convenient state variables for studying system decomposition using coherent groups.

5.3 Localizability and Decomposability

In dynamic networks, coherent groups are candidates as areas for aggregation. To prepare for the investigation of this possibility, we examine in this section the conditions under which the local variables z can be decoupled.

We start by examining the conditions for decomposing one coherent group. Suppose that group α has n_α states coherent with respect to σ_α. From the group, we choose $x_i = x_{r\alpha}$ as the reference state and form $(n_\alpha-1)$ differences $x_j - x_i$ where x_j are the other states in the group with the notation (5.2.22)

$$z^\alpha = G_\alpha x_{ref} = [-L_{g\alpha} \quad I_p'] \begin{bmatrix} x_r^1 \\ x_r^2 \end{bmatrix} \qquad (5.3.1)$$

where z^α is of dimension $p = n_\alpha-1$,

$$L_{g\alpha} = [0 \quad u_\alpha' \quad 0], \quad I_p' = [0 \quad I_p \quad 0], \qquad (5.3.2)$$

are $p \times \rho$, $p \times (n-\rho)$ matrices, respectively, and I_p is a $p \times p$ identity matrix.

Definition 5.3.1: Group α of system (5.2.1) is said to be localizable if and only if there exists an $A_{d\alpha}$ such that

$$\dot{z}^\alpha = A_{d\alpha} z^\alpha. \qquad (5.3.3)$$

The modes of $A_{d\alpha}$, σ_α^c, are called the local modes.

The notion of localizability is identical to aggregability with respect to matrix G_α of (5.3.1). We use localizability to describe (5.3.3) since the z variables are local variables and do not have the interpretation of aggregated quantities.

Lemma 5.3.1: Group α of system (5.2.1) is localizable if and only if its states are coherent with respect to σ_α and

$$n_\alpha + r_\alpha = n + 1 \qquad (5.3.4)$$

where n_α is the number of states in group α and r_α is the number of modes in σ_α.

Proof: If group α is localizable, then $r_\alpha = n-(n_\alpha-1)$ modes of A, which we denote by σ_α, are unobservable from z. Let V^α be an $(n \times r_\alpha)$ σ_α-eigenbasis matrix. Since $G_\alpha V^\alpha = 0$, the rows of V^α corresponding to the states in group α are equal, and hence group α is a coherent group. Conversely, if the rows of the $(n \times r_\alpha)$ matrix V^α corresponding to group α are equal, then r modes of A are unobservable from z. If (5.3.4) is satisfied, the number of observable modes in z is $n-r_\alpha = n_\alpha-1$, which is equal to the dimension of z. This guarantees that group α is localizable. $\square$

In example (5.2.8), the only coherent group $\{x_1, x_2, x_3\}$ is localizable since

$$r_1 = 3 \quad , \quad n_1 = 3 \quad , \quad n = 5 \tag{5.3.5}$$

satisfy (5.3.4).

Since V^α is of rank r_α, there cannot be more than $n-(r_\alpha-1)$ states in group α, that is,

$$n_\alpha \leq n-(r_\alpha-1) \tag{5.3.6}$$

or

$$n_\alpha + r_\alpha \leq n + 1 . \tag{5.3.7}$$

Hence, for a coherent group to be localizable, n_α is required to take its maximum possible value. This implies that no other states are coherent with respect to the same set of modes. Equation (5.3.4) shows the trade-off between the numbers of modes and states in a coherent group for localizability. A smaller group would require its states to be coherent to a larger number of modes, while a smaller number of modes in σ_α would require a larger coherent group.

When a system has more than one coherent group, the localizability conditions can be applied independently to each group. As an example, let the modal matrix of a 5-state system be

$$\begin{array}{c} \\ x_1 \\ x_2 \\ x_3 \\ x_4 \\ x_5 \end{array} \begin{array}{ccccc} \lambda_1 & \lambda_2 & \lambda_3 & \lambda_4 & \lambda_5 \\ \left[\begin{array}{ccccc} a & b & c & * & * \\ a & b & c & * & * \\ a & b & c & * & * \\ * & d & e & f & g \\ * & d & e & f & g \end{array}\right] \end{array} \qquad (5.3.8)$$

where λ_i are the eigenvalues, and $*$ are entries which make the matrix nonsingular, but whose exact values are unimportant for our discussion. Group 1 = $\{x_1, x_2, x_3\}$ is a σ_1-coherent group where $\sigma_1 = \{\lambda_1, \lambda_2, \lambda_3\}$ and satisfies (5.3.4). Hence, it is localizable and its local modes are $\sigma_1^c = \{\lambda_4, \lambda_5\}$. Likewise, group 2 = $\{x_4, x_5\}$ is σ_2-coherent where $\sigma_2 = \{\lambda_2, \lambda_3, \lambda_4, \lambda_5\}$ and satisfies (5.3.4), and it is localizable with local mode $\sigma_2^c = \{\lambda_1\}$.

When, as in the above example, both the groups and the local modes are disjoint, the system is called <u>multi-localizable</u>; that is, more than one local model of the type (5.3.3) can be obtained. Each local model observes only the local modes. Thus, the conditions required for multi-localizability may not be easily satisfied. In some applications we do not require the local variables from different coherent groups to be decoupled. In these cases, the multi-localizability conditions can be relaxed.

<u>Definition 5.3.2</u>: Let the states of (5.2.1) be divided into ρ_1 disjoint groups and ρ_2 single states. Then (5.2.1) is said to be <u>decomposable</u> if and only if the local variables z = Gx of (5.2.22) decouples from the system; that is, there exists a matrix A_d such that

$$\dot{z} = A_d z \ . \qquad (5.3.9)$$

<u>Theorem 5.3.1</u>: System (5.2.1) is decomposable if and only if with respect to r modes σ_a there are ρ_1 coherent groups and ρ_2 non-coherent states, and

$$\rho = \rho_1 + \rho_2 = r \ . \qquad (5.3.10)$$

<u>Proof</u>: If (5.2.1) is decomposable, only $(n-\rho)$ modes are observable from the local variables z whose dimension is $(n-\rho)$. Let σ_a be the set of $r=\rho$ unobservable modes and V a σ_a-eigenbasis matrix. Since GV = 0, the rows of V corresponding to the same group are identical, implying that the groups are coherent with respect to σ_a. Conversely, if all the groups are coherent with respect to σ_a, then (5.3.10) is satisfied and the σ_a-modes are

unobservable. If the number $(n-\rho)$ of z variables is also equal to the number of observable modes $(n-r)$, that is (5.3.9) is satisfied, (5.2.1) is decomposable. □

As an illustration, consider again example (5.3.8). Both groups 1 and 2 are coherent with respect to $\sigma_a = \{\lambda_2, \lambda_3\}$ which is the intersection of σ_1 and σ_2. Since $\rho = 2$ and $r = 2$, condition (5.3.10) is satisfied. Hence, the system with modal matrix (5.3.8) is decomposable. We point out that multi-localizability of all the coherent groups is a sufficient condition for decomposability. In that case, A_d is block diagonal with blocks of dimensions $n_\alpha-1$, $\alpha = 1,2,\ldots,\rho_1$, which is illustrated by example (5.3.8). However, decomposability does not necessarily imply that any of the coherent groups are localizable.

To obtain the decomposed model when $\rho = r$, we use the transformation

$$\begin{bmatrix} x_r^1 \\ z \end{bmatrix} = \begin{bmatrix} I_r & 0 \\ -L_g & I_{n-r} \end{bmatrix} \begin{bmatrix} x_r^1 \\ x_r^2 \end{bmatrix} \tag{5.3.11}$$

whose inverse is

$$\begin{bmatrix} x_r^1 \\ x_r^2 \end{bmatrix} = \begin{bmatrix} I_r & 0 \\ L_g & I_{n-r} \end{bmatrix} \begin{bmatrix} x_r^1 \\ z \end{bmatrix}. \tag{5.3.12}$$

Applying (5.3.11) and (5.3.12) to (5.2.1), which has been partitioned as

$$\begin{bmatrix} \dot{x}_r^1 \\ \dot{x}_r^2 \end{bmatrix} = \begin{bmatrix} A_{11} & A_{12} \\ A_{21} & A_{22} \end{bmatrix} \begin{bmatrix} x_r^1 \\ x_r^2 \end{bmatrix} , \tag{5.3.13}$$

we obtain

$$\begin{bmatrix} \dot{x}_r^1 \\ \dot{z} \end{bmatrix} = \begin{bmatrix} A_{11}' & A_{12} \\ R(L_g) & A_{22}' \end{bmatrix} \begin{bmatrix} x_r^1 \\ z \end{bmatrix} , \tag{5.3.14}$$

where

$$R(L_g) = A_{22}L_g - L_gA_{11} - L_gA_{12}L_g + A_{21}, \tag{5.3.15}$$

$$A_{11}' = A_{11} + A_{12}L_g, \qquad A_{22}' = A_{22} - L_g A_{12}. \qquad (5.3.16)$$

For decomposability, the Riccati equation satisfies

$$R(L_g) = 0 \qquad (5.3.17)$$

and hence the decomposed model is

$$\dot{z} = A_d z = A_{22}' z . \qquad (5.3.18)$$

The modes of A_{22}' are σ_a^c. In general, the local variables in one coherent group are coupled to the local variables of the other coherent groups.

Theorem 5.3.1 establishes the relationship between decomposability and coherency. Its result is also important for using the coherent groups as areas for aggregation.

5.4 Coherency-Based Aggregation

In Chapter 4 and up to now in this chapter, we have presented two model reduction approaches: an aggregation approach where the dominant modes are retained, and a coherency approach where the local modes are retained. In this section we show that for dynamic networks, these seemingly different approaches are complementary techniques.

Let us examine when coherency is possible in first order dynamic networks

$$M\dot{x} = Kx \qquad (5.4.1)$$

and second order dynamic networks

$$M\ddot{x} = -D\dot{x} + Kx \qquad (5.4.2)$$

with uniform area damping, both of which are expressed in the potential form. Recall from Theorem 4.5.1 that if the r areas are aggregable with respect to the center of inertia variable y, then there exists an eigenbasis matrix in the form of a partition matrix U. Under this condition, U is a basis matrix of the aggregate modes σ_a. Since the rows of U corresponding to the states in an area are identical, the states in the same area are coherent with respect to the σ_a-modes. Similarly, when the r areas are aggregable, diag(U,U) is a σ_a-eigenbasis matrix of (5.4.2) when it is rewritten in the form (4.6.21). Thus, the states in the same areas are also coherent.

On the other hand, for (5.4.1), if there are ρ_1 coherent groups and ρ_2 non-coherent states with respect to r modes σ_a, and $\rho_1 + \rho_2 = r$, then the σ_a-eigenbasis matrix V has r groups of identical rows. Using the reference ordering such that the first r rows of V are distinct, we partition V into

$$V = \begin{bmatrix} V_1 \\ V_2 \end{bmatrix} \tag{5.4.3}$$

where the rxr matrix V_1 is nonsingular. From the unobservability condition in Lemma 5.2.1 and the result of Theorem 5.3.1,

$$GV = [-L_g \ I_{n-r}] \begin{bmatrix} V_1 \\ V_2 \end{bmatrix} = 0, \tag{5.4.4}$$

implying that

$$V_2 V_1^{-1} = L_g \ . \tag{5.4.5}$$

Since V is a basis matrix of the σ_a-eigenspace, the partition matrix in the reference ordering

$$V V_1^{-1} = \begin{bmatrix} I_r \\ L_g \end{bmatrix} = U_{ref} \tag{5.4.6}$$

is also a basis matrix of the σ_a-eigenspace. The areas defined by U_{ref} are aggregable with respect to the center of inertia variables y. The steps to show that a ρ_1 coherent groups and ρ_2 non-coherent states, $\rho_1 + \rho_2 = r$, form r aggregable areas of (5.4.2) are similar.

Combining these observations, we obtain the following coherency-based aggregation result for C_a defined by (4.5.6).

Theorem 5.4.1: An area partition of a dynamic network expressed in the potential form is aggregable with respect to $y = C_a x$ if and only if the states in the same areas are coherent with respect to r modes σ_a and the number of areas is equal to r. Furthermore, σ_a are also the modes of $M_a^{-1} K_a$.

Theorem 5.4.1 can also be shown using the condition $R(L_g) = 0$ (5.3.15) for decomposable systems. This condition is identical to the structural condition for aggregation given in (4.5.36). (To show that they are equivalent, we simply have to transpose (4.5.36).)

As an illustration of Theorem 5.4.1, in the RC-circuit example (4.5.21), (4.5.22), an eigenbasis matrix V corresponding to σ_a = {0, -5p/c} is

$$
V = \begin{bmatrix} 1 & 1 \\ 1 & 1 \\ 1 & 1 \\ 1 & -1.5 \\ 1 & -1.5 \end{bmatrix} , \tag{5.4.7}
$$

which implies that x_1, x_2 and x_3 are coherent, and x_4 and x_5 are coherent. Partitioning the system into area 1 = $\{x_1, x_2, x_3\}$ and area 2 = $\{x_4, x_5\}$ ensures that the areas are aggregable, since there are two modes in σ_a and two coherent areas, thus verifying the aggregability results in Chapter 4.

Theorem 5.4.1 proposes the use of coherency to find areas. For dynamic networks in the potential form, coherency as defined in Definition 5.2.1 is suitable since the states are appropriately scaled. For dynamic networks in the storage form (4.2.34) and (4.2.35), we modify the coherency criterion to

Definition 5.4.1: The states ξ_i and ξ_j of dynamic networks in the storage form are coherent with respect to the σ_a-modes if and only if ξ_0 = $\xi(0)$ in the σ_a-eigenspace implies that

$$
z_k = \xi_j/m_j - \xi_i/m_i = 0 \tag{5.4.8}
$$

for all t_d, where m_i and m_j are the inertias of the i-th and j-th storage elements.

Definitions 5.4.1 and 5.2.1 are equivalent since x_i and x_j of a dynamic network in the potential form are coherent if and only if ξ_i and ξ_j are coherent when the same network is expressed in the storage form. The condition that an area partition of a dynamic network in storage form is aggregable is similar to that in Theorem 5.4.1, that is, if and only if the areas in the same areas are coherent according to Definition 5.4.1, and the numbers of areas and the modes in σ_a are equal.

The aggregation results of Theorem 4.5.1, Corollary 4.5.1 and Theorem 5.4.1 are all equivalent. Theorem 4.5.1 states the result in terms of the null space of the internal connections. Corollary 4.5.2 is an interpretation in terms of the external connections and Theorem 5.4.1 is an interpretation in terms of the system dynamics. Furthermore, Theorem 5.4.1 indicates that a procedure to find the areas is to examine the rows of an eigenbasis matrix of the aggregate modes. It also indicates that the areas must be partitioned according to coherency. Any other choice of areas will not result in aggregation.

To complete the analysis, we combine the results of Theorems 5.3.1 and 5.4.1 to form the transformation

$$
\begin{bmatrix} y \\ \\ z \end{bmatrix} = \begin{bmatrix} C_a \\ \\ G \end{bmatrix} x_{ref} = \begin{bmatrix} M_a^{-1}M_1 & M_a^{-1}L_g^TM_2 \\ \\ -L_g & I_{n-r} \end{bmatrix} \begin{bmatrix} x_r^1 \\ \\ x_r^2 \end{bmatrix} , \qquad (5.4.9)
$$

whose inverse is

$$
\begin{bmatrix} x_r^1 \\ \\ x_r^2 \end{bmatrix} = \begin{bmatrix} I_r & -M_a^{-1}L_g^TM_2 \\ \\ L_g & I_{n-r} - L_g M_a^{-1}L_g^TM_2 \end{bmatrix} \begin{bmatrix} y \\ \\ z \end{bmatrix} . \qquad (5.4.10)
$$

As a result of the transformation, the dynamic network model (5.4.1) is decoupled into two subsystems

$$
\dot{y} = M_a^{-1}K_a y , \qquad (5.4.11)
$$

$$
\dot{z} = (M_2^{-1}K_{22} - L_g M_1^{-1}K_{12}) z , \qquad (5.4.12)
$$

where (5.4.11) is the aggregate model describing the dynamics due to the σ_a-modes, and (5.4.12) is the local model describing the dynamics due to the σ_a^c-modes.

5.5 Identification of Near-Coherent States

The coherency condition (5.2.5) may not be exactly satisfied in dynamic network models of real systems. If (5.2.5) is applied to a real dynamic network, there will be, in general, more coherent groups than the number of modes in σ_a. This means that the groups cannot directly be used as areas for aggregation. Consequently, we treat some groups as near-coherent such that the total number of near-coherent groups is equal to the number of modes in σ_a. The areas formed by these near-coherent groups will be near-aggregable, and the perturbation results in Section 4.7 are applicable. In this section we examine an eigenspace characterization of near-coherency, which motivates the development of a grouping algorithm.

Definition 5.5.1: The states x_i and x_j are near-coherent with respect to σ_a if and only if there exists a σ_a-eigenbasis matrix of $O(1)$ such that

$$w_i - w_j = O(\epsilon) \tag{5.5.1}$$

where w_i and w_j are the i-th and j-th rows of V and ϵ is a small parameter.

For a system with near-coherent groups, we write the σ_a-eigenbasis matrix V as

$$V = V_0 + \epsilon V_\epsilon \tag{5.5.2}$$

such that if the i-th and j-th rows of V satisfy (5.5.1), then the i-th and j-th rows of V_0 are identical. Let us regard the rows w_i of V as vectors in the r-dimensional space χ. Thus, groups of near-identical row vectors of V form clusters, each of which is contained in a cone (Figure 5.5.1). For a good grouping the cones are narrow and well separated from each other.

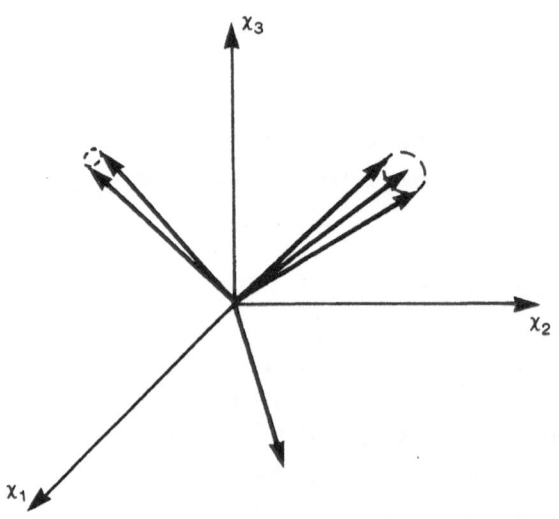

Figure 5.5.1 Clusters of row vectors of V depicting coherent groups.

The clusters depend on the representation of σ_a-eigenbasis in V. Consider the eigenbasis representation

$$V = [v_1 \ v_2 \ \cdots \ v_r] = \begin{bmatrix} w_1 \\ w_2 \\ \cdot \\ \cdot \\ \cdot \\ w_n \end{bmatrix} \tag{5.5.3}$$

where $v_1 = [1 \ 1 \ \cdots \ 1]^T$ is the eigenvector of the zero eigenvalue. If we regard w_i as points in the r-dimensional space with coordinates $(x_1, \ x_2, \ \cdots, \ x_r)$, then all the points w_i, $i=1, 2, \ldots, r$, lie on the hyperplane $x_1 = 1$.

Let us illustrate this subspace representation with the three machine power system (4.3.18). An eigenbasis matrix for the eigenvalues 0 and -75.5 of $M^{-1}K$ in the form (5.5.3) is

$$V = \begin{bmatrix} 1 & -0.287 \\ 1 & 0.827 \\ 1 & 0.483 \end{bmatrix} = \begin{bmatrix} w_1 \\ w_2 \\ w_3 \end{bmatrix}. \tag{5.5.4}$$

The row vectors of (5.5.4) are plotted in Figure 5.5.2a which shows that w_2 and w_3 are more clustered than w_1 and w_3.

Not all clusters are as easily identified as in Figure 5.5.2a. In the hypothetical two area, six state system in Figure 5.5.3, it may appear that there are three, instead of two, clusters. However, the coherency-based aggregation requires that the number of areas be equal to the number of modes in σ_a. Figure 5.5.3 shows that even in the case of an aggregation with respect to only two modes the clustering based on a direct numerical comparison may be difficult.

To more clearly reveal the clusters of row vectors, we pick one reference vector from each cluster and use it as a coordinate in a new r-dimensional coordinate system. Denoting V_1 as the matrix containing these r reference rows and V_2 as the matrix containing the remaining n-r row vectors, this process is equivalent to the transformation in (5.4.6)

$$\begin{bmatrix} V_1 \\ V_2 \end{bmatrix} V_1^{-1} = \begin{bmatrix} I_r \\ V_2 V_1^{-1} \end{bmatrix} = \begin{bmatrix} I_r \\ L \end{bmatrix} = V_L \tag{5.5.5}$$

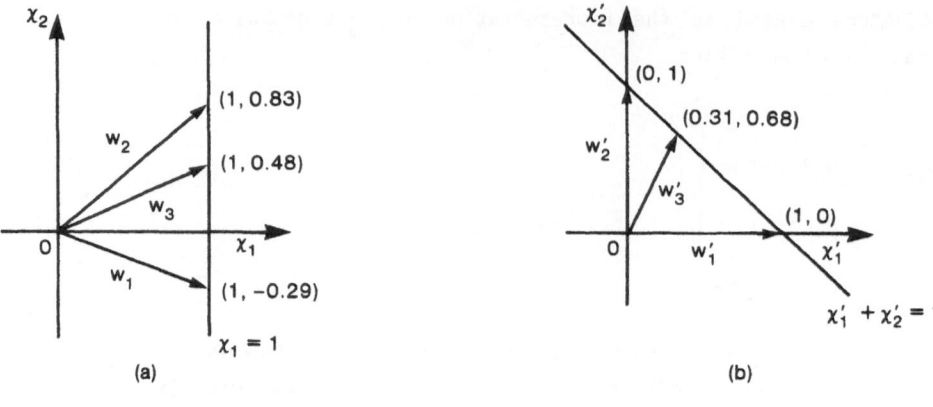

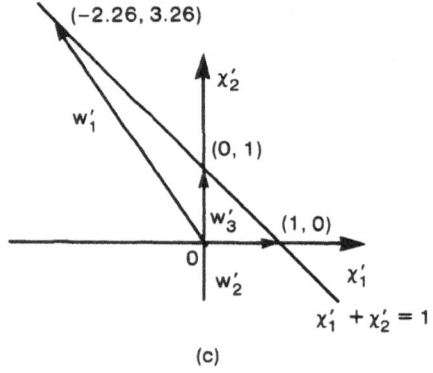

Figure 5.5.2   Row vectors of V for the three machine system. In (a), the V matrix has the column vector $[1\ 1\ \ldots\ 1]^T$. In (b) and (c) the rows of V_L are used as coordinates. The clusters are more apparent in (b) than in (c).

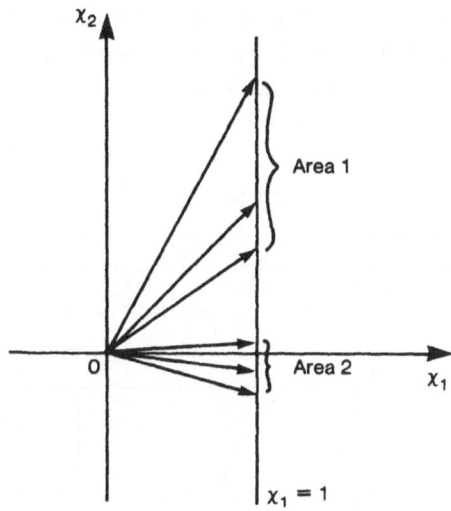

Figure 5.5.3   Row vectors of V for six state system.   The vectors for Area 1 appear to be in two groups.

such that the rows of L are the coordinates of the other n-r row vectors in the new coordinate system χ'. This transformation is possible provided that V_1 is nonsingular. Let us denote by S_L the set of matrices L for all possible choices of references V_1. We do not distinguish between L's which differ only in a permutation of their rows. If the system has r near-coherent areas, that is, (5.5.2) is satisfied, then

$$V_L = \begin{bmatrix} I_r \\ L_g \end{bmatrix} + \begin{bmatrix} 0 \\ 0(\varepsilon) \end{bmatrix} = U + 0(\varepsilon), \tag{5.5.6}$$

where L_g is a grouping matrix and U is a partition matrix. In other words, there exists an L,

$$L = L_g + 0(\varepsilon) , \tag{5.5.7}$$

in S_L such that every row of L contains only one entry which is close to 1 while the other entries are close to zero. Hence, the row vectors of L now cluster about the unit coordinate vectors which are the rows of I_r. There is one cluster to each row of I_r.

Table 5.5.1 gives the L's for the three machine system with different choices of the reference vectors x^1. The L for the third choice is plotted in Figure 5.5.2b and for the second choice in Figure 5.5.2c.

Table 5.5.1

3 machine system with different sets of tentative
reference states. (P1) chooses reference states x^1 to minimize
$\|L-L_g\|$, while (P2) chooses x^1 to minimize $\|L\|$.
The solution to both (P1) and (P2) is $x^1 = \{x_1, x_2\}$.

x^1	L	L_g	$\|L-L_g\|$	$\|L\|$	$\sigma(A_a)$
x_1, x_3	[-0.44 1.44]	[0 1]	0.88	1.88	0.0, - 81.1
x_2, x_3	[-2.26 3.26]	[0 1]	4.52	5.52	0.0, -100.8
x_1, x_2	[0.31 0.69]	[0 1]	0.62	1.00	0.0, - 81.1

The advantage of using the basis matrix in the form (5.5.6) is that we have a set of well-separated vectors, namely, the rows of I_r, to be used as reference vectors. Our coherency grouping approach is then to find a set of reference vectors such that the rows of L are clustered about the rows of I_r, that is, L is close to a matrix L_g. The coherency identification problem is posed as:

(P1) find reference states and L_g to minimize $\|L-L_g\|$.

In (P1) we use the matrix row norm

$$\|A\| = \max_i \sum_{j=1}^{n} |A_{ij}|.$$ (5.5.8)

Systems with near-coherent areas will have small $\|L-L_g\|$, and the grouping of the other states with the reference states will be determined by L_g.

Let us use the norm criterion in (P1) to find the reference states and areas for the three machine example. For each set of tentative reference states we compute L and L_g to minimize $\|L-L_g\|$. The minimum of $\|L-L_g\|$ is found to be 0.62 (Table 5.5.1). The minimum norm criterion indicates that x_1 and x_2

are the reference states, and according to L_g, x_3 is grouped with x_2. This result is consistent with the areas found from inspecting Figure 5.5.2b. On the other hand, the norm condition indicates that x_2 and x_3 are a bad choice for reference vectors, and Figure 5.4.2c shows no apparent clusters. Note that $\|L-L_g\|$ for the first choice is not significantly larger than minimum $\|L-L_g\|$. Furthermore, using x_1 and x_3 as the reference states and assigning x_2 to the same group as x_3, the resulting coherency groups are the same as that found from minimum $\|L-L_g\|$. Thus the minimization procedure for systems with clearly separated coherency groups is robust. The choice of areas from the minimum norm condition is also consistent with the choice indicated by the eigenvalue approximation of the aggregate model.

5.6 A Coherency Grouping Algorithm

In the 3 machine example, we have solved for Problem (P1) by examining all possible choices of reference states. For large scale systems, the complete enumeration procedure is computationally infeasible. To avoid this exhaustive search procedure, we find a suboptimal solution to (P1) requiring only a finite number of steps.

The following result motivates the suboptimal solution method.

<u>Lemma 5.6.1</u>: Let V be an eigenbasis matrix for the σ_a-modes of a dynamic network. Then, every element L in S_L satisfies

$$\sum_{j=1}^{r} L_{ij} = 1, \qquad i = 1,2,\ldots,n-r , \tag{5.6.1}$$

that is, the summation of the entries in each row of L is equal to 1.

<u>Proof</u>: Since $L = V_2 V_1^{-1}$, the transformation

$$\begin{bmatrix} x_r^1 \\ z \end{bmatrix} = \begin{bmatrix} I_r & 0 \\ -L & I_{n-r} \end{bmatrix} \begin{bmatrix} x_r^1 \\ x_r^2 \end{bmatrix} , \tag{5.6.2}$$

where z is not necessarily the difference of x, applied to (5.3.13) results in the upper-block-diagonal system

$$\begin{bmatrix} \dot{x}_r^1 \\ \dot{z} \end{bmatrix} = \begin{bmatrix} A_{11} + A_{12} L & A_{12} \\ 0 & A_{22} - L A_{12} \end{bmatrix} \begin{bmatrix} x_r^1 \\ z \end{bmatrix} . \tag{5.6.3}$$

Let v be an eigenvector of $A_{11}+A_{12}L$. Then

$$v' = \begin{bmatrix} I_r & 0 \\ L & I_{n-r} \end{bmatrix} \begin{bmatrix} v \\ 0 \end{bmatrix} = \begin{bmatrix} v \\ Lv \end{bmatrix} \qquad (5.6.4)$$

is an eigenvector of A for the same eigenvalue. Since the n-vector $v' = [1\ 1...1]^T$ is the eigenvector of the zero eigenvalue, from (5.6.4), we obtain v as the r-vector $[1\ 1...1]^T$ and Lv as the (n-r)-vector $[1\ 1...1]^T$. Thus (5.6.1) is obtained by writing Lv, which is a summation of the entries of the rows of L, in scalar form. □

An interpretation of Lemma 5.6.1 is that if we regard the rows w_i' of

$$V_L = \begin{bmatrix} I_r \\ L \end{bmatrix} = \begin{bmatrix} w_1' \\ w_2' \\ . \\ . \\ . \\ w_n' \end{bmatrix} \qquad (5.6.5)$$

as points having the coordinates $(x_1',\ x_2',\ ...,\ x_r')$, then (5.6.5) implies that these points lie on the hyperplane

$$\sum_{i=1}^{r} x_i' = 1 . \qquad (5.6.6)$$

The hyperplane (5.6.6) in the $(x_1',\ x_2',\ ...,\ x_r')$ coordinate system is a transformation of the hyperplane $x_1=1$ in the $(x_1,\ x_2,\ ...,\ x_r)$ coordinate system. The three machine system example verifies (5.6.6) as Figures 5.5.2b and 5.5.2c show that all the points lie on the line $x_1' + x_2' = 1$.

A direct consequence of Lemma 5.6.1 is that the norm of L is bounded from below.

Corollary 5.6.1: Every element L of the set S_L satisfies

$$\|L\| \geq 1 . \qquad (5.6.7)$$

If the areas are coherent, then $L = L_g$ achieves the minimum norm $\|L\|=1$. If the areas are near-coherent, then the row vectors of L are clustered about the unit coordinate vectors, and hence, $\|L\| \approx 1$. Thus of all the solutions L in S_L, we seek those with their norms close to 1. Hence, as a more practical alternative to (P1), we pose the following optimization problem:

(P2) find reference states to minimize $\|L\|$ and L_g to minimize $\|L - L_g\|$.

For the three machine system example, the solution to (P2) yields the reference states as x_1 and x_2, and the grouping of x_3 with x_2. Thus, for this example the solutions to (P1) and (P2) are identical. Note that in this case $L = [0.32\ 0.68]$ achieves $\|L\| = 1$ even though $L \neq L_g$. It illustrates that the minimum $\|L\|=1$ is achieved not only when $L=L_g$, but also when all the entries of L are non-negative. Because L can have negative entries, $\|L\|=1$ may not be achieved. The solution of (P2) favors an L in which positive elements dominate, that is, whose row vectors tend to be in the positive "quadrant" of the r-dimensional space. Then these vectors can be grouped with the closest unit coordinate vectors.

We now develop a procedure to find an L with a norm close to 1 without searching through all L in S_L. From Lemma 5.6.1, if minimum $\|L\| = 1$ is achieved for a system, then all the entries of L are non-negative. When r=3, the unit coordinates are edges of the unit cube. Then, minimum $\|L\| = 1$ implies that all the row vectors of L are contained in the cube. The unit cube becomes a parallelepiped in the coordinate system corresponding to V of (5.4.3). The row vectors of V_1 are the edges of the parallelepiped which contains the row vectors of V_2 if minimum $\|L\| = 1$. The volume of the V_1-parallelepiped is given by the Gramian [19]

$$G(V_1) = \det(V_1 V_1^T) = (\det(V_1))^2 \tag{5.6.8}$$

which also serves as a measure of the linear independence of the row vectors of V_1. That is, for a given set of vectors in V_1 with fixed length, $G(V_1)$ is largest when the vectors are orthogonal, and is zero if they are linearly dependent. For r>3, the V_1-parallelepiped is the r-dimensional polytope formed by the row vectors of V_1, and the Gramian (5.6.8) is a generalized measure of the "volume" of the V_1-parallelepiped.

The reference vectors which achieve $\|L\| = 1$ can then be found from the rows of V which maximize $G(V_1)$, that is, the rows of V that maximize the volume of the V_1-parallelepiped. Otherwise, if some row vectors of V_2 lie outside of the V_1-parallelepiped, then L has some negative entries and $\|L\| \neq 1$. This problem can be stated as one of finding a permutation P for the basis matrix V to maximize

$$G(V_1') = G(V,P) \tag{5.6.9}$$

where

$$V' = \begin{bmatrix} V_1' \\ \\ V_2' \end{bmatrix} = PV. \tag{5.6.10}$$

The permutation P that achieves the minimum norm is independent of the choice of the basis V.

Lemma 5.6.2: If the permutation P* maximizes G(V,P), that is, if $G(V,P*) \geq G(V,P)$ for all permutations P, then for any other basis representation W = VQ where Q is nonsingular, P* also maximizes G(W,P), that is, $G(W,P*) \geq G(W,P)$.

Proof: Since $G(W,P) = (\det Q)^2 G(V,P)$, P* which maximizes G(V,P) also maximizes G(W,P). □

Systems with near-coherent areas seldom yield $\|L\|=1$. However, if the clusters about the unit coordinate vectors are enclosed in narrow cones, to maximize $G(V_1)$, a vector must be picked from each cluster. While the minimization of $\|L\|$ requires examining many elements of S_L, an approximation to finding V_1 which maximizes $G(V_1)$ can be obtained by Gaussian elimination.

Let p_i denote the pivot of the i-th step in the Gaussian elimination of the rows of V. Then

$$G(V_1') = (p_1 p_2 \ldots p_r)^2 . \tag{5.6.11}$$

Thus maximizing $G(V_1')$ is equivalent to finding a permutation P for a given V such that the product of the pivots (5.6.11) is maximized. The commonly used Gaussian elimination with complete pivoting [52] is an approximate method of finding the optimal P. In the first step it searches for the largest pivot p_1. In the second step it searches for the largest pivot p_2 among the remaining n-1 rows of V. Thus it maximizes the individual pivots but does not necessarily maximize the overall product of the pivots. In the same sense, maximizing $G(V_1')$ involves finding the set of most linearly independent vectors from V, whereas Gaussian elimination with complete pivoting is an approximate method for this purpose.

Applying Gaussian elimination with complete pivoting to V, the rows and columns of V are permuted such that the (1,1) entry of the resulting V is the entry largest in magnitude. Permuting the rows of V is equivalent to changing the ordering of the states. The (1,1) entry of V is used as the pivot for performing the first step of the Gaussian elimination. Then the largest entry is chosen from the remaining $(n-1)x(r-1)$ submatrix of the reduced V as the pivot for the next elimination step. The elimination terminates in r steps and the states corresponding to the first r rows of the final reduced V matrix are designated as the reference states. Rows having small entries will not be used as the pivot because the small entries are the result of elimination with almost identical rows already used as pivoting rows. Thus, this procedure does not put two near-coherent states together as reference states.

Let us illustrate the Gaussian elimination procedure on the 3 machine system example. The column vectors in V of (5.5.4) are first normalized such that the length of the vectors are unity to obtain

$$
\begin{array}{c} x_1 \\ x_2 \\ x_3 \end{array}
\begin{bmatrix} 0.577 & -0.287 \\ 0.577 & 0.827 \\ 0.577 & 0.483 \end{bmatrix} . \tag{5.6.12}
$$

The largest number in (5.6.12) is the (2,2) entry. We exchange the first and second rows and the first and second columns to obtain

$$
\begin{array}{c} x_2 \\ x_1 \\ x_3 \end{array}
\begin{bmatrix} 0.827 & 0.577 \\ -0.287 & 0.577 \\ 0.483 & 0.577 \end{bmatrix} . \tag{5.6.13}
$$

Then the (1,1) entry is used as the pivot to eliminate the remainder of the first column, resulting in

$$
\begin{array}{c} x_2 \\ x_1 \\ x_3 \end{array}
\begin{bmatrix} 0.827 & 0.577 \\ 0 & 0.831 \\ 0 & 0.239 \end{bmatrix} . \tag{5.6.14}
$$

The largest number below the first row is the (2,2) entry. The procedure terminates here because all the pivots have been found and the reference states are x_2 and x_1, which agree with our earlier analysis.

For the set of reference states found by the elimination procedure the corresponding L is readily computed from

$$V_1^T L^T = V_2^T \tag{5.6.15}$$

using the LU decomposition of V_1 obtained from the Gaussian elimination. Then an L_g is found to minimize $\|L - L_g\|$ and assign the remaining $(n-r)$ states to the areas.

We summarize the coherency grouping algorithm as follows:

Step 1: Choose the number of groups and the modes σ_a.

Step 2: Compute a basis matrix V of the σ_a-eigenspace for a given ordering of the state variables.

Step 3: Apply Gaussian elimination with complete pivoting to V and obtain the set of reference states.

Step 4: Compute L for the set of reference states chosen in step 3.

Step 5: Construct the matrix L_g which defines the states in each area.

The main computation burden of the algorithm is in Step 2. Since $M^{-1}K$ is similar to the symmetric matrix $M^{-1/2}KM^{-1/2}$, symmetric eigenvalue programs can be used to simplify the computation. A further simplication occurs if σ_a are the slowest modes of the system. When $r < n/4$, partial eigenvalue and eigenvector computation techniques are superior to complete eigenvalue and eigenvector computation techniques [62]. For large scale dynamic networks with sparse structures, special techniques, such as Lanczo's algorithm [14,15], which use sparsity are able to substantially reduce computation time and memory requirement. Using the Lanczo's algorithm in [14], the coherency grouping algorithm has been applied to a 1700 bus, 400 machine power system. The techniques and results will be published in the near future.

5.7 Power System Examples

We illustrate the coherency grouping algorithm on two power systems. The first system is a 48 machine model of the Northeastern U.S. and Ontario, Canada (Figure 5.7.1) [9,42]. The second system is a 42 machine model of the western portion of the United States (Figure 5.7.2) [9]. The dots denote the geographical locations of the machines. In both cases we will identify the areas using nonsymmetric K matrices, that is, the conductance terms G_{ij} are retained.

In the model of the first system, most of the details in New England and New York are retained, while the rest of the system is extremely reduced. From the linearized electromechanical model, we extract the nxn system matrix by eliminating the machine speed variable (see Section 4.3). This matrix is given in Appendix A. Note that the $M^{-1}K$ matrix has some small off-diagonal negative entries which are due to the G_{ij} terms. Since they are small, we make no attempt to eliminate these terms and work directly with this matrix.

To use the algorithm, we first specify that we want nine areas with respect to the nine slowest modes. From this point on the algorithm proceeds automatically giving the following results. In step 2 a basis for the 9-dimensional slow subspace is computed. In step 3 the Gaussian elimination is performed and the set of reference machines is found to be 5, 39, 44, 34, 48, 41, 17, 29, 36. In step 4 L is computed and is given in Table 5.7.1. In step 5, the largest entry in each row, which is underlined in Table 5.7.1, is used to assign the corresponding machine to an area; that is, this entry is approximated by 1 and all other entries in the row by zero. As a result the following grouping of machines into areas is obtained:

Area 1:   1, 2, 3, 4, 5, 6, 7, 8, 9
Area 2:   39, 42
Area 3:   43, 44, 45, 46
Area 4:   34, 35
Area 5:   48
Area 6:   32, 37, 38, 40, 41
Area 7:   13, 14, 15, 16, 17, 18, 19, 20, 21, 22, 23, 24, 25, 26, 31, 47
Area 8:   10, 27, 28, 29, 30
Area 9:   11, 12, 33, 36.

The areas are shown in Figure 5.7.1. Note that the areas are geographically contiguous. Some areas contain machines that are geographically far away such as machines 33 and 36 in Area 9 and machines 43 and 44 in Area 3. However, careful examination of the transmission line data in [9] shows that these machines are strongly coupled.

Table 5.7.1

L for the 48 machine system

	5	39	44	34	48	41	17	29	36
1.	0.56	-0.00	-0.04	-0.01	-0.00	-0.00	0.05	0.42	0.02
2.	0.60	-0.00	-0.04	-0.01	-0.00	-0.00	0.05	0.38	0.02
3.	0.83	-0.00	-0.01	-0.01	0.00	-0.00	0.03	0.15	0.01
4.	0.83	-0.00	-0.01	-0.00	0.00	-0.00	0.03	0.14	0.01
6.	0.84	-0.00	-0.02	-0.01	-0.00	-0.00	0.03	0.15	0.01
7.	0.83	-0.00	-0.02	-0.01	-0.00	-0.00	0.03	0.16	0.01
8.	0.85	-0.00	-0.01	0.01	0.00	-0.00	0.05	0.11	0.02
9.	0.58	-0.00	-0.01	-0.01	0.00	-0.01	0.10	0.30	0.04
10.	0.18	-0.00	0.03	-0.03	0.01	-0.01	0.28	0.43	0.13
11.	0.07	-0.01	-0.03	-0.15	0.00	-0.04	0.21	0.28	0.66
12.	0.08	-0.01	-0.02	-0.12	0.00	-0.03	0.21	0.27	0.62
13.	0.10	-0.00	-0.01	-0.03	0.00	-0.02	0.51	0.32	0.12
14.	0.11	-0.00	0.02	-0.02	0.01	-0.01	0.46	0.32	0.12
15.	0.04	-0.00	-0.01	-0.02	-0.00	-0.02	0.78	0.17	0.06
16.	0.02	0.01	-0.00	0.03	0.00	0.01	0.77	0.10	0.06
18.	0.02	0.00	0.00	0.02	0.01	0.01	0.78	0.09	0.06
19.	0.03	0.01	0.03	0.04	0.02	0.02	0.67	0.10	0.08
20.	0.03	0.01	0.02	0.03	0.02	0.01	0.72	0.10	0.06
21.	0.02	0.00	0.11	0.02	0.08	0.00	0.63	0.09	0.05
22.	0.03	0.00	0.09	0.02	0.07	0.01	0.63	0.10	0.06
23	0.06	0.00	0.05	-0.00	0.01	-0.01	0.62	0.19	0.07
24.	0.09	0.00	0.21	-0.01	0.04	-0.01	0.37	0.24	0.06
25.	0.11	-0.00	0.17	-0.02	0.03	-0.01	0.36	0.30	0.07
26.	0.10	-0.00	0.09	-0.03	0.02	-0.02	0.42	0.33	0.09
27.	0.07	-0.00	0.12	-0.00	0.01	-0.00	0.05	0.73	0.02
28.	0.02	-0.00	0.03	-0.00	0.00	-0.00	0.01	0.93	0.00
30.	0.04	-0.00	0.06	-0.00	0.00	-0.00	0.02	0.88	0.01
31.	0.02	0.05	0.00	0.13	0.01	0.10	0.48	0.06	0.15
32.	0.00	0.24	-0.00	0.09	0.04	0.41	0.16	-0.01	0.07
33.	0.00	0.04	-0.00	0.28	0.00	0.10	0.25	0.02	0.31
35.	0.00	0.01	-0.00	0.87	-0.00	0.02	0.05	0.00	0.05
37.	0.00	0.32	0.01	0.05	0.09	0.40	0.09	-0.01	0.04
38.	0.00	0.38	0.00	0.04	0.06	0.41	0.08	-0.01	0.03
40.	0.00	0.28	-0.00	0.05	0.00	0.56	0.09	-0.01	0.03
42.	0.00	0.47	0.00	0.03	0.03	0.39	0.06	-0.01	0.02
43.	0.01	0.00	0.73	-0.00	0.11	0.00	0.02	0.13	0.00
45.	0.02	-0.00	0.60	-0.00	0.12	-0.00	0.18	0.07	0.02
46.	0.00	0.00	0.89	0.01	0.07	0.01	0.01	0.01	0.00
47.	0.02	0.00	0.26	0.01	0.21	0.00	0.37	0.08	0.04

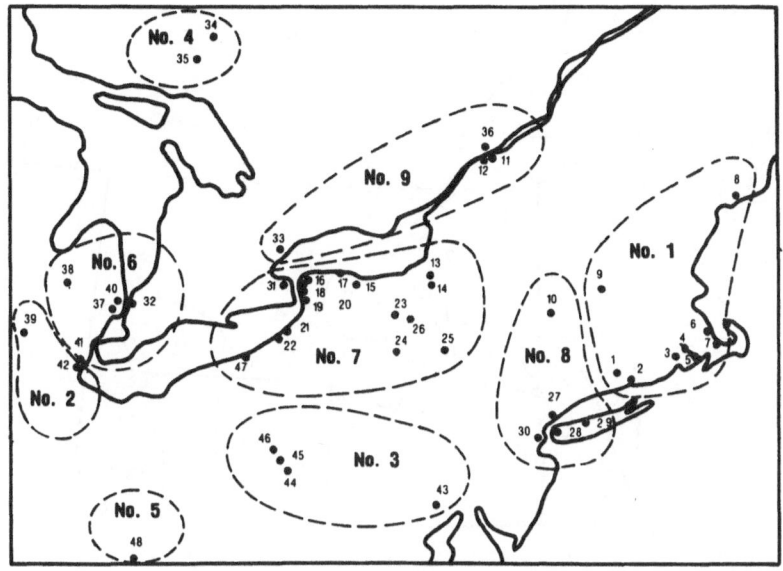

Figure 5.7.1   Coherent areas of the 48 machine system of the Northeastern U.S.
and Ontario, Canada

To evaluate the grouping of the machines into areas, we examine the
approximation of L by L_g. First, we give an evaluation in an average sense. The
average value of the entries of L in Table 5.7.1 which have been approximated by 1
is 0.63 and the average value of the entries which have been approximated by 0 is
0.05. Although 0.63 is not close to 1, it is large compared to 0.05. However, the
largest two entries for machines 10, 14, 24, 25, 26, 32, 33, 37, 38, 42 and 47 are
quite close to each other. For example, for machine 33, they are 0.28 and 0.31.
All these machines are on the borders of their areas. The rows of L indicate that
each of these machines could belong to either one of the two areas. For reasons of
convenience, such as consistency with the administrative boundaries of the areas,
these machines can be grouped with the other area without incurring much additional
error. For this system, we keep the areas as listed above and verify them with an
eigenvalue test and time responses in Chapters 6 and 8.

The second system, the western portion of the United States, is of interest
because of its wide geographical area and unique "doughnut" structure [13]. The
model contains a hypothetical high voltage dc transmission system with seven
terminals. Relative to the time-scales of the electromechanical modes, the
dynamics associated with the dc system can be assumed infinitely fast and
represented by algebraic equations.

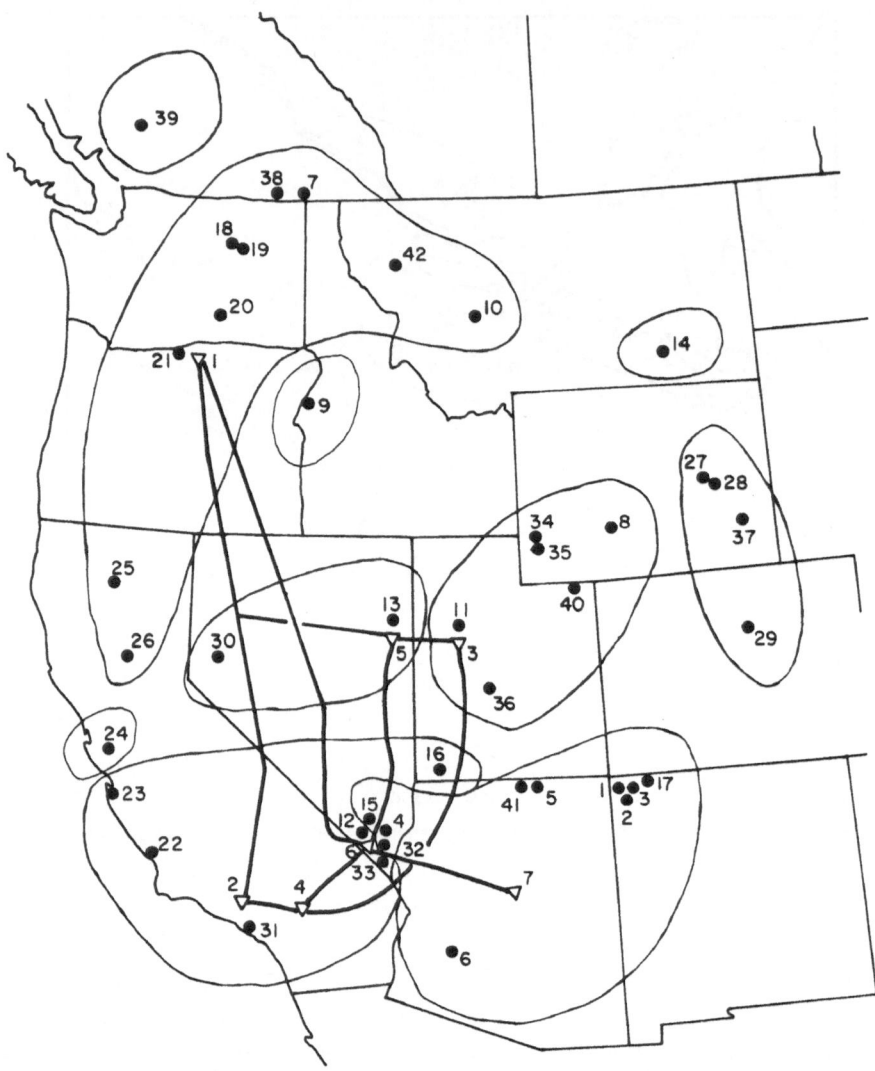

Figure 5.7.2 42 machine system 10-area partition

To obtain the areas we linearize the system and neglect damping. For this system, we specify the number of areas to be 10 and σ_a to be the 10 slowest modes in the first step of the algorithm. In the second step, a basis for the 10-dimensional slow subspace is computed. Gaussian elimination is performed on this basis, and the set of reference machines is found to be 29, 30, 14, 31, 24, 6, 19, 35, 9 and 39. The matrix L is solved for in the fourth step of the algorithm, and approximated by an L_g matrix in the fifth step. The resulting areas are shown in Figure 5.7.2. These analytically derived areas agree with physical intuition and experience. As an illustration, observe that machines 4, 15, and 32 are not in the same area as machines 12, 16, and 33. Although they are geographically close, there is limited transmission capacity between these two groups of machines in the actual system.

In this system most machines are grouped with sufficient accuracy. As an example, the rows of L corresponding to machines 2, 13 and 21 are shown in Table 5.7.2, where the underlined entries are those approximated by one and all other entries by zero. Assignment of some machines, for example, machine 22, is not as distinct. The row in L corresponding to machine 22 only has 0.4524 as its entry in area 4 and that for area 5 is 0.1987. This area partition will also be further examined in the next chapter.

5.8 Conclusions

We have proposed a coherency criterion which requires the states to be coherent with respect to only a selected set of modes. This criterion results in disturbance-independent coherent groups. For dynamic networks, the coherent groups found according to this criterion form aggregable areas, which verifies the heretofore heuristic coherency-based aggregation technique used in power system analysis. For models of real systems, we have developed a grouping algorithm to identify near-coherent states which form near-aggregable areas. The algorithm is efficient and has shown to be applicable to large scale power systems with as many as 400 machines and 1700 buses.

In this chapter, we have dealt with coherency with respect to a selected set of modes. In the next chapter, we examine coherency with respect to the slowest modes. As will be shown, this leads to areas that are weakly connected.

Table 5.7.2

Selected rows of L_d for 42 machine system

Area Number

Machine	1	2	3	4	5
2	0.4486E-01	0.2503E-01	0.4029E-02	0.5055E-01	-0.1644E-02
13	-0.3036E-02	<u>0.7507</u>	-0.5785E-02	-0.8574E-01	-0.9172E-01
21	0.2184E-02	0.4671E-02	0.3114E-01	0.3299E-01	0.6884E-01
22	0.1785E-02	0.8283E-02	0.4801E-02	<u>0.4524</u>	0.1987

	6	7	8	9	10
2	<u>0.8011</u>	0.3382E-02	0.6928E-01	0.3568E-02	-0.1172E-03
13	0.1379	-0.5802E-01	0.3998	-0.4355E-01	-0.3696E-03
21	0.1851E-01	<u>0.7550</u>	0.1628E-01	0.4627E-01	0.2403E-01
22	0.1808	0.1236	0.1081E-01	0.1663E-01	0.2174E-02

CHAPTER 6

SLOW COHERENCY AND WEAK CONNECTIONS

6.1 Introduction

A question which remains to be answered is the selection of σ_a-modes for coherency-based aggregation of dynamic networks. In a realistic model, there is, in general, freedom to choose the σ_a-modes, since near-coherency is usually possible with respect to more than one set of σ_a-modes. In this chapter, we examine coherency with respect to a set of the slowest modes of a system. A fundamental property of this choice of modes is that the areas of the system are partitioned along the weakest boundaries. This results in the time-scale separation of the aggregate model from the local models and the decoupling among the local models. These models simplify the analysis and control process since hierarchical and decentralized techniques can be used.

The fundamental relationship between weak connections and time-scales is discussed in early works by Simon and Ando [50]. They pointed out that in most large scale physical and economic systems, there exist groups of strongly interacting units (machines, commodities, etc.), such that the interaction between units in the same group is much stronger than the interaction of units from different groups. Short run behavior of such systems can be studied by analyzing individual groups as isolated subsystems. However, in the long run, this decomposition is, in general, wrong. Even very weak interactions between groups may become significant after long enough periods of time. To study the long term behavior, each group is represented by an aggregate variable. The interconnection of these variables from different groups form the aggregate model. Simon, et al., support this aggregation approach with a linear analysis and many convincing examples from diverse fields [49,50]. Some examples have also been discussed in Chapter 1.

It is somewhat surprising that in system theory, the aggregation concept has lost its time-scale and weak coupling content [2,56]. Other aggregation approaches using diagonal dominance, such as vector Lyapunov functions [48], also fail to exploit the relationship between weak coupling and time-scales. It is only recently that this relationship has been used in the aggregation of power systems [27,38] and Markov chains [26,40]. In [37,66] these linear results are extended to nonlinear models of power systems. The next chapter develops the time-scale results for a broader class of nonlinear systems. This chapter uses the results in

Chapters 3 to 5 to provide an analytical basis of the weak connections and time-scales in linear dynamic networks.

A physical evidence of weak connections is "slow coherency." It has been frequently observed in real physical systems that, in the long run, units in the same group are coherent with respect to the slow modes. For example, in power systems, fast non-coherent motions are typically confined to machines close to a disturbance. However, groups of machines remote from the disturbance often exhibit slow-coherent motions [51,41]. In this case, the slow aggregate represents the motions of the coherent groups of machines.

We show that slow coherency occurs in dynamic networks when the connections between the areas are weak. Dynamic networks with this property are in the weak connection form (3.5.17), a class of singularly perturbed systems whose time-scales are nonexplicit. As indicated in Section 3.5, the study of this type of two time-scale systems is nontrivial - although the weak connections can be neglected in the fast time-scale, they represent strong coupling between the center of inertia variables in the slow time-scale.

Dynamic networks with weak connections have properties that are important in practical applications. First, the fast transients within an area are decoupled from the fast transients in other areas, second, the fast transients have a negligible effect on the slow aggregate, and third, the coherency and aggregability conditions are satisfied not due to tuned inertias and connections but, more realistically, to weak connections. A further advantage of slow coherency and weak connections is that, as properties not depending on linearity, they can be extended to nonlinear systems as shown in Chapter 7. If necessary, the effect of the weak connections can be introduced into the slow aggregate and the fast local models by performing a first order correction with the singular perturbation method.

In Section 6.2, we obtain a relationship between time-scales and weak connections, which is illustrated by an example. In Section 6.3, we assume that the external connections of a dynamic network are weak compared to the internal connections and use the results in Chapter 3 to establish time-scales. Section 6.4 describes an empirical reduction procedure which is verified by an asymptotic analysis in Section 6.5. Section 6.6 examines slow coherency in real power system models.

6.2 Time-Scales and Weak Coupling

We start by showing through an example that coherency in a dynamic network may be possible with respect to more than one set of σ_a-modes. What is important is that the external connections are weakest when the coherency is with respect to the slowest modes. This is a general property of dynamic neworks with multiple coherencies.

Consider the RC-circuit (Figure 6.2.1)

$$\dot{x} = \begin{bmatrix} -(p+q) & p & 0 & q \\ p & -(p+q) & q & 0 \\ 0 & q & -(p+q) & p \\ q & 0 & p & -(p+q) \end{bmatrix} \quad x = Ax \quad (6.2.1)$$

where the x variables are the capacitor voltages, the capacitances are all equal to 1 and the "non-touching" connections are identical

$$1/R_{12} = 1/R_{34} = p ,$$
$$\qquad (6.2.2)$$
$$1/R_{23} = 1/R_{14} = q .$$

The eigenvalues of the A matrix of (6.2.1) are $\sigma(A) = \{0, -2q, -2p, -2(p+q)\}$, and the corresponding eigenvectors are

$$\begin{bmatrix} 1 \\ 1 \\ 1 \\ 1 \end{bmatrix}, \begin{bmatrix} 1 \\ 1 \\ -1 \\ -1 \end{bmatrix}, \begin{bmatrix} 1 \\ -1 \\ -1 \\ 1 \end{bmatrix}, \begin{bmatrix} 1 \\ -1 \\ 1 \\ -1 \end{bmatrix} \quad . \qquad (6.2.3)$$

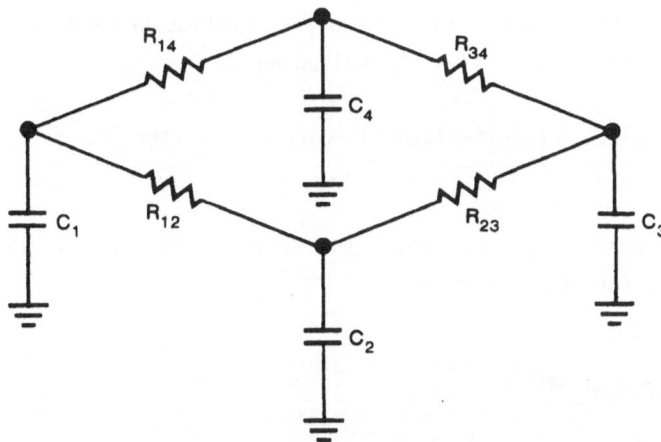

Figure 6.2.1   An RC-circuit example illustrating multiple coherencies. All the capacitors are identical and $R_{12} = R_{34}$, $R_{14} = R_{23}$.

Note that the voltages of all the capacitors are coherent with respect to the 0 eigenvalue. There are two coherent groups of capacitors with respect to each of the remaining three eigenvalues. For example, for the eigenvalue $-2q$, the states x_1 and x_2 are coherent, and x_3 and x_4 are coherent. As a result, there are three choices of σ_a each containing two modes and resulting in two coherent groups (Table 6.2.1). By the coherency-based aggregation result in Theorem 5.4.1, these groups can be used as areas for aggregation. A remarkable fact is that in all three choices the magnitude of the nonzero mode equals the sum of the external connections. Therefore, the weaker the external connections, the closer this mode is to zero. On the other hand, the stronger the external connections, the farther this mode is from zero, as is the case of $\sigma_a = \sigma_3$ where the states within the areas are not even connected.

Table 6.2.1

Coherent groups for RC-circuit (6.2.1)

σ_a	coherent groups
$\{0, -2q\} = \sigma_1$	$\{x_1, x_2\}$, $\{x_3, x_4\}$
$\{0, -2p\} = \sigma_2$	$\{x_1, x_4\}$, $\{x_2, x_3\}$
$\{0, -2(p+q)\} = \sigma_3$	$\{x_1, x_3\}$, $\{x_2, x_4\}$

This example, although quite artificial, demonstrates a general property of dynamic networks. To express it we need a convenient measure of the strength of connections between the areas in cases where inertias are not identical. We assume that a dynamic network satisfies the following.

Assumption 6.2.1: The off-diagonal entries of the connection matrix K are nonnegative.

Under this assumption, the (α,β)-th entries of the aggregate matrix K_a, $k_{\alpha\beta}^a$, and hence, the scalar quantity

$$s = \sum_{\alpha=1}^{r} \sum_{\beta=1}^{r} k_{\alpha\beta}^a/m_{a\alpha}, \quad \alpha \neq \beta \qquad (6.2.4)$$

are nonnegative where $m_{a\alpha}$ is the aggregate inertia of area α. Moreover s is a monotonically increasing function of the external connections; that is, s increases when any off-diagonal entry of K^E increases. Taking s as a measure of the strength of connections between the areas, we establish the relationship between weak connections and the σ_a-modes as follows.

Theorem 6.2.1: Let the aggregability condition (4.5.27) be satisfied in a dynamic network with respect to the r slowest modes $\sigma_a = \sigma_1$ and also with respect to another set of r modes $\sigma_a = \sigma_2$. Then under Assumption 6.2.1, the strength of connections s_1 between the σ_1-coherent areas is weaker than the strength of connections s_2 between the σ_2-coherent areas, that is $s_1 < s_2$, where s_1 and s_2 are given by (6.2.4).

Proof: Since K_a is a network matrix,

$$k_{\alpha\alpha}^a = -\sum_{\beta=1}^{r} k_{\alpha\beta}^a, \quad \beta \neq \alpha. \tag{6.2.5}$$

Therefore

$$s = -\sum_{\alpha=1}^{r} k_{\alpha\alpha}^a / m_{\alpha\alpha} = - \text{ trace }(A_a) \tag{6.2.6}$$

where trace (A_a) denotes the sum of the diagonal entries of $A_a = M_a^{-1} K_a$ and is equal to the sum of the eigenvalues λ_α in σ_a, that is,

$$\text{trace }(A_a) = \sum_{\alpha=1}^{r} \lambda_\alpha . \tag{6.2.7}$$

Since all the eigenvalues λ_α are nonpositive and the sum of the eigenvalues in σ_1 is smaller in magnitude than that of σ_2, it follows that $s_1 < s_2$. $\square$

Theorem 6.2.1 is a consequence of the fact that the diagonal entries of A_a contain information about the strength of external connections. In the RC-circuit of Figure 6.2.1, with $\sigma_1 = \{0, -2q\}$,

$$A_a = \begin{bmatrix} -q & q \\ q & -q \end{bmatrix}, \tag{6.2.8}$$

that is, trace $(A_a) = -2q = -s_1$. If $q<p$, then σ_1 contains the two slowest modes and the connections between the areas are weaker than those of either $\sigma_2 = \{0, -2p\}$ or $\sigma_3 = \{0, -2(p+q)\}$. Theorem 6.2.1 motivates the

study of dynamic networks with weak external connections, which will be used to develop the slow coherency concept.

6.3 Slow Coherency

The areas found in the coherency-based aggregation are determined by the σ_a-modes. For long term studies of dynamic networks, it is desirable to make the aggregate model represent the slow time-scale. This requires finding coherent groups with respect to the slowest modes in the system.

Definition 6.3.1: The states x_i and x_j of a system $\dot{x} = Ax$ are <u>slow coherent</u> if and only if they are coherent with respect to a set of r slowest modes σ_s of the system.

If the areas formed by the slow-coherent groups satisfy the aggregability condition, then the aggregate modes are also σ_s. This is illustrated by the RC-circuit of Figure 6.2.1 where $\sigma_s = \sigma_1$, and the states $\{x_1, x_2\}$ and $\{x_3, x_4\}$ form slow-coherent areas.

From Theorem 6.2.1, the areas defined by slow coherency have the weakest external connections. This result suggests an area partition along the weak boundaries such that the connections are strong within an area but are weak between the areas. In this case let us scale the external connections by the small parameters ϵ such that

$$K = K^I + \epsilon K^E . \tag{6.3.1}$$

Physically ϵ could denote that external connections are smaller in magnitude than internal connections, or that the number of internal connections is much larger than that of external connections.

Letting q=ϵ in the RC-circuit of Figure 6.2.1, we obtain

$$\dot{x} = \left(\begin{bmatrix} -p & p & 0 & 0 \\ p & -p & 0 & 0 \\ 0 & 0 & -p & p \\ 0 & 0 & p & -p \end{bmatrix} + \epsilon \begin{bmatrix} -1 & 0 & 0 & 1 \\ 0 & -1 & 1 & 0 \\ 0 & 1 & -1 & 0 \\ 1 & 0 & 0 & -1 \end{bmatrix} \right) x. \tag{6.3.2}$$

The eigenvalues of (6.3.2) are $\{0, -2\epsilon, -2p, -2(p+\epsilon)\}$ and the pair 0 and -2ϵ are separated from $-2p$ and $-2(p+\epsilon)$. This type of time-scale separation holds for any dynamic network

$$\dot{x} = dx/d\tau = M^{-1} (K^I + \epsilon K^E) x = (A_0 + \epsilon A_1) x \qquad (6.3.3)$$

whose areas are weakly connected. The time derivative in (6.3.3) is interpreted to be with respect to the fast time variable τ. Since A_0 is singular, system (6.3.3) is a nonexplicit model as the slow variables are not readily identifiable. In fact, because of the special structures of M and K^I, (6.3.3) is in the weak connection form whose time-scale separation has already been discussed in Section 3.5. We now use the results in Section 3.5 to show that the states in the areas are slow coherent.

In the sequential ordering $x = x_{seq}$, at $\epsilon = 0$, (6.3.3) becomes

$$dx/d\tau = M^{-1} K^I x = A_0 x \qquad (6.3.4)$$

where K^I and A_0 are in block diagonal form with r diagonal blocks where $n > r > 1$. Thus, the system separates into r disconnected areas. Since each diagonal block of K^I has a zero eigenvalue, K^I has r zero eigenvalues and

$$K^I U_{seq} = 0 , \qquad (6.3.5)$$

where U_{seq} is the partition matrix in sequential notation. Thus

$$\dim N(K^I) = \dim N(A_0) = r > 1. \qquad (6.3.6)$$

Furthermore, the range of each diagonal block of K^I has dimension $(n_\alpha - 1)$, that is

$$\dim R(K^I) = \dim R(A_0) = n - r \geq 1. \qquad (6.3.7)$$

Since K^I has r zero eigenvalues, (6.3.6) and (6.3.7) imply that

$$R(A_0) \oplus N(A_0) = R^n. \qquad (6.3.8)$$

<u>Theorem 6.3.1</u>: System (6.3.3) has r small eigenvalues of $O(\epsilon)$ and $(n-r)$ eigenvalues of $O(1)$; that is, it has two time-scales.

<u>Proof</u>: Since (6.3.4) satisfies Assumption 3.3.1 because of (6.3.6), (6.3.7) and (6.3.8), the result follows from Theorem 3.3.1. □

The trajectory of system (6.3.4) stays on a dynamic manifold F which is a translate of $R(A_0)$. If the $O(1)$ eigenvalues have negative real parts, the trajectory converges to the equilibrium manifold S defined by $N(A_0)$ which is spanned by the columns of U. For $\varepsilon \neq 0$, the trajectory of system (6.3.3) moves rapidly along F until it is close to S. Then it slowly slides along S. On S, the coherent states are identical.

Theorem 6.3.2: If system (6.3.3) has ρ_1 areas with more than one state and ρ_2 single-state areas, $\rho_1 + \rho_2 = r$, as defined by the partition matrix U which satisfies $K^I U = 0$, then with respect to the r small eigenvalues of $O(\varepsilon)$, system (6.3.3) has ρ_1 near-coherent groups and ρ_2 non-coherent states.

Proof: Since U satisfies (6.3.5), there exists U_ε such that the columns of $U + \varepsilon U_\varepsilon$ span the slow eigenspace of system (6.3.3). Thus, with respect to slow modes, there are ρ_1 near-coherent groups of states and ρ_2 non-coherent states according to Definition 5.5.1. □

For second order dynamic networks with small damping

$$Md^2x/d\tau^2 = -\varepsilon Ddx/d\tau + (K^I + \varepsilon K^E)x, \tag{6.3.9}$$

the following results, similar to those for first order dynamic networks, are easily obtained.

Corollary 6.3.1: System (6.3.9) has 2r small eigenvalues of $O(\sqrt{\varepsilon})$ and $2(n-r)$ eigenvalues of $O(1)$; that is, it has two time-scales.

Corollary 6.3.2: If system (6.3.9) has ρ_1 areas with more than one state and ρ_2 single-state areas, $\rho_1 + \rho_2 = r$, as defined by the partition matrix U which satisfies $K^I U = 0$, then with respect to the 2r small eigenvalues of $O(\sqrt{\varepsilon})$, system (6.3.9) has ρ_1 near-coherent groups and ρ_2 non-coherent states.

For system (6.3.9), the time-scale separation is in terms of frequency. The εD term in (6.3.9) contributes only $O(\varepsilon)$ damping to the fast oscillatory modes in τ-scale, and $O(\sqrt{\varepsilon})$ damping to the slow oscillatory modes in t-scale. Thus, the damping does not significantly affect the oscillatory nature of these modes.

Theorems 6.3.1 and 6.3.2 and Corollaries 6.3.1 and 6.3.2 illuminate several important properties of dynamic networks with weak connections. The parameter ε serves as a measure of the separation of the slow and fast time-scales as well as a measure of the strength of connections. This two-fold nature of ε has practical significance. When the weak boundaries of a system are given, the states in the same areas are slow coherent. Since the number of slow modes and the number of areas are equal, the areas are near-aggregable. The aggregability condition (4.5.27) is approximately satisfied not because the external connections are tuned, but because they are weak. When the weak boundaries of a system are not given, we first examine the spectrum of the system and determine the slow and fast time-scales. Then the slow-coherent areas, found using the grouping algorithm in Chapter 5 with respect to the slow eigenspace, are weakly connected.

Areas found from slow coherency have several useful properties. Weak connection is a system property which is independent of operating conditions. A linearized system may satisfy the tuned aggregability condition (4.5.27) at one operating condition but not at another operating condition. However, systems with weak connections will approximately satisfy the aggregability condition (4.5.27) at all operating conditions. This is important in the study of nonlinear systems such as power systems. Although the small eigenvalues of the linearized model may change with operating conditions, the slow eigenspace will remain roughly unchanged, and will yield the same areas. Other properties include the decoupling of the aggregate and local models, and the robustness of eigenvalue approximations, which are the subject of the next two sections.

Let us illustrate Theorems 6.3.1 and 6.3.2 with the 5 capacitor RC-circuit in Figure 4.2.1 where

$$R_{12} = R_{23} = R_{45} = 1$$

$$R_{14} = R_{15} = R_{25} = R_{34} = 1/\varepsilon \qquad (6.3.10)$$

$$C_i = 1, \quad i = 1,2,\ldots,5,$$

$$\varepsilon = 0.1.$$

The eigenvalues of this circuit with parameters (6.3.10) are $\{0, -0.328, -1.152, -2.195, -3.126\}$ and the eigenspace corresponding to the small eigenvalues 0 and -0.328 is spanned by the columns of

$$
\begin{bmatrix}
1.0 & 0 \\
1.083 & -0.083 \\
1.130 & -0.130 \\
0 & 1 \\
-0.003 & 1.003
\end{bmatrix}
=
\begin{bmatrix}
1 & 0 \\
1 & 0 \\
1 & 0 \\
0 & 1 \\
0 & 1
\end{bmatrix}
+ 0.1
\begin{bmatrix}
0 & 0 \\
0.83 & -0.83 \\
1.30 & -1.30 \\
0 & 0 \\
-0.03 & 0.03
\end{bmatrix} . \qquad (6.3.11)
$$

Therefore, the states which are the capacitor voltages of the areas $\{x_1,\ x_2,\ x_3\}$ and $\{x_4,\ x_5\}$ are slow coherent. On the other hand, if ϵ is not given, we simply compute an eigenbasis matrix and use it to find the areas. The separation of the small and large eigenvalues guarantees that the areas are weakly connected.

6.4 An Empirical Reduction Procedure

To motivate the subsystem decomposition analysis of dynamic networks with weak connections, we present in this section an empirical reduction procedure.

For weakly connected systems (6.3.3), the natural first step is to neglect the weak connections, that is, set $\epsilon = 0$, to obtain (6.3.4). Since K^I is block-diagonal, (6.3.4) is separated into

$$dx^\alpha/d\tau = M_\alpha^{-1}K_\alpha^I x^\alpha \ , \ \alpha = 1,2,\ldots,r, \tag{6.4.1}$$

where x^α is the state, M_α the inertia matrix, and K_α^I the internal connection matrix of the α-th area. The systems of (6.4.1) are expressed in the fast time-scale and the slow time-scale appears as the zero eigenvalues in the systems. These decoupled systems describe the fast dynamics which model the flow between storage elements within the areas.

The systems of (6.4.1) are in the absolute reference frame. They can also be modeled in the local reference frame by choosing one state from each system as the reference and expressing the dynamics of the other states in the same system with respect to the reference. Using x_1^α as the reference, we write $x_i^\alpha - x_1^\alpha$ in vector form as

$$z^\alpha = [-u_\alpha'\ I_{n_\alpha-1}]x^\alpha = G_\alpha x^\alpha \tag{6.4.2}$$

and let

$$x^\alpha = M_\alpha G_\alpha^T(G_\alpha M_\alpha G_\alpha^T)^{-1}z^\alpha = G_\alpha^+ z^\alpha \ . \tag{6.4.3}$$

Then (6.4.1) becomes

$$dz^\alpha/d\tau = G_\alpha M_\alpha^{-1}K_\alpha^I G_\alpha^+ z^\alpha, \tag{6.4.4}$$

whose dimension is smaller than that of (6.4.1) by one, and which does not retain the zero eigenvalue.

Assuming the connections between the areas $\{x_1, x_2, x_3\}$ and $\{x_4, x_5\}$ are weak in the RC-circuit in Figure 4.2.1, the fast dynamics are described by two separate circuits: one includes capacitors C_1, C_2 and C_3, and the other includes capacitors C_4 and C_5 (Figure 6.4.1).

To obtain the slow time-scale model, we scale all the connections by ε such that the weak external connections εK^E become K^E and the internal connections K^I become K^I/ε. The process strengthens the internal connections and in the limit the states within an area are rigidly connected; that is, the nodes within an area collapse to a single node. For example, as the resistance between C_1, C_2 and C_3 in the five capacitor circuit of Figure 4.3.1 becomes zero, the three capacitors are connected in parallel. This process adds up the storage elements in an area into an equivalent storage element located at the area node, and the connections between two areas into an equivalent connection between the two area nodes. The reduced model is the aggregate model given by

$$dy/dt = M_a^{-1} K_a y \qquad\qquad (6.4.5)$$

where, as described in Chapter 4, the variables y are the center of inertia states of the areas, M_a is the aggregate inertia matrix and K_a is the aggregate connection matrix. The aggregate model describes the slow dynamics which are the flow between the areas. For the RC-circuit example in Figure 4.2.1, the aggregate model is given in Figure 6.4.2.

We use the RC-circuit example in Figures 6.4.1 and 6.4.2 for a numerical illustration. The fast dynamics are described by the local models

$$(d/d\tau) \begin{bmatrix} x_1 \\ x_2 \\ x_3 \end{bmatrix} = \begin{bmatrix} -1 & 1 & 0 \\ 1 & -2 & 1 \\ 0 & 1 & -1 \end{bmatrix} \begin{bmatrix} x_1 \\ x_2 \\ x_3 \end{bmatrix} \qquad\qquad (6.4.6)$$

$$(d/d\tau) \begin{bmatrix} x_4 \\ x_5 \end{bmatrix} = \begin{bmatrix} -1 & 1 \\ 1 & -1 \end{bmatrix} \begin{bmatrix} x_4 \\ x_5 \end{bmatrix} \qquad\qquad (6.4.7)$$

and the slow dynamics are described by the aggregate model

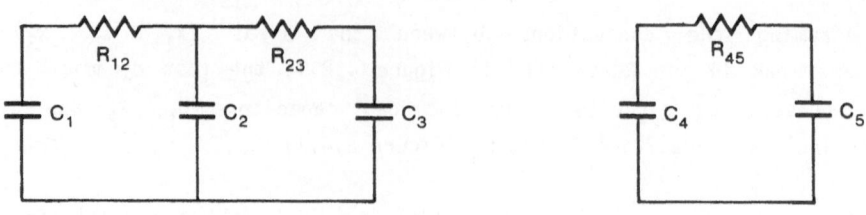

Figure 6.4.1   Local models of the RC-circuit in Figure 4.2.1 are obtained
by disconnecting the resistors between these models.

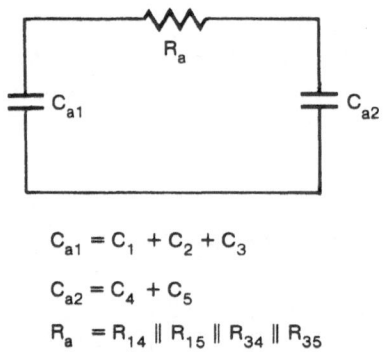

$$C_{a1} = C_1 + C_2 + C_3$$

$$C_{a2} = C_4 + C_5$$

$$R_a = R_{14} \parallel R_{15} \parallel R_{34} \parallel R_{35}$$

Figure 6.4.2   Aggregate model of the RC-circuit in Figure 4.2.1 is
obtained by shorting the resistors between C_1, C_2 and
C_3, and between C_4 and C_5.

$$dy/dt \quad = \quad \begin{bmatrix} 3 & 0 \\ 0 & 2 \end{bmatrix}^{-1} \begin{bmatrix} -4 & 4 \\ 4 & -4 \end{bmatrix} \quad y$$

$$= \quad \begin{bmatrix} -4/3 & 4/3 \\ 2 & -2 \end{bmatrix} \quad y \; . \tag{6.4.8}$$

To eliminate the zero eigenvalues in the local models, we rewrite (6.4.6) and (6.4.7) as

$$d/d\tau \quad \begin{bmatrix} x_2 - x_1 \\ x_3 - x_1 \end{bmatrix} = \begin{bmatrix} -3 & 1 \\ 0 & -1 \end{bmatrix} \begin{bmatrix} x_2 - x_1 \\ x_3 - x_1 \end{bmatrix}, \tag{6.4.9}$$

$$d/d\tau \quad [x_5 - x_4] = [-2] [x_5 - x_4], \tag{6.4.10}$$

where x_1 and x_4 are chosen as the reference states for the areas. The fast eigenvalues of (6.4.9) in τ-scale are -1 and -3, the fast eigenvalue of (6.4.10) in τ-scale is -2, and the slow eigenvalues of (6.4.7) in t-scale are 0 and -3.33. They compare well with the exact eigenvalues -1.152, -3.126, -2.195, 0, and -0.328 in τ-scale since $\tau = t/\varepsilon = 10t$.

The empirical reduction procedure will be verified by an asymptotic analysis in the next section. The asymptotic analysis provides an order of magnitude estimate of the approximation achieved by the reduced models. In cases when reduced models more accurate than those of (6.4.4) and (6.4.5) are required, the asymptotic analysis also provides a method for improving on the approximation.

6.5 Time-Scale Modeling Methodology

In the physical reduction procedure given in the last section, we have alluded to the ideas of fast and slow time-scales, aggregate and local models, slow coherent states and fast local dynamics, and weak and strong connections. These ideas have been developed mostly separately. In this section, we propose a time-scale modeling methodology that encompasses all these ideas to verify the empirical reduction procedure.

The time-scale modeling methodology for dynamic networks starts by transforming a dynamic network with weak connections, which is a non-explicit two-time-scale system, into an explicit form which clearly displays the slow and fast variables. Recall that in Section 3.3, this transformation is obtained using the null space and the range space of A_0. For dynamic networks, the transformation comes readily from aggregation and coherency. From the explicit form, slow and fast subsystems, each having its own physical meaning, are obtained, which approximate the full system. Weak connections can be accounted for in the subsystems to improve on the approximation.

We start by constructing the slow and the fast variables. Recall that the null space of $M^{-1}K^I$ is spanned by the columns of the partition matrix U. Since the aggregation matrix C_a satisfies $C_a U = I_r$, that is, $C_a M^{-1}K^I = 0$, the aggregate variables

$$y = C_a x \qquad\qquad (6.5.1)$$

are used as the slow variables.

To obtain the fast variables, we have to choose a matrix representation of the left range space of $M^{-1}K^I$. Since the areas are near-coherent with respect to the slow modes, we pick one state from each area as the reference state and take the differences between all the other states with the reference state in the same area. These (n-r) difference states can be written in vector form as

$$z = Gx \qquad\qquad (6.5.2)$$

where x is in the sequential ordering and

$$G = \text{diag} (G_1, G_2, \ldots, G_r), \qquad\qquad (6.5.3)$$

where G_α, $\alpha = 1,2,\ldots,r$, are given by (6.4.2). The z variables are fast because the slow dynamics are poorly observable in z, that is,

$$GU = 0. \qquad\qquad (6.5.4)$$

The inverse of the transformation (6.5.1), (6.5.2)

$$\begin{bmatrix} y \\ z \end{bmatrix} = \begin{bmatrix} C_a \\ G \end{bmatrix} x \qquad\qquad (6.5.5)$$

is given by

$$x = [U \ G^+] \begin{bmatrix} y \\ z \end{bmatrix} \tag{6.5.6}$$

where

$$G^+ = M^{-1}G^T (GM^{-1}G^T)^{-1} = \text{diag} (G_1^+, G_2^+, \ldots, G_r^+). \tag{6.5.7}$$

Applying (6.5.5) and (6.5.6) to the weakly connected dynamic network (6.3.3) we obtain

$$\begin{bmatrix} dy/d\tau \\ dz/d\tau \end{bmatrix} = \begin{bmatrix} \varepsilon A_{11} & \varepsilon A_{12} \\ \varepsilon A_{21} & A_{22} + \varepsilon A_{22}' \end{bmatrix} \begin{bmatrix} y \\ z \end{bmatrix} \tag{6.5.8}$$

where

$$A_{11} = M_a^{-1}U^T K^E U = M_a^{-1}K_a \tag{6.5.9}$$

$$A_{12} = M_a^{-1}U^T K^E G^+ \tag{6.5.10}$$

$$A_{21} = GM^{-1}K^E U \tag{6.5.11}$$

$$A_{22} = GM^{-1}K^I G^+ \tag{6.5.12}$$

$$A_{22}' = GM^{-1}K^E G^+. \tag{6.5.13}$$

Since rank $(A_0 + \varepsilon A_1) = (n-r)$ at $\varepsilon = 0$, then

$$\text{rank} \begin{bmatrix} \varepsilon A_{11} & \varepsilon A_{12} \\ \varepsilon A_{21} & A_{22} + \varepsilon A_{22}' \end{bmatrix} \tag{6.5.14}$$

is also $(n-r)$ at $\varepsilon = 0$. Thus, rank $(A_{22}) = (n-r)$, and A_{22} is nonsingular. Hence, (6.5.8) is a singularly perturbed system expressed in the fast time-scale τ and in separated form. In the slow time-scale t, (6.5.8) becomes

$$(d/dt) \begin{bmatrix} y \\ \varepsilon z \end{bmatrix} = \begin{bmatrix} A_{11} & A_{12} \\ \varepsilon A_{21} & A_{22} + \varepsilon A_{22}' \end{bmatrix} \begin{bmatrix} y \\ z \end{bmatrix} \tag{6.5.15}$$

which indicates that y and z are weakly coupled.

Neglecting the $\epsilon A'_{22}$ and off-diagonal block terms A_{12} and ϵA_{21}, the singularly perturbed system (6.5.15) in separated form decomposes into the slow subsystem

$$dy_s/dt = A_{11}y_s = M_a^{-1}K_a y_s, \quad y_s(0) = y(0) \tag{6.5.16}$$

and the fast subsystem

$$dz_f/d\tau = A_{22}z_f = GM^{-1}K^I G^+ z_f, \quad z_f(0) = z(0). \tag{6.5.17}$$

The A_{22} matrix is block diagonal with

$$G_\alpha M_\alpha^{-1} K_\alpha^I G_\alpha^+ \tag{6.5.18}$$

as its α-th diagonal block. Thus, (6.5.17) decouples into

$$dz_f^\alpha/d\tau = G_\alpha M_\alpha^{-1} K_\alpha^I G_\alpha^+ z_f^\alpha, \quad \alpha = 1,2,\dots,r, \tag{6.5.19}$$

which are identical to the local models obtained in (6.4.4). The slow subsystem is an aggregate model and also has the structure of a dynamic network. The following results are direct applications of Corollary 3.3.1.

Theorem 6.5.1: The slow and fast modes of (6.5.15), σ_s and σ_f, are approximated by

$$\sigma_s = \sigma(A_{11}) + 0(\epsilon) \tag{6.5.20}$$

$$\sigma_f = \sigma(A_{22}/\epsilon) + 0(1), \tag{6.5.21}$$

and if $\mathrm{Re}\{\lambda(A_{22})\} \leq -\rho_0 < 0$, where ρ_0 is a scalar independent of ϵ, then the states of (6.5.15) are approximated by

$$y(t) = y_s(t) + 0(\epsilon), \tag{6.5.22}$$

$$z(t) = z_f(t) + 0(\epsilon) . \tag{6.5.23}$$

Theorem 6.5.1 verifies the empirical reduction procedure in Section 6.4. The separation of time-scales has resulted in a decomposition in which parts from every subsystem are put together to form a slow core (y-variables) while the rest of each subsystem forms a <u>fast residue</u> (z^α-variables). The slow core describes the system-wide slow behavior due to the weak connections between the subsystems. The fast residues describe the local dynamics which, due to the strong connections within the subsystems, are significant in the short run. If the fast residues are asymptotically stable, then the z^α variables quickly reach their quasi-steady state equilibrium ($z^\alpha_s = 0$). This decomposition is an analytical form of Simon and Ando's procedure in their classical 1961 paper [50] from which we quote:

"(1) We can somehow classify all the variables ... into a small number of groups;

(2) We can study the interactions within the groups as though the interaction among groups did not exist;

(3) We can define indices representing groups and study the interaction among these indices without regard to the interactions within each group."

Step (1) corresponds in our case to identifying weak connections. Step (2) corresponds to our disconnected fast models (6.5.19), except that we have further removed the slow motion from each subsystem. Step (3) corresponds to the definition of our slow variables y_α as "indices" representing subsystems and the study of the system-wide dynamics through the slow core (6.5.16).

In the RC-circuit example with parameters (6.3.10), the areas are $\{x_1, x_2, x_3\}$ and $\{x_4, x_5\}$ and we use x_1 and x_4 as the reference states. The transformation (6.5.5) is given by

$$C_a = \begin{bmatrix} 1/3 & 1/3 & 1/3 & 0 & 0 \\ 0 & 0 & 0 & 1/2 & 1/2 \end{bmatrix}; \tag{6.5.24}$$

$$G = \begin{bmatrix} -1 & 1 & 0 & 0 & 0 \\ -1 & 0 & 1 & 0 & 0 \\ 0 & 0 & 0 & -1 & 1 \end{bmatrix}. \tag{6.5.25}$$

The inverse transformation (6.5.6) is given by

$$U = \begin{bmatrix} 1 & 0 \\ 1 & 0 \\ 1 & 0 \\ 0 & 1 \\ 0 & 1 \end{bmatrix}, \tag{6.5.26}$$

$$
G^{+} = \begin{bmatrix} -1/3 & -1/3 & 0 \\ 2/3 & -1/3 & 0 \\ -1/3 & 2/3 & 0 \\ 0 & 0 & -1/2 \\ 0 & 0 & 1/2 \end{bmatrix} . \tag{6.5.27}
$$

The slow subsystem (6.5.16) is identical to (6.4.8). The fast subsystem in block diagonal form is

$$
\varepsilon dz_f/dt = \left[\begin{array}{cc|c} -3 & 1 & 0 \\ 0 & -1 & 0 \\ \hline 0 & 0 & -2 \end{array} \right] z_f , \tag{6.5.28}
$$

which illustrates the separation of the area difference variables, and is equivalent to the combination of (6.4.9) and (6.4.10). The eigenvalue approximations of the subsystems are the same as those of (6.4.8), (6.4.9) and (6.4.10).

Subsystems (6.5.16) and (6.5.17) are the simplest models obtained through the use of the singular perturbation techniques. Since (6.5.15) has two time-scales, the subsystems (6.5.16) and (6.5.17) can be improved by an iterative process such as the one given in Section 3.3. For dynamic networks with weak connections, iterative improvements usually are not necessary. However, in some applications, it may be desirable to take one iteration step in correcting the effect of weak connections in systems (6.5.16) and (6.5.17).

Using the expressions (3.3.25) and (3.3.26) for one iteration step, we obtain, through the substitution of appropriate quantities into the expressions,

$$
dy_{s\varepsilon}/dt = (A_{11} - \varepsilon A_{12}(A_{22} + \varepsilon A_{22}')^{-1}A_{21})y_{s\varepsilon} = A_{11\varepsilon}y_{s\varepsilon},
$$

$$
y_{s\varepsilon}(0) = y(0) - \varepsilon A_{12}(A_{22} + \varepsilon A_{22}')^{-1}z(0), \tag{6.5.29}
$$

$$
\varepsilon dz_{f\varepsilon}/dt = (A_{22} + \varepsilon A_{22}')z_{f\varepsilon}, \quad z_{f\varepsilon}(0) = z(0) - \varepsilon(A_{22} + \varepsilon A_{22}')^{-1}A_{21}y(0). \tag{6.5.30}
$$

Corollary 3.3.2 leads to the following result.

Theorem 6.5.2: The slow and fast modes of (6.5.15), σ_s and σ_f, are approximated by

$$\sigma_s = \sigma(A_{11\epsilon}) + 0(\epsilon^2) \tag{6.5.31}$$

$$\sigma_f = \sigma((A_{22} + \epsilon A_{22}')/\epsilon) + 0(\epsilon), \tag{6.5.32}$$

and if Re $\{\lambda(A_{22})\} \le -\rho_0 < 0$, where ρ_0 is a positive scalar independent of ϵ, then

$$y(t) = y_{s\epsilon}(t) + \epsilon A_{12}(A_{22} + \epsilon A_{22}')^{-1} z_{f\epsilon}(t) + 0(\epsilon^2), \tag{6.5.33}$$

$$z(t) = -\epsilon(A_{22} + \epsilon A_{22}')^{-1} A_{21} y_{s\epsilon}(t) + z_{f\epsilon}(t) + 0(\epsilon^2). \tag{6.5.34}$$

The subsystems (6.5.29) and (6.5.30) differ from (6.5.16) and (6.5.17) in that a secondary effect of weak connections is introduced. In the slow subsystem (6.5.29) the ϵ dependent term accounts for the effect of the fast contribution $z_{f\epsilon}$ in the slow state y. This term will be small compared to A_{11} which is due to the strong coupling of the weak connections in the slow time-scale. For the fast subsystem (6.5.30), the weak connections between the local models are retained. Thus, the local models are no longer decoupled.

The time-scale decomposition of slow and fast subsystems is also applicable to second order dynamic networks. We will not repeat the derivation but will illustrate with power system examples in the next section.

For the RC-circuit example with parameters (6.3.10),

$$A_{11\epsilon} = \begin{bmatrix} -0.132 & 0.132 \\ 0.198 & -0.198 \end{bmatrix}, \tag{6.5.35}$$

$$(A_{22} + \epsilon A_{22}')/\epsilon = \begin{bmatrix} -3.133 & 0.967 & 0.05 \\ -0.033 & -1.133 & 0.05 \\ 0.1 & -0.1 & -2.2 \end{bmatrix}. \tag{6.6.36}$$

Thus, the slow and fast eigenvalues of the subsystems are 0, -0.330, -1.148, -2.195 and -3.125, which are excellent approximations of the accurate eigenvalues 0, -0.328, -1.152, -2.195 and -3.126.

In conclusion, we propose a time-scale modeling methodology for dynamic networks, which consists of the following steps:

1. Identify slow coherent areas either by recognition of weak connections or by using the grouping algorithm in Section 5.6.

2. Obtain the slow and fast variables y and z.

3. Use the subsystems (6.5.16) and (6.5.17) to model the slow and fast dynamics separately.

4. If necessary, use the subsystems (6.5.29) and (6.5.30) for more accurate modeling of the slow and fast dynamics.

The methodology will be illustrated in the next section with power system models. A nonlinear counterpart of this methodology will be given in the next chapter.

6.6 Slow Coherency in Power System Examples

The partition of systems into weakly connected areas is more physical than using the tuned aggregability conditions because it ensures that the states within each area will be strongly connected. In power systems, this results in contiguous areas which are a physically meaningful decomposition. For large power systems, it is often cumbersome to identify the weak connections manually. Instead, we use the grouping algorithm by setting σ_a to be the slowest modes, since it is an automated means of finding the areas. For systems with no clear separation in time-scale, we find the largest gap between two successive eigenvalues λ_r and λ_{r+1}, where

$$|\lambda_i| \le |\lambda_{i+1}|, \quad i = 1,2,\ldots,n, \tag{6.6.1}$$

and let

$$\varepsilon = |\lambda_r|/|\lambda_{r+1}| , \tag{6.6.2}$$

$$\sigma_a = \sigma_s = \{\lambda_1, \lambda_2, \ldots, \lambda_r\}. \tag{6.6.3}$$

This procedure ensures that the connections between the areas will be weak. In this section, we use the three machine system example in Figure 4.3.1, the 48 machine model of the Northeastern U.S. system in Figure 5.7.1, and the 42 machine model of the Western U.S. system in Figure 5.7.2 to illustrate that the connections between slow coherent areas are weak, and to show the eigenvalue approximation of the slow and fast subsystems.

The eigenvalues for the three machine system (4.3.18) without damping are 0, 0, $\pm$ j8.689 and $\pm$ j13.349 and there is a separation between the first and second oscillatory modes with $\varepsilon = |-8.689|/|-13.349| = 0.651$. Specifying coherency with respect to the two pairs of the slow modes, we have found in Chapter 5 that the areas are area 1 = $\{x_1\}$, and area 2 = $\{x_2, x_3\}$. Let us verify this choice by examining the strength of external connections s (6.2.4). Table 6.6.1

shows the values of s for different partitions. Clearly, s is smallest for the partition $\{x_1\}$ and $\{x_2, x_3\}$.

Table 6.6.1

External connections for different choices of areas

Area Partitions	External Connections, s
$\{x_1, x_2\}$, $\{x_3\}$	197.3
$\{x_1, x_3\}$, $\{x_2\}$	166.0
$\{x_1\}$, $\{x_2, x_3\}$	151.1

Let us examine the eigenvalue approximation achieved by the aggregate and local models with damping included. The aggregate model has been obtained earlier in Chapter 4. For completeness, we shall repeat it here. With

$$U = \begin{bmatrix} 1 & 0 \\ 0 & 1 \\ 0 & 1 \end{bmatrix},$$

$$M_a = \begin{bmatrix} 0.05 & 0 \\ 0 & 0.035 \end{bmatrix},$$

$$C_a = \begin{bmatrix} 1 & 0 & 0 \\ 0 & 0.068 & 0.32 \end{bmatrix},$$

$$G = \begin{bmatrix} 0 & -1 & 1 \end{bmatrix},$$

$$G^+ = \begin{bmatrix} 0 \\ -0.32 \\ 0.68 \end{bmatrix},$$

$$\tag{6.6.4}$$

the aggregate model is

$$\ddot{y}_s = -M_a^{-1} U^T D U \dot{y}_s + M_a^{-1} U^T K^E U y_s = -M_a^{-1} D_a \dot{y}_s + M_a^{-1} K_a y_s$$

$$= \begin{bmatrix} -0.203 & 0 \\ 0 & -0.186 \end{bmatrix} \dot{y}_s + \begin{bmatrix} -23.2 & 23.2 \\ 57.9 & -57.9 \end{bmatrix} y_s. \tag{6.6.5}$$

The aggregate modes are 0, -0.198 and $-0.0953 \pm j9.00$. There is no fast local model for area 1 since it has only one state. The fast local model for area 2 is

$$\ddot{z}_f = GM^{-1}DG^{+}\dot{z}_f + GM^{-1}KG^{+}z_f$$

$$= -0.175\,\dot{z}_f - 176.13\,z_f \quad , \tag{6.6.6}$$

where $z_f = x_3 - x_2$, whose mode is $-0.0876 \pm j13.3$. The slow modes and the fast mode are close to the modes 0, -0.198, $-0.092 \pm j8.804$, and $-0.0858 \pm j13.403$ of the original system (4.3.17).

The approximation achieved by the aggregate and local models is already very good, and there is no need for further improvement. Here we make one correction step for illustrative purposes. To carry out corrections for second order dynamic networks, we have to express them as systems of first order differential equations and then use (6.5.29) and (6.5.30). For the slow subsystem (6.5.29), denoting

$$y_{s1}' = y_{s1}, \; y_{s2}' = \dot{y}_{s1}, \; y_{s3}' = y_{s2}, \; y_{s4}' = \dot{y}_{s2}, \tag{6.6.7}$$

we obtain

$$\begin{bmatrix} \dot{y}_{s\epsilon1}' \\[4pt] \dot{y}_{s\epsilon2}' \\[4pt] \dot{y}_{s\epsilon3}' \\[4pt] \dot{y}_{s\epsilon4}' \end{bmatrix} = \begin{bmatrix} 0 & 1 & 0 & 0 \\[4pt] -22.6 & -0.203 & 22.6 & 0.000484 \\[4pt] 0 & 0 & 0 & 1 \\[4pt] 56.6 & 0 & -56.5 & -0.187 \end{bmatrix} \begin{bmatrix} y_{s\epsilon1}' \\[4pt] y_{s\epsilon2}' \\[4pt] y_{s\epsilon3}' \\[4pt] y_{s\epsilon4}' \end{bmatrix} \tag{6.6.8}$$

whose modes are 0, -0.198, $-0.0959 \pm j8.89$. Denoting

$$z_{f1}' = z_{f1}, \; z_{f2}' = \dot{z}_{f1}, \tag{6.6.9}$$

the fast subsystem (6.5.30) is

$$\begin{bmatrix} \dot{z}_{f\epsilon1}' \\[4pt] \dot{z}_{f\epsilon2}' \end{bmatrix} = \begin{bmatrix} 0.00121 & 1.0 \\[4pt] -176.0 & -0.175 \end{bmatrix} \begin{bmatrix} z_{f\epsilon1}' \\[4pt] z_{f\epsilon2}' \end{bmatrix} \tag{6.6.10}$$

whose mode is $-0.0870 \pm j13.3$. Note that the introduction of the terms 0.000484 in (6.6.7) and 0.00121 in (6.6.8) changes the interpretation of the fast and slow variables and hence the representation of (6.6.7) and (6.6.8) as equivalent dynamic networks. In this case, the improvement in the approximation by (6.6.8) and (6.6.10) over the approximation by (6.6.5) and (6.6.6) is small.

For the 48 machine system, we also take damping into consideration. The largest gap between the eigenvalues occurs between the eighth smallest complex eigenvalue $-0.2604 \pm j5.2806$ and the ninth smallest complex eigenvalue $-0.1131 \pm j6.0530$, that is, $\varepsilon = 5.2806/6.0530 = 0.8724$. Therefore, the number of areas is chosen to be nine, since there is a pair of slow non-oscillatory modes 0 and -0.4846 corresponding to the system frequency and angle. The nine areas have already been found in Section 5.6.

For this system, we use a different approach to examine the external connections since it is difficult to examine them for all possible combinations of the 48 states into nine areas. Table 6.6.2 shows the strength of connections in matrix form between the nine areas. Each entry $\gamma_{\alpha\beta}$ of the table is the total of all connections of k_{ij}/m_i over all states i in area α and state j in area β. The diagonal entry $\gamma_{\alpha\alpha}$ is the total internal connection of area α. The sum of the values for each area is normalized to 100%. Entries less than 1% are not listed in the table. Every off-diagonal entry except for γ_{26} is smaller than the corresponding diagonal entry which is the total internal coupling. Entry γ_{55} is of no interest since area 5 consists of only one machine. Moreover, every diagonal entry, except for γ_{22} and γ_{44}, is larger than the sum of off-diagonal entries in the corresponding row. Thus this area partition results in weakly connected areas.

Table 6.6.2

Strength of connection between areas for 48 machine system

Areas	1	2	3	4	5	6	7	8	9
1	83	-	1	-	-	-	4	11	-
2	-	34	-	-	4	59	2	-	1
3	-	-	75	-	9	-	6	8	-
4	-	-	-	47	-	5	11	-	37
5	-	4	56	-	*	30	6	3	-
6	-	25	1	-	7	57	5	-	3
7	3	-	12	-	4	2	66	6	5
8	6	-	4	-	-	-	10	77	3
9	3	-	1	6	-	5	25	8	51

Tables 6.6.3 and 6.6.4 show the eigenvalue approximation for the slow time-scale and the fast time-scale. The aggregate modes approximate the slowest modes to within 28%, and with a correction for the weak connections, approximate the slowest modes to within 12%. The fast modes of the local models of the areas 1

and 2 are listed in Table 6.6.4. Since many eigenvalues are very close, to compare the fast models, we first match the eigenvectors of the local models and the full model according to their directions [63]. The fast modes of area 1 approximate the accurate eigenvalues to within 17.3%, while the fast eigenvalue of area 2 is almost 40% off the accurate eigenvalue. The latter case is already noted in the connection table which shows that there are significant interactions between areas 2 and 6. With a correction for weak connections included, the fast modes are approximated to within 1.5%.

For the 42 machine system, we examine the eigenvalue approximation achieved by the 10-area partition in Section 5.7. The separation between the 9th and the 10th smallest complex eigenvalue is ϵ = 5.2366/5.8366 = 0.90. Table 6.6.5 shows the slow and fast time-scale approximation by the aggregate and local models with a correction for weak connections included. The worst error is less than 8.7%.

Table 6.6.3

Slow time-scale approximation of 48 machine system

Accurate	Aggregate Model	Aggregate Model with Weak Connection Corrections
0.0	0.0	0.0
-.4846	-.4842	-.4845
-.2486 + j1.678	-.2499 + j1.835	-.2491 + j1.684
-.1860 ∓ j2.528	-.1893 ∓ j2.720	-.1854 ∓ j2.548
-.2429 ∓ j3.056	-.2441 ∓ j3.337	-.2457 ∓ j3.094
-.1879 ∓ j3.327	-.1766 ∓ j3.696	-.1816 ∓ j3.388
-.2703 ∓ j4.435	-.2470 ∓ j5.202	-.2716 ∓ j4.412
-.1995 ∓ j4.707	-.2339 ∓ j5.308	-.1986 ∓ j4.893
-.2015 ∓ j5.049	-.2195 ∓ j5.745	-.2135 ∓ j5.286
-.2604 ∓ j5.281	-.2108 ∓ j6.748	-.2363 ∓ j5.929

Table 6.6.4

Fast time-scale approximation of 48 machine system for areas 1 and 2

Area	Accurate	Local Model	Local Model with Weak Connection Correction
1	-.1131 + j6.053	-.1135 + j5.306	-.1134 + j6.053
	-.0984 ∓ j6.819	-.0943 ∓ j5.641	-.1050 ∓ j6.715
	-.0963 ∓ j7.294	-.0940 ∓ j6.734	-.0963 ∓ j7.280
	-.0919 ∓ j8.310	-.0919 ∓ j7.037	-.0919 ∓ j8.310
	-.1170 ∓ j8.858	-.1146 ∓ j7.216	-.0115 ∓ j8.821
	-.1045 ∓ j9.173	-.1022 ∓ j8.685	-.1045 ∓ j9.173
	-.1044 ∓ j9.797	-.1043 ∓ j9.367	-.1044 ∓ j9.797
	-.1404 ∓ j15.281	-.1399 ∓ j14.715	-.1402 ∓ j15.279
2	-.2945 + j9.717	-.2980 + j5.957	-.2949 + j9.660

Table 6.6.5

Eigenvalue approximation of 42 machine system.

Only two eigenvalues of the fast time-scales are shown.

Time-Scale	Accurate	Aggregate and Local Models with Weak Connection Correction
Slow	0.0 -.4540 -.2170 + j1.6382 -.2025 $\mp$ j2.0205 -.1786 $\mp$ j2.5840 -.1921 $\mp$ j2.7962 -.1546 $\mp$ j3.2541 -.2578 $\mp$ j3.4137 -.1872 $\mp$ j4.1504 -.1802 $\mp$ j4.3461 -.2137 $\mp$ j4.8186	0.0 -.4538 -.2253 + j1.6588 -.2145 $\mp$ j2.0478 -.1793 $\mp$ j2.5972 -.1914 $\mp$ j2.8284 -.1546 $\mp$ j3.2799 -.2753 $\mp$ j3.5367 -.1877 $\mp$ j4.2068 -.1914 $\mp$ j4.6042 -.2498 $\mp$ j5.2366
Fast	-.2122 + j5.8428 -.2820 $\mp$ j6.5424	-.2079 + j5.8366 -.1562 $\mp$ j6.4951

6.7 Conclusions

We have developed a time-scale methodology for the modeling of linear dynamic networks. The assumption here, which is satisfied by many real systems, is that the areas within a dynamic network are weakly connected. Under this assumption, the dynamic network exhibit two time-scales, of which the slow time-scale behavior can be captured by the aggregate model which represents the motions between the areas, and the fast time-scale behavior can be captured by the local models which represent the motions within the individual areas. The aggregate model and the decoupled local models are useful for decentralized and hierarchical control design.

The extension of the two time-scale methodology to nonlinear dynamic networks will be studied in the next chapter.

CHAPTER 7

NONLINEAR DYNAMIC NETWORKS

7.1 Introduction

The study of dynamic networks often requires nonlinearities to be retained. An example is the transient stability study of a power system subject to a disturbance, where the electrical power output of a synchronous machine is a nonlinear function of rotor angles [1]. In this chapter we will develop a time-scale modeling methodology for nonlinear dynamic networks. The methodology is similar to that for linear dynamic networks because the time-scale properties of a dynamic network are due to its structure and are not restricted by linearity assumptions.

We begin by developing a transformation for expressing a nonlinear two-time-scale system with singular $\partial g/\partial z$ into the explicit form (2.2.7), (2.2.8). In Chapter 3 a set of slow and fast variables is obtained for a linear two-time-scale system using a transformation from the equilibrium and dynamic manifolds. The concept of equilibrium and dynamic manifolds is now extended to nonlinear systems. As in the linear case, these manifolds, which are in general nonlinear, serve as a coordinate-free characterization of time-scales, and can be used to obtain predominantly slow and fast variables.

The class of dynamic networks considered in this chapter, which includes the electromechanical model of power systems, has nonlinear connection characteristics. The areas, and internal and external connections defined in Chapter 4 for linear dynamic networks are equally applicable to these nonlinear dynamic networks. With weak external connections we can readily construct the equilibrium and dynamic manifolds and show that a nonlinear dynamic network has two time-scales. Despite the nonlinearities in the model, the transformation leading to the explicit form is linear since the manifolds are linear. The time-scale separation allows the decomposition of a dynamic network into nonlinear aggregate and local models. The equilibrium of the reduced models can be chosen so that it is equal to the equilibrium of the original model. This choice improves on the approximations achieved by the reduced models.

In Section 7.2 we develop manifolds for expressing a nonlinear two-time-scale system into the explicit form. Nonlinear dynamic networks are discussed in Section 7.3 and time-scales in weakly connected networks are shown using the manifolds. The decomposition into aggregate and local models are discussed in Section 7.4. A small power system is used in Section 7.5 to illustrate the application of the time-scale modeling methodology to the nonlinear electromechanical model.

7.2 Conservation and Equilibrium Properties in Nonlinear Systems

In nonlinear systems, we can no longer use the wide separation of eigenvalues as a characterization of time-scales since the notion of modes is nonexistent. However, characterization via the conservation and equilibrium properties introduced in Chapter 3 for linear systems is still applicable. As in the linear case, these properties lead to a new set of variables in which the time-scales are explicit.

Let us reexamine already known time-scale properties of the nonlinear singularly perturbed model in explicit form (2.2.7), (2.2.8). Writing (2.2.7), (2.2.8) in the fast time-scale τ, we obtain

$$dy/d\tau = \epsilon \, f(y,z,\epsilon),$$
$$dz/d\tau = g(y,z,\epsilon), \qquad\qquad (7.2.1)$$

where y are r slow states and z are (n-r) fast states. For clarity, we have denoted the ϵ-dependence of f and g and assumed that they do not depend explicitly on time.

Setting $\epsilon=0$ we obtain the auxiliary system

$$dy/d\tau = 0,$$
$$dz/d\tau = g(y,z,0), \qquad\qquad (7.2.2)$$

which has the following two important properties.

Conservation Property: An r-dimensional function of the state

$$\psi(y,z) = y \qquad\qquad (7.2.3)$$

remains at its initial value

$$\psi(y(0), z(0)) = y(0), \qquad\qquad (7.2.4)$$

that is, it is conserved during the motion of (7.2.2).

Equilibrium Property: System (7.2.2) possesses a set of non-isolated (continuum) equilibrium points defined by an (n-r)-dimensional function

$$\varphi(y,z) = 0 \qquad\qquad (7.2.5)$$

which is given by

$$\varphi(y,z) = g(y,z,0) = 0. \tag{7.2.6}$$

The equilibria defined by (7.2.6) are the quasi-steady states to which the fast transients of (7.2.1) will converge if they are asymptotically stable.

The trajectories of the auxiliary system (7.2.2) approximate the trajectories of the explicit model (7.2.1) in the fast time-scale. With the conservation property, a trajectory of (7.2.2) stays on the dynamic manifold defined by

$$F = \{y,z : y = y(0)\}. \tag{7.2.7}$$

If the fast dynamics are asymptotically stable, the trajectory converges to and terminates on the equilibrium manifold defined by

$$S = \{y,z : g(y,z,0)=0\}. \tag{7.2.8}$$

For the explicit model (7.2.1), y remains almost constant in the fast time-scale, therefore, the boundary layer trajectory remains close to F. If the fast dynamics are asymptotically stable, then the trajectory converges to S. When it gets close to the intersection of F and S, that is, the system is in quasi-steady state, it begins to slide slowly along S. Thus, the two-time-scale behavior of (7.2.1) is described in terms of a fast motion on the dynamic manifold due to the conservation property and a slow motion on the equilbrium manifold due to the equilibrium property.

We now proceed to use the conservation and equilibrium properties to characterize time-scales in non-explicit models with an n-dimensional state x

$$\epsilon \, dx/dt = dx/d\tau = h(x,\epsilon) \tag{7.2.9}$$

defined in a domain $Ex[0,\epsilon_0]$ in which the function h is assumed to be continuously differentiable with respect to x and ϵ. In τ-scale at $\epsilon=0$, (7.2.9) becomes the auxiliary system

$$dx/d\tau = h(x,0). \tag{7.2.10}$$

<u>Assumption 3.2.1</u>: System (7.2.10) satisfies the following conditions for the existence of manifolds S and F.

<u>Equilibrium Manifold S</u>: The set

$$S = \{x : h(x,0) = 0, \ x \text{ in } E\} \tag{7.2.11}$$

defines a ν-dimensional continuously differentiable manifold, $\nu \geq 1$. Hence, there exists a ρ-dimensional continuously differentiable function $\varphi(x)$ with $\rho=n-\nu$ and rank $(\partial\varphi/\partial x) = \rho$ for all x in E such that

$$\varphi(x) = 0 \qquad \text{if and only if} \qquad h(x,0) = 0, \tag{7.2.12}$$

that is, in the domain of interest E, every equilibrium of (7.2.10) satisfies $\varphi(x)=0$ and every x satisfying $\varphi(x)=0$ is an equilibrium of (7.2.10).

<u>Dynamic Manifold F</u>: There exists a ν-dimensional continuously differentiable function $\psi(x)$ such that for any initial condition x(0) in E, the ρ-dimensional manifold

$$F_{x(0)} = \{x : \psi(x) - \psi(x(0)) = 0, \text{ rank } (\partial\psi/\partial x) = \nu\} \tag{7.2.13}$$

is an invariant manifold of (7.2.10), that is, a trajectory originating in $F_{x(0)}$ remains in $F_{x(0)}$,

$$\psi(x(\tau)) - \psi(x(0)) = 0, \text{ for all } \tau \geq 0. \tag{7.2.14}$$

As in the linear case, for notational simplicity, we will frequently omit the subscript in $F_{x(0)}$ and use F to denote a dynamic manifold, with the understanding that F is dependent on initial conditions.

Moreover, for all x(0) in E, manifolds S and F are not tangent to each other, that is, for all x in the intersection of S and F

$$\text{rank} \begin{bmatrix} \partial\varphi/\partial x \\ \partial\psi/\partial x \end{bmatrix} = n. \tag{7.2.15}$$

<u>Theorem 7.2.1</u>: Under Assumption 7.2.1, the change of coordinates

$$y = \psi(x) \quad , \quad z = \varphi(x) \tag{7.2.16}$$

transforms (7.2.9) into a singularly perturbed model in the explicit separated form with $\partial g/\partial z$ at $\varepsilon=0$ nonsingular and $z_s(t)=0$, where z_s is the slow part of z.

<u>Proof</u>: The τ-derivative of ψ with respect to (7.2.10) is

$$d\psi/d\tau = (\partial\psi/\partial x)(dx/d\tau) = (\partial\psi/\partial x) h(x,0) = 0. \tag{7.2.17}$$

Using the mean value theorem in ε for each component of h, the t-derivative of y with respect to (7.2.9) is

$dy/dt = (1/\varepsilon)(\partial\psi/\partial x) \, h(x,\varepsilon) = (\partial\psi/\partial x)(\partial h/\partial \varepsilon),$ (7.2.18)

implying that y is a slow variable. Using the inverse transformation $x=\gamma(y,z)$ of (7.2.16) which exists because of (7.2.15) and taking the t-derivative of $z=\varphi(x)$ with respect to (7.2.9), we obtain

$\varepsilon(dz/dt) = (\partial\varphi/\partial x) \, h(x,\varepsilon) = (\partial\varphi/\partial x) \, h(\gamma(y,z), \, \varepsilon) = g(y,z,\varepsilon).$ (7.2.19)

We show that $(\partial g/\partial z)$ at $\varepsilon=0$ is nonsingular by contradiction. Assuming that it is singular, the equilibrium manifold of (7.2.18), (7.2.19) has dimension greater than ν which is a contradiction because (7.2.16) is a nonsingular transformation. Finally, since x is in S if and only if $x = \gamma(y,0)$, it follows that

$h(\gamma(y,0),0)=0$ and $g(y,0,0) = 0,$ (7.2.20)

implying that $z_s(t) = 0.$ □

The intuitive idea behind this theorem is illustrated by Figure 7.2.1. If the equilibrium manifold S is attractive, the trajectories of the auxiliary system (7.2.10), which are confined to some F because of the conservation property, converge to S, and when $\tau \to \infty$, they terminate at the intersection of F and S. Consequently, the trajectories of the original system (7.2.9) rapidly approach S, staying in a boundary layer close to F, and then slowly continue their motions close to S. Since the trajectories are initially close to F, the quantity $\psi(x)$ stays almost constant during this interval; thus it qualifies as a predominantly slow variable. On the other hand, the quantity $\varphi(x)$ is large if the trajectory starts far away from S and rapidly diminishes when the trajectory approaches S. Thus, it qualifies as a predominantly fast variable.

As an illustration, we consider the nonlinear system

$dx_1/d\tau = -\varphi_1(x) + (x_1 + x_3) \, \varphi_2(x) - \varepsilon x_1,$

$dx_2/d\tau = -2x_2 \, \varphi_2(x) - \varepsilon x_2^3,$ (7.2.21)

$dx_3/d\tau = \varphi_1(x) + (x_1 + x_3) \, \varphi_2(x) - \varepsilon x_3,$

defined over

$E= \{(x_1, x_2, x_3) : x_1 > 1 , x_2 > 0.5, x_3 > 0.5\},$ (7.2.22)

where $\varphi_1(x)$ and $\varphi_2(x)$ are continuously differentiable functions defined over E. Setting $\varepsilon=0$ in (7.2.21), we obtain

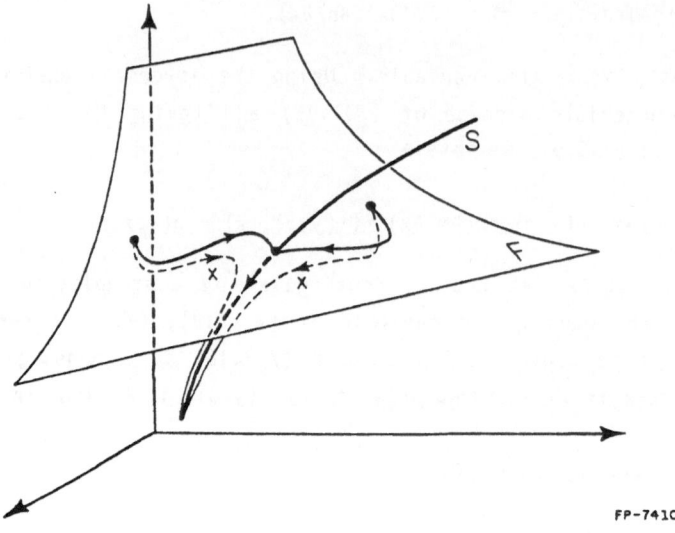

FP-7410

Figure 7.2.1 Equilibrium (S) and dynamic (F) manifolds
of a three state two-time-scale system

$$dx_1/d\tau = -\varphi_1(x) + (x_1 + x_3)\,\varphi_2(x),$$

$$dx_2/d\tau = -2x_2\varphi_2(x),$$ (7.2.23)

$$dx_3/d\tau = \varphi_1(x) + (x_1 + x_3)\,\varphi_2(x),$$

for which

$$\varphi_1(x) = 0 \quad , \quad \varphi_2(x) = 0$$ (7.2.24)

define the equilibrium manifold S. It is easily verified that the dynamic manifold is defined by $\psi(x) = \psi(x(0))$ where

$$\psi(x) = (x_1 + x_3)x_2.$$ (7.2.25)

The equilibrium manifold and a dynamic manifold of this system are shown in Figure 7.2.1 where the functions φ_1, φ_2 have been chosen as

$$\varphi_1(x) = x_1 - x_3 \quad , \quad \varphi_2(x) = x_2^2 - x_3 - x_1 + 1.$$ (7.2.26)

Thus, system (7.2.21) can be put into the explicit separated form using

$$y = \psi(x)$$ (7.2.27)

as the slow variable and

$$z_1 = \varphi_1(x) \quad , \quad z_2 = \varphi_2(x)$$ (7.2.28)

as the fast variables since the determinant of

$$\begin{bmatrix} \partial\psi/\partial x \\ \partial\varphi_1/\partial x \\ \partial\varphi_2/\partial x \end{bmatrix} = \begin{bmatrix} x_2 & x_1+x_2 & x_3 \\ 1 & 0 & -1 \\ -1 & 2x_2 & -1 \end{bmatrix}$$ (7.2.29)

is $2(x_1 + x_2 + x_2x_3 + x_2^2)$, which is positive for all x in E (7.2.22), implying that (7.2.29) is of full rank.

The manifolds can also be used to investigate time-scales in oscillatory systems written as a system of second order differential equations

$$\varepsilon d^2x/dt^2 = d^2x/d\tau^2 = h(x,\varepsilon)$$ (7.2.30)

where x is an n-vector and h is assumed to be continuously differentiable with respect to x and ε in a domain $Ex[0,\varepsilon_0]$. In τ-scale we set $\varepsilon=0$ to obtain the auxiliary system

$$d^2x/d\tau^2 = h(x,0). \tag{7.2.31}$$

For (7.2.31), we assume that there exist a set S given by (7.2.11) which defines a ν-dimensional continuously differentiable $\psi(x)$ which satisfies (7.2.12), where $\rho = n - \nu$. Furthermore, there exists a ν-dimensional continously differentiable function $\psi(x)$ with the property

$$d\psi(x)/d\tau = d\psi(x)/d\tau|_{\tau=0} = c_0, \text{ rank } (\partial\psi/\partial x) = \nu. \tag{7.2.32}$$

The functions $\varphi(x)$ and $\psi(x)$ also satisfy (7.2.15). The motion of (7.2.31) for all x in S is one of constant velocity because

$$d^2x/d\tau^2 = 0. \tag{7.2.33}$$

In addition, the trajectory of (7.2.31) is confined to the moving plane

$$F = \{x : \psi(x) = c_0\tau + c_1\}. \tag{7.2.34}$$

For c_0 small, F drifts away slowly. When $\epsilon \neq 0$ as in (7.2.30), F oscillates about the origin.

In the case when both ψ and φ are linear functions of x, we can construct the slow variables

$$y = \psi(x) \tag{7.2.35}$$

and the fast variables

$$z = \varphi(x) \tag{7.2.36}$$

for the nonexplicit model (7.2.30). With respect to the auxiliary system (7.2.31),

$$d^2\psi/d\tau^2 = d(d\psi/d\tau)/d\tau = d((\partial\psi/\partial x)(dx/d\tau))/d\tau$$
$$= (\partial\psi/\partial x)(d^2x/d\tau^2) = (\partial\psi/\partial x) h(x,0) = 0. \tag{7.2.37}$$

Thus, with respect to the nonexplicit model (7.2.30),

$$d^2y/dt^2 = (\partial\psi/\partial x)(d^2x/dt^2) = (\partial\psi/\partial x) h(x,\epsilon)/\epsilon$$
$$= (\partial\psi/\partial x)(\partial h/\partial \epsilon), \tag{7.2.38}$$

implying that y is slow. The steps to show that z is fast are similar to those given in Theorem 7.2.1 for (7.2.9).

7.3 Time-Scales in Nonlinear Dynamic Networks

An assumption used in the study of dynamic networks in Chapter 2 is that the flow f_{ij} from node i to node j depends linearly on the potential difference $(x_i - x_j)$ between nodes i and j. In this section, we consider dynamic networks whose flow f_{ij} is governed by a nonlinear function $f_{ij}(x_i - x_j)$ of the potential difference between nodes i and j. This class of nonlinearity more accurately models some physical processes, for example, the flow of current in RC-circuits with nonlinear resistors, the transfer of momenta in mass-spring systems with nonlinear springs, and the transfer of angular momenta between machines in power systems. When the external connections are weak, we show that the linear transformation used for linear dynamic networks also separates the time-scales in nonlinear dynamic networks.

We assume that the flow in the interconnections are continuously differentiable functions of the potential differences across the interconnections satisfying

$$f_{ij}(x_i - x_j) = -f_{ji}(x_j - x_i). \tag{7.3.1}$$

This assumption is equivalent to saying that there are neither sources nor sinks along the interconnections. Nonlinear dynamic networks are then modeled in the potential form by either the system of first order equations

$$m_i \dot{x}_i = \sum_{\substack{j=1 \\ j \neq i}}^{n} - f_{ij}(x_i - x_j) + p_i \tag{7.3.2}$$

or the system of second order equations

$$m_i \ddot{x}_i = - d_i \dot{x}_i + \sum_{\substack{j=1 \\ j \neq i}}^{n} - f_{ij}(x_i - x_j) + p_i \tag{7.3.3}$$

where x_i, m_i are the potential and inertia of the i-th storage element, and p_i is the net injection at the i-th node. The damping d_i for second order dynamic networks is assumed to be small. If nodes i and j are not connected, then $f_{ij} = 0$. To avoid repetition, we will not consider the storage form of (7.3.2) and (7.3.3) where the stored quantities $\xi_i = m_i x_i$ are used as the state variables.

We point out that since (7.3.1) is satisfied,

$$\partial f_{ij}/\partial x_j = \partial f_{ji}/\partial x_i. \tag{7.3.4}$$

Thus, the linearized models of (7.3.1) and (7.3.2) have properties (4.2.15) and (4.2.16) of linear dynamic networks.

The notions defined in Chapter 4 for linear dynamic networks are also applicable to nonlinear dynamic networks. Areas are sets of states such that every state x_i is in one and only one set. Similarly, the set containing the indices of the states in area α is denoted by J_α. The flow f_{ij} is said to be internal if the states x_i and x_j are in the same area, and external if otherwise. For the ensuing analysis, we assume that x is in the sequential ordering such that the nxr partition matrix U is

$$U = U_{seq} = \text{diag}(u_1,\ldots,u_r), \tag{7.3.5}$$

where u_α is an n_α-vector with all entries equal to one.

In nonlinear dynamic networks an area partition is meaningful when the connections between the areas are weak. This could be due to relatively soft springs or large impedances. We rescale the external flow f_{ij} as

$$f_{ij} = \varepsilon g_{ij} \tag{7.3.6}$$

where ε is a small parameter. Using the summation notation in (4.4.17) and (4.4.18), the model of a weakly connected dynamic network (7.3.2) is

$$m_i dx_i/d\tau = \underset{j,j\neq i}{\Sigma^\alpha} - f_{ij}(x_i - x_j) + \varepsilon \underset{\substack{\beta=1 \\ \beta\neq\alpha}}{\overset{r}{\Sigma}} \underset{j}{\Sigma^\beta} - g_{ij}(x_i - x_j) + p_i(\varepsilon), \tag{7.3.7}$$

where x_i is in area α. As in the linear case, the time variable of (7.3.2) is taken to be the fast time τ. The net injection at node i, $p_i(\varepsilon)$, is assumed to be a continuously differentiable function of ε.

A fundamental property of weakly connected networks is that neglecting the weak connection terms εg_{ij}, system (7.3.7) decomposes into r isolated areas

$$m_i dx_i/d\tau = \underset{j,j\neq i}{\Sigma^\alpha} - f_{ij}(x_i - x_j) + p_i(0), \quad i \text{ in } J_\alpha, \ \alpha = 1,2,\ldots,r. \tag{7.3.8}$$

<u>Assumption 7.3.1</u>: Each of the r areas formed by setting $\varepsilon=0$ in (7.3.7) has an equilibrium state.

In the case of power systems, Assumption 7.3.1 requires that every area, when isolated from the rest of the system, has its own load flow. To satisfy this requirement, the injections $p_i(\varepsilon)$ are considered functions of ε. Then $p_i(\varepsilon) - p_i(0)$ is the flow to the other areas and for each area,

$$\sum_i^\alpha p_i(0) = 0, \ i \ \text{in} \ J_\alpha, \ \alpha = 1,2,\ldots,r, \tag{7.3.9}$$

since there is no sink or source in the branches. The choice of the dependence of p_i on ε and its impact on the accuracy of the reduced models will be discussed later.

Dynamic networks are a class of nonlinear systems in which equilibrium and dynamic manifolds can be found directly. In each area α we select a reference state $x_i = x_1^\alpha$ and form the $(n_\alpha - 1)$ differences

$$s_j = x_j^e - x_i^e = x_j^e - (x_1^\alpha)^e, \tag{7.3.10}$$

where j is in J_α and $j \neq i$, and x_j^e, x_i^e are the values of x_j, x_i at an equilibrium $(x^\alpha)^e$ of the area α model (7.3.8).

Theorem 7.3.1: System (7.3.8) has an equilibrium manifold S described by

$$\varphi_k(x) = x_j - x_i - s_j = 0, \ x_i = x_1^\alpha, \ k = k_\alpha + 1, \ \ldots, \ k_\alpha + n_\alpha - 1,$$
$$k_\alpha = \sum_{m=1}^{\alpha-1} (n_m - 1), \tag{7.3.11}$$

for all j in J_α and $j \neq i$, and all areas $\alpha=1,2,\ldots,r$. The dynamic manifold F for a given initial condition $x(0)$ is

$$\psi_\alpha(x) - \psi_\alpha(x(0)) = 0, \ \alpha=1,2,\ldots,r, \tag{7.3.12}$$

where ψ_α is the area α center of inertia variable

$$\psi_\alpha(x) = \sum_j^\alpha m_j x_j / \sum_j^\alpha m_j. \tag{7.3.13}$$

Furthermore,

$$y_\alpha = \psi_\alpha(x), \ z_k = \varphi_k(x), \ \alpha = 1,2,\ldots,r, \ k = 1,2,\ldots,n-r, \tag{7.3.14}$$

are the slow and the fast variables satisfying Theorem 7.2.1.

Proof: Any x satisfying

$$x_j - x_p = x_j^e - x_p^e \qquad (7.3.15)$$

for all j, p in J_α, $\alpha=1,2,\ldots,r$, is an equilibrium of (7.3.7). Thus, φ_k in (7.3.11) constitutes an equilibrium manifold since

$$x_j - x_p = (x_j - x_1^\alpha) - (x_p - x_1^\alpha) = s_j - s_p$$
$$= x_j^e - x_p^e \ . \qquad (7.3.16)$$

Writing (7.3.8) at an equilibrium

$$0 = -[\sum_{p,p\neq j}^\alpha f_{jp}(x_j^e - x_p^e) + p_j(0)] \ , \ j \ \text{in} \ J_\alpha, \ \alpha=1,2,\ldots,r, \qquad (7.3.17)$$

we obtain, because of (7.3.9),

$$\sum_j^\alpha m_j(dx_j/d\tau) = 0 \quad , \quad \alpha=1,2,\ldots,r. \qquad (7.3.18)$$

The dynamic manifold (7.3.12) is obtained by integrating and scaling (7.3.18). Finally, the transformation (7.3.14) is an application of Theorem 7.2.1. □

Although the model (7.3.8) is nonlinear, both the equilibrium manifold (7.3.11) and the dynamic manifold (7.3.12) are linear, leading to a linear transformation separating the time-scales. Manifold S is linear because the right-hand side of (7.3.8) is a function of a linear combination (the differences) of the states as opposed to being a function of the states individually. Manifolds F are linear because the conservation property is linear. In the case of RC-circuits, the conservation property expresses Kirchhoff's current law and in the case of power systems, the conservation of angular momentum. These physical laws are linear even when some elements of the network have nonlinear characteristics.

The time-scale separation results in Theorem 7.3.1 can be extended to second order dynamic networks with small damping and weakly connected areas

$$m_i \ d^2x_i/d\tau^2 = - \ \epsilon d_i \ dx_i/d\tau +$$
$$\sum_{j,j\neq i}^\alpha - f_{ij}(x_i - x_j) + \epsilon \sum_{\substack{\beta=1 \\ \beta\neq\alpha}}^r \sum_j^\beta -g_{ij}(x_i - x_j) + p_i(\epsilon), \qquad (7.3.19)$$

where x_i is in area α. It is straightforward to show that for (7.3.19) with $\epsilon=0$,

$$m_i \, d^2x_i/d\tau^2 = \sum_{j,j\neq i}^{\alpha} -f_{ij}(x_i - x_j) + p_i(0) \, , \text{ i in } J_\alpha, \, \alpha = 1,2,\ldots,r, \qquad (7.3.20)$$

the manifold S is given by (7.3.11) provided that (7.3.20) satisfies Assumption 7.3.1. From (7.2.34), the manifold F is given by

$$\psi_\alpha(x) = d\psi_\alpha(x)/d\tau\big|_{\tau=0} \, \tau + c_\alpha, \, \alpha = 1,2,\ldots,r, \qquad (7.3.21)$$

where ψ_α is given by (7.3.13) and c_α is a constant. For d_i small, the fact that $y_\alpha = \psi_\alpha(x)$ is slow and $z_k = \varphi_k(x)$ is fast follows from (7.2.30) to (7.2.36).

7.4 Slow and Fast Subsystems

To rewrite the transformation (7.3.14) in matrix form we define the $(n-r) \times n$ difference matrix $G = \text{diag}(G_1,\ldots,G_r)$ where

$$G_\alpha = \begin{bmatrix} -1 & 1 & 0 & . & . & . & . & 0 \\ -1 & 0 & 1 & . & . & . & . & 0 \\ . & . & . & . & . & . & . & . \\ -1 & 0 & 0 & . & . & . & . & 1 \end{bmatrix} = [-u_\alpha' \quad I_{n_\alpha-1}] \qquad (7.4.1)$$

is an $(n_\alpha-1) \times n_\alpha$ matrix with two non-zero elements per row. With the states x in the sequential ordering, that is, the states x in the same area appear consecutively in x with the reference state first, and $C_a = (U^T M U)^{-1} U^T M$, the transformation (7.3.14) in vector form is

$$\begin{bmatrix} y \\ z \end{bmatrix} = \begin{bmatrix} C_a \\ G \end{bmatrix} x - \begin{bmatrix} 0 \\ s \end{bmatrix} \qquad (7.4.2)$$

where s is an $(n-r)$-vector with components s_k. The inverse of (7.4.2) is

$$x = [U \quad G^+] \begin{bmatrix} y \\ z+s \end{bmatrix} \qquad (7.4.3)$$

where $G^+ = M^{-1}G^T(GM^{-1}G^T)^{-1}$. Recall that every row of U has one entry 1 and the rest 0, whence

$$x_j = y_\alpha + w_j(z+s), \text{ for all j in } J_\alpha, \, \alpha=1,2,\ldots,r, \qquad (7.4.4)$$

where w_j is the j-th row of G^+. After simple manipulation, we obtain the transformed model

$$m_{a\alpha} \, dy_\alpha/d\tau = \epsilon \, [- \sum_{\substack{\beta=1 \\ \beta \neq \alpha}}^{r} g^{\alpha\beta}(y, z+s) + p^\alpha] \, , \qquad (7.4.5)$$

$$dz_k/d\tau = (1/m_j)[-f^j(z+s) + p_j(\epsilon)] - (1/m_i)[-f^i(z+s) + p_i(\epsilon)]$$

$$- \epsilon \, [(1/m_j) \sum_{\substack{\beta=1 \\ \beta \neq \alpha}}^{r} g_j^\beta (y,z+s) - (1/m_i) \sum_{\substack{\beta=1 \\ \beta \neq \alpha}}^{r} g_i^\beta(y,z+s)] \, , \qquad (7.4.6)$$

where

j is in J_α , $j \neq i$, $x_i = x_1^\alpha$,

$$g^{\alpha\beta} = \Sigma^\beta_p \, \Sigma^\alpha_q \, g_{pq}(y_\alpha - y_\beta + (w_p - w_q)(z+s)) \, , \ \alpha \neq \beta \, ,$$

$$\epsilon p^\alpha = \Sigma^\alpha_q (p_q(\epsilon) - p_q(0)) = \Sigma^\alpha_q \, p_q(\epsilon) \, , \qquad (7.4.7)$$

$$f^j = \Sigma^\alpha_q \, f_{jq}((w_j - w_q)(z+s)) \, ,$$

$$g_j^\beta = \Sigma^\beta_p \, g_{jp}((y_\alpha - y_\beta) + (w_j - w_p)(z+s)).$$

The injection ϵp^α is the total flow from area α to the other areas, and the quantity $g^{\alpha\beta}$ is the flow from area α to area β. The quantity f^j is the flow from node j to all the other nodes in the same area, while g_j^β is the flow from node j to the nodes in area β.

In the original state description (7.3.7) areas cannot be considered weakly coupled because over a longer period their interaction through weak connections becomes significant. In the transformed description the fast-time area models in z variables are weakly coupled, as indicated by (7.4.6), and the long term area interaction is approximately described by (7.4.5), that is, the aggregate variables y alone. The fundamental difference between this and the original model is that the decoupled z-equations, obtained by setting $\epsilon=0$ in (7.4.6), no longer have a continuum of equilibrium points, since they are now expressed in the relative reference frame.

The definition of slow coherency as given in Section 6.3 is based on a modal decomposition and is not directly applicable to nonlinear systems. Since we have shown that the two-time-scale properties remain valid for nonlinear systems, we will use them for the following generalization of the notion of slow coherency.

Definition 7.4.1: States x_i, x_j of (7.3.7) are said to be slow coherent if $x(0)$ in S implies

$$x_i(t) - x_j(t) = \text{constant, for all } t \geq 0. \tag{7.4.8}$$

States x_i and x_j are said to be near slow coherent if there exists a bounded function of time $\gamma(t)$ such that if $x(0)$ in S then

$$x_i(t) - x_j(t) = \text{constant} + \epsilon\, \gamma(t), \text{ for all } t \geq 0. \tag{7.4.9}$$

An area is slow coherent if any two states in the area are near slow coherent.

The following theorem relates weakly connected areas and slow-coherent areas extending the corresponding results in Section 6.3.

Theorem 7.4.1: If ϵ is sufficiently small, system (7.4.6) has r near slow-coherent areas specified by U.

Proof: From Theorem 7.3.1, if j,p are in J_α,

$$x_j - x_p = (x_j - x_1^\alpha) - (x_p - x_1^\alpha) = z_j - z_p + s_j - s_p. \tag{7.4.10}$$

If $x(0)$ is in S, $z(0) = \varphi(x(0)) = 0$ which, when combined with (7.2.20) and (2.2.14), (2.2.15), implies that $z_s(t) = O(\epsilon)$. Then (7.4.9) follows from (7.4.10). $\square$

Model (7.4.5), (7.4.6) is in the explicit form (2.2.7), (2.2.8). Hence, letting $\epsilon \rightarrow 0$,

$$p^\alpha = \lim_{\epsilon \to 0} \sum_j^\alpha p_j(\epsilon)/\epsilon \tag{7.4.11}$$

and using the results of Theorems 7.3.1 and 7.4.1 that $z_s = 0$, the slow subsystem is

$$m_{a\alpha}\, dy_{s\alpha}/dt = - \sum_{\substack{\beta=1 \\ \beta \neq \alpha}}^{r} g^{\alpha\beta}(y_s, s) - p^\alpha, \quad \alpha = 1,2,\ldots,r. \tag{7.4.12}$$

The fast subsystem is

$$dz_{fk}/d\tau = (1/m_j)\, [-f^j(z_f + s) - p_j(0)] - (1/m_i)\, [-f^i(z_f + s) - p_i(0)],$$

$$j \text{ in } J_\alpha, \; j \neq i, \; x_i = x_1^\alpha, \; \alpha = 1,2,\ldots,r. \tag{7.4.13}$$

The slow model (7.4.12) and the fast models (7.4.13) are decoupled. The slow subsystem represents an aggregate dynamic network with storage element inertias $m_{a\alpha}$, net injections p^α, and interconnection characteristics $g^{\alpha\beta}$. Since the sums in (7.4.13) involve only the nodes from the same area, the z-equations for two different areas are decoupled, that is, the fast models (7.4.13) are local in the sense that they involve quantities from one area only. Thus, each area uses its local model and at the same time provides the data to and receives results from the aggregate model. This multi-modeling decomposition helps in the formulation of decentralized controls [24].

In (7.3.7) and in subsequent derivations it was assumed that the dependence of the injections $p_i(\varepsilon)$ on ε is known. In a realistic situation ε has a specific value and the injections are constant. The dependence on ε is an asymptotic tool guaranteeing that the isolated areas formed by $\varepsilon \to 0$ have a well-defined equilibrium. Therefore, for any function $p(\varepsilon)$ satisfying (7.3.9), Assumption 7.3.1 holds and the quantities s_j in (7.3.10) are well defined. Furthermore, the freedom in choosing $p(\varepsilon)$ can be utilized to improve on the accuracy of reduced models in realistic systems where ε may not be very small.

Note that for $\varepsilon \to 0$, the equilibria of (7.4.12), (7.4.13) are generally different from the equilibria of (7.4.5), (7.4.6). It has been observed in numerical experiments that the approximation of the time response improves when the equilibria of the reduced models (7.4.12), (7.4.13) are closer to the equilibria of the original model (7.4.5), (7.4.6). Consequently, it is desirable, particularly if the system response is oscillatory, and if the reduced models (7.4.12), (7.4.13) are used for stability analysis, to make the two equilibria as close as possible. The following corollaries provide guidance in this direction.

Corollary 7.4.1: Let x^E be an equilibrium of (7.3.7). Then the equilibria of (7.4.12), (7.4.13) are equal to the equilibria of (7.4.5), (7.4.6) if and only if

$$s = G\, x^E. \qquad\qquad (7.4.14)$$

Proof: First note that by Theorems 7.3.1 and 7.4.1 $z_f = 0$ is the equilibrium of (7.4.13), regardless of the choice of s. From (7.4.2) the equilibrium of (7.4.6) corresponding to x^E is

$$z^E = G\, x^E - s \qquad\qquad (7.4.15)$$

which is made zero by (7.4.14). Setting z=0 in (7.4.5) to obtain (7.4.12) does not alter the equilibrium because $z^E = 0$. The choice (7.4.14) is unique because (7.4.15) is linear in s. $\square$

Corollary 7.4.1 shows that there is a unique s for which the equilibria of the exact and approximate systems are equal. Since by definition $s=Gx^e$, the choice of

$$x^e = x^E, \qquad\qquad (7.4.16)$$

ensures that

$$y^E = y^e, \ z^E = z^e \qquad\qquad (7.4.17)$$

are satisfied. The next corollary gives a necessary condition on $p_i(\varepsilon)$ such that (7.4.16) is satisfied. <u>Boundary nodes</u> are nodes to which external connections are attached.

<u>Corollary 7.4.2</u>: Condition (7.4.16) is satisfied only if

$$p_{j\varepsilon} = p_j(\varepsilon) - p_j(0) = \sum_{\substack{\beta=1 \\ \beta\neq\alpha}}^{r} g_j^\beta(y^E, s), \qquad\qquad (7.4.18)$$

that is, the net injection at boundary nodes is adjusted by the interarea flow while it is left unaltered at non-boundary nodes.

<u>Proof</u>: For (7.3.7) in equilibrium

$$\sum_{j,j\neq i}^\alpha f_{ij}(x_i^E - x_j^E) = -\varepsilon \sum_{\substack{\beta=1 \\ \beta\neq\alpha}}^{r} \sum_j^\alpha g_{ij}(x_i^E - x_j^E) + p_i(\varepsilon), \qquad\qquad (7.4.19)$$

and for (7.3.8) in equilibrium

$$\sum_{j,j\neq i}^\alpha f_{ij}(x_i^e - x_j^e) = p_i(0). \qquad\qquad (7.4.20)$$

Hence, (7.4.18) is necessary for (7.4.16) to be true. □

The designation of $p_j(\varepsilon)$ into $p_j(0)$ and $p_{j\varepsilon}$ according to (7.4.18) is unique. It lets the injections $p_{j\varepsilon}$ at the boundary nodes be equal to the flows to the other areas. At the internal nodes, nodes which have no connections to other areas, $p_{j\varepsilon}=0$. Thus, (7.4.18) does not alter the flow inside an area, which is the physical explanation of Corollary 7.4.2. When the small parameter ε is not readily identifiable, Corollary 7.4.2 would determine the injections to external areas.

The results in Theorem 7.4.1 and Corollaries 7.4.1 and 7.4.2 for first order dynamic networks (7.3.7) are likewise applicable to second order dynamic networks (7.3.19), which can also be decomposed into slow and fast subsystems similar to (7.4.12) and (7.4.13). We will not repeat the derivation but instead will illustrate the decomposition with the nonlinear electromechanical model of power systems in the next section.

To summarize, we have presented time-scale modeling results for weakly connected nonlinear dynamic networks, which are parallel to those for linear dynamic networks. These results are combined into a time-scale modeling methodology for nonlinear dynamic networks, which consists of the following steps:

1. Identify slow-coherent areas.
2. Construct the slow and fast variables y and z.
3. Compute an equilibrium point x^E.
4. Use the slow subsystem (7.4.12) to model the aggregate dynamics, and the fast subsystems (7.4.13) to model the local dynamics.

For small scale dynamic networks, slow-coherent areas can be found by manually locating the weak connections. For large scale systems, a more practical scheme is to first linearize the system and then use the grouping algorithm to identify the slow-coherent areas. The steps of the time-scale modeling methodology will be illustrated with a small power system in the next section. In certain applications where higher accuracy is needed, we may need to compute a time-varying quasi-equilibrium x^E. We may also need to introduce some weak connections into the subsystems. These topics are discussed with regard to realistic power systems in the next chapter.

We remark that the results in the last and this section have been developed assuming linear storage elements. For systems such as water distribution networks with nonlinear storage elements, the reduction procedure is still applicable after some modifications. Assuming that the stored quantity is a strictly monotonic function of the potential, the dynamics of the network are described by an equation analogous to (7.3.2) in which m_i is now a function of x_i. The area center of inertia (7.3.13) becomes

$$\psi_\alpha(x) = \sum_i^\alpha m_i(x_i)x_i / \sum_i^\alpha m_i(x_i) \tag{7.4.21}$$

and the dynamic manifold is no longer linear. The equilibrium manifold, however, is still given by (7.3.11).

7.5 Application to Electromechanical Model

As an illustration of the time-scale modeling methodology, we consider the nonlinear electromechanic model for an n machine power system.

$$(2H_i/\Omega)\ddot{\delta}_i = (\tilde{d}_i/\Omega)\dot{\delta}_i + (P_{mi} - P_{ei}), \quad i = 1,2,\ldots,n, \tag{7.5.1}$$

where H_i is the inertia constant, $\tilde{d}_i$ the damping constant, P_{mi} the mechanical input power, P_{ei} the electrical output power of machine i and Ω the base frequency. Neglecting the off-diagonal conductance terms G_{ij} in the admittance matrix

$$Y = G + jB \tag{7.5.2}$$

we model P_{ei} as

$$P_{ei} = P_{ei}^B = \sum_{\substack{j=1 \\ j \neq i}}^{n} v_i v_j B_{ij} \sin(\delta_i - \delta_j) + v_i^2 G_{ii}. \tag{7.5.3}$$

For (7.5.1) we assume that the damping $\tilde{d}_i$ is small and scale $\tilde{d}_i/\Omega$ as ϵd_i where ϵ is a small parameter. Furthermore, we assume that the connections between the areas are weak, that is, we can decompose B into

$$B = B^I + \epsilon B^E \tag{7.5.4}$$

where B^I is the internal susceptance matrix for connections within an area and B^E is the weak external susceptance matrix for connections between the areas. Then we rewrite P_{ei} as

$$P_{ei}^B = \sum_{j,j=1}^{\alpha} v_i v_j B_{ij} \sin(\delta_i - \delta_j) + v_i^2 G_{ii} + \epsilon \sum_{\substack{\beta=1 \\ \beta \neq \alpha}}^{r} \sum_{j}^{\beta} v_i v_j B_{ij}^E \sin(\delta_i - \delta_j),$$

$$= P_{ei}^{IB} + v_i^2 G_{ii} + \epsilon \sum_{\substack{\beta=1 \\ \beta \neq \alpha}}^{r} P_{ei\beta}^{EB} \tag{7.5.5}$$

such that P_{ei}^{IB} is the flow of power from node i to the nodes in the same area and $\epsilon P_{ei\beta}^{EB}$ is the flow from node i to the nodes in area β.

In the new notation we rewrite (7.5.1) as

$$m_i \ d^2\delta_i/dt^2 = -ed_i d\delta_i/d\tau - P_{ei}^{IB} - \epsilon \sum_{\substack{\beta=1 \\ \beta \neq \alpha}}^{r} P_{ei\beta}^{EB} + (P_{mi} - v_i^2 G_{ii}) \tag{7.5.6}$$

where $m_i = 2H_i/\Omega$ and the time-derivative in (7.5.1) is taken to be with respect to the fast time τ. Note that (7.5.6) is in the form (7.3.19) of a weakly connected nonlinear dynamic network where

$$\delta_i = x_i$$

$$P_{ei}^{IB} = \sum_{j,j \neq i}^{\alpha} f_{ij} (x_i - x_j) \ , \ f_{ij} (x_i - x_j) = v_i \ v_j \ B_{ij}^{I} \sin (\delta_i - \delta_j)$$

$$P_{ei\beta}^{EB} = \sum_{j}^{\beta} g_{ij} (x_i - x_j) \ , \ g_{ij} (x_i - x_j) = v_i \ v_j \ B_{ij}^{E} \sin (\delta_i - \delta_j)$$

$$P_i = P_{mi} + v_i^2 \ G_{ii}. \tag{7.5.7}$$

Note that $f_{ij} = f_{ji}$ and $g_{ij} = g_{ji}$ since $B_{ij}^{E} = B_{ji}^{E}$. Thus, (7.5.6) has two time-scales and can be decomposed into the slow and fast subsystems.

We use the aggregate variables which are the centers of angles

$$y_\alpha = \sum_i^{\alpha} m_i \ \delta_i/m_{a\alpha} \tag{7.5.8}$$

as the slow variables and the difference variables which are the relative angles with respect to the reference angles

$$z_k = \delta_j - \delta_i - s_j, \ j \ \text{in} \ J_\alpha \ , \ j \neq i, \ \delta_i = \delta_1^{\alpha} \ ,$$

$$k = k_\alpha + 1, \ \ldots, \ k_\alpha + n_\alpha - 1, \ k_\alpha = \sum_{m=1}^{\alpha-1} (n_m - 1) \tag{7.5.9}$$

as the fast variables. For the slow variables,

$$m_{a\alpha} \ d^2 y_\alpha/d\tau^2 = \sum_i^{\alpha} m_i \ d^2\delta_i/d\tau^2$$

$$= \epsilon \ d_{a\alpha} dy_\alpha/d\tau + d_{a\alpha}'(dy_\alpha/d\tau, \ dz^\alpha/d\tau) - \epsilon \sum_{\substack{\beta=1 \\ \beta \neq \alpha}}^{r} P_{e\beta}^{B\alpha} + \epsilon P_m^\alpha, \tag{7.5.10}$$

where

$$d_{a\alpha} = \sum_i^{\alpha} d_i, \tag{7.5.11}$$

$$d'_{a\alpha} = \sum_i^\alpha (d_a m_i/m_{a\alpha} - d_i)\, d\delta_i/d\tau$$

$$= \sum_i^\alpha (d_a m_i/m_{a\alpha} - d_i)\, d/d\tau\, (y_\alpha - w_i z^\alpha), \tag{7.5.12}$$

$$P^{\beta\alpha}_{e\beta} = \sum_i^\alpha P^{EB}_{ei\beta}\, (y, z + s), \tag{7.5.13}$$

$$\varepsilon P^\alpha_m = \sum_i^\alpha (P_{mi} - v_i^2 G_{ii}). \tag{7.5.14}$$

The damping $d_{a\alpha}$ has the meaning of an aggregate damping, and $d'_{a\alpha}$ is zero when the area damping is uniform, that is, when d_i satisfies Assumption 4.6.1. $P^{\beta\alpha}_{e\beta}$ is the flow of power from area α to area β, and εP^α_m is the net injection of area α, which is the summation of all the injections in area α and assumed to be small. The summation of P^{EB}_{ei} terms is identically zero.

For systems with almost uniform damping, $d'_{a\alpha}$ is small and can be neglected. Furthermore, we let z=0 which is its quasi-steady state value. Then (7.5.10) reduces to the aggregate model which when expressed in the slow time-scale is

$$d^2 y_a/dt^2 = \sqrt{\varepsilon}\, d_{a\alpha}\, dy/dt - \sum_{\substack{\beta=1 \\ \beta\neq\alpha}}^r P^{\beta\alpha}_{e\beta}\, (y,s) + P^\alpha_m . \tag{7.5.15}$$

This model represents the motion of the centers of angles as determined by the exchange of power between the areas, and is oscillatory with $O(\sqrt{\varepsilon})$ damping.

For the fast variable,

$$d^2 z_k/d\tau^2 = - \varepsilon(d_j/m_j)\, d/d\tau\, (y_\alpha - w_j\, (z^\alpha - s)) - P^{IB}_{ej} + P_{mj} - v_j^2 G_{jj}$$

$$+ \varepsilon(d_i/m_i) d/d\tau\, (y_\alpha - w_i\, (z^\alpha - s)) + P^{IB}_{ei} - P_{mi} + v_i^2 G_{ii}$$

$$- \varepsilon \sum_{\substack{\beta=1 \\ \beta\neq\alpha}}^r (P^{EB}_{ej\beta} - P^{EB}_{ei\beta}),\ j \text{ in } J_\alpha,\ j\neq i,\ x_i = x_1^\alpha. \tag{7.5.16}$$

If the area damping is uniform and the flow between the areas is neglected in the fast time-scale, (7.5.16) reduces to

$$d^2 z_k/d\tau^2 = - \varepsilon\, (d_{a\alpha}/m_{a\alpha})\, dz_k/d\tau - (P^{IB}_{ej} - P^{IB}_{ei})$$

$$+ (P_{mj} - P_{mi} - v_j^2 G_{jj} + v_i^2 G_{ii}). \tag{7.5.17}$$

System (7.5.17) describes the dynamics within an area which are fast, and is oscillatory with $O(\epsilon)$ damping. It is decoupled from the other areas since P_{ej}^{IB} and P_{ei}^{IB} are functions of z^{α} only. The subsystems (7.5.15) and (7.5.17) can be used to approximate (7.5.6) to a finite time T.

The time-scale modeling methodology is illustrated using a five machine example. In the power system of Figure 7.5.1,

$$H_i = 0.5 \text{ pu, } i=1,2,\ldots,5,$$

$$V_i = 1.0 \text{ pu, } i=1,2,\ldots,5,$$

$$B_{12} = B_{23} = B_{45} = 10.0 \text{ pu,}$$
(7.5.18)

$$B_{34} = B_{25} = B_{15} = B_{14} = 1.0 \text{ pu.}$$

Damping is neglected in this example. The net injections p_i and the resulting steady state angles (pre-fault angles) are given in columns 1 and 2 of Table 7.5.1.

Table 7.5.1

Injections and Pre-Fault and Post-Fault Angles

Injections pu	Pre-Fault Angles, radians	Post-Fault Angles, radians
$p_1 = -2.80$	$\delta_1 = 0.0$	$\delta_1 = 0.0$
$p_2 = -0.77$	$\delta_2 = 0.171$	$\delta_2 = 0.215$
$p_3 = 1.86$	$\delta_3 = 0.391$	$\delta_3 = 0.458$
$p_4 = 3.62$	$\delta_4 = 0.723$	$\delta_4 = 1.042$
$p_5 = -1.91$	$\delta_5 = 0.456$	$\delta_5 = 0.730$

Note that since the susceptances B_{34}, B_{25}, B_{15}, B_{14} are much smaller than the rest, the system is divided into two weakly connected areas $J_1 = \{1,2,3\}$, $J_2 = \{4,5\}$. We designate states x_2 and x_5 as the references for the areas.

Suppose now that line B_{14} is tripped and we want to simulate the resulting oscillations using the reduced models (7.5.15), (7.5.17). The post-fault load flow (column 3 of Table 7.5.1) gives

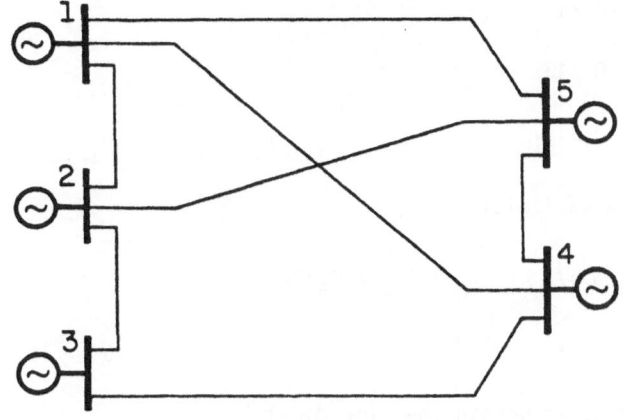

FP-7506

Figure 7.5.1   Five machine power system example. The external
connections between machines 1, 2 and 3, and
machines 4 and 5 are weak.

$$s_1 = \delta_1^e - \delta_2^e = -0.215,$$

$$s_3 = \delta_3^e - \delta_2^e = 0.243, \qquad\qquad (7.5.19)$$

$$s_4 = \delta_4^e - \delta_5^e = 0.312.$$

Defining the new variables

$$y_1 = (\delta_1 + \delta_2 + \delta_3)/3 \;, \quad y_2 = (\delta_4 + \delta_5)/2,$$

$$z_1 = \delta_1 - \delta_2 - s_1 \;, \quad z_2 = \delta_3 - \delta_2 - s_3 \;, \quad z_3 = \delta_4 - \delta_5 - s_4, \qquad (7.5.20)$$

and letting $\varepsilon \to 0$, we obtain the slow model

$$d^2 y_{s1}/dt^2 = -0.33 \sin(y_{s1} - y_{s2} - 0.068) - 0.33 \sin(y_{s1} - y_{s2} + 0.147)$$

$$- 0.33 \sin(y_{s1} - y_{s2} + 0.078) - 0.57,$$

$$\qquad (7.5.21)$$

$$d^2 y_{s2}/dt^2 = -0.5 \sin(y_{s2} - y_{s1} - 0.078) - 0.5 \sin(y_{s2} - y_{s1} - 0.147)$$

$$- 0.5 \sin(y_{s2} - y_{s1} + 0.068) + 0.86,$$

and the fast models

$$d^2 z_{f1}/d\tau^2 = -20 \sin(z_{f1} - 0.215) - 10 \sin(z_{f2} + 0.243) - 1.85,$$

$$d^2 z_{f2}/d\tau^2 = -20 \sin(z_{f2} + 0.243) - 10 \sin(z_{f1} - 0.215) + 2.69,$$

$$\qquad (7.5.22)$$

and

$$d^2 z_{f3}/d\tau^2 = -20 \sin(z_{f3} + 0.312) + 6.14. \qquad\qquad (7.5.23)$$

Note that (7.5.21) is decoupled from (7.5.22), (7.5.23). The aggregate model (7.5.21) represents the oscillations of the aggregate angles y_1, y_2 against each other, whereas the local models (7.5.22), (7.5.23) represent the intermachine oscillations in areas 1 and 2, respectively. Figures 7.5.2 to 7.5.5 are simulations of the original system and the slow and fast subsystems with initial conditions equal to the pre-fault equilibrium. Figures 7.5.2 and 7.5.3 show the exact (solid

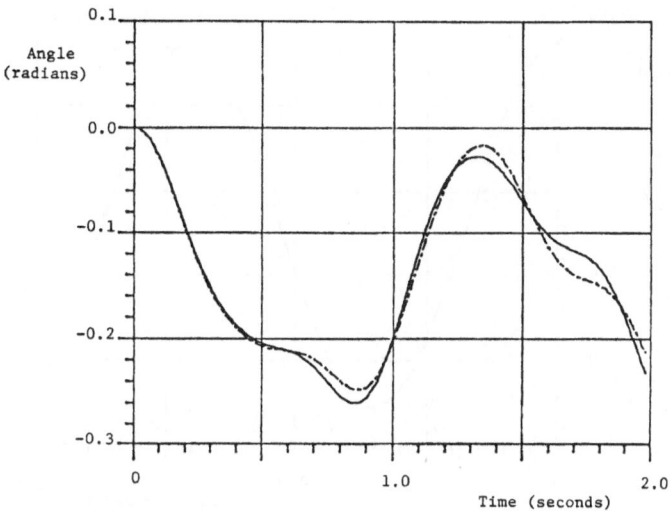

Figure 7.5.2 Exact (solid line) and approximate
(dotted line) responses of δ_1

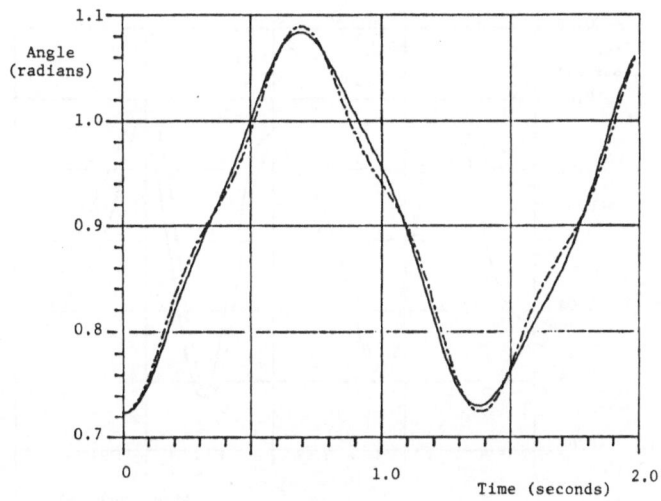

Figure 7.5.3 Exact (solid line) and approximate
(dotted line) responses of δ_4

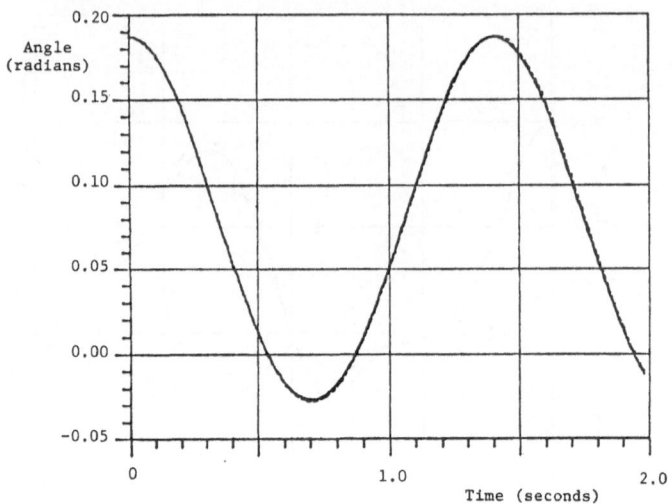

Figure 7.5.4   Exact (dotted line) and approximate
(solid line) responses of y_1.

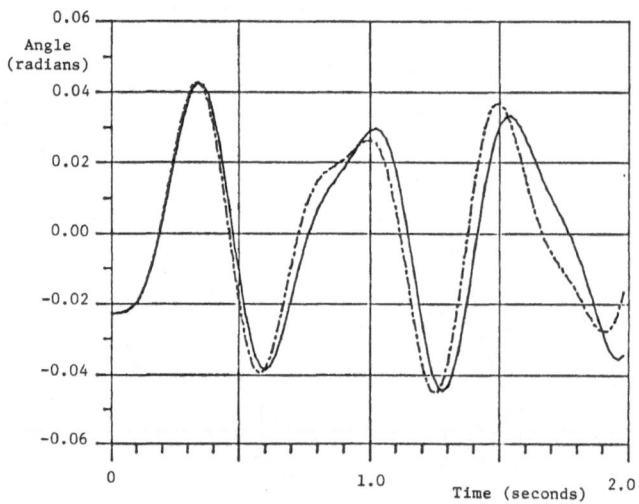

Figure 7.5.5   Exact (dotted line) and approximate
(solid line) responses of z_2.

lines) and approximate (dotted lines) responses of angles δ_1 and δ_4, whereas Figures 7.5.4 and 7.5.5 show exact (dotted lines) and approximate (solid lines) responses of the transformed variables y_1, z_2. Note that the generator angles are mixed variables, whereas y_1 is predominantly slow and z_2 is predominantly fast.

The approximations achieved by the slow and fast subsystems are excellent initially. As expected, larger discrepancies are observed after a longer period. Simulations of two realistic power systems including damping will be illustrated in the next chapter.

7.6 Conclusions

The ultimate utility of the linear results in Chapters 4, 5 and 6 depends on their applicability to nonlinear systems. From physical laws or empirical evidence it is clear that time-scale properties are not restricted to linear systems. What classes of nonlinear models preserve their multi-time-scale behavior present in their linearized approximations? Which aggregate and local variables should be chosen to make this behavior explicit? This chapter answers such questions using coordinate-free characterization of singular perturbations and relating it to conservation and equilibrium properties. This results in an explicit singular perturbation model for which a time-scale modeling methodology is available. Applying this approach to the nonlinear electromechanical power system model, we have extended dynamic energy balance and coherency-based aggregation idea to this class of nonlinear dynamic networks. Further nonlinear generalizations of aggregation and coherency seem possible. Networks with both storage and non-storage nodes should be considered. Also important are storage elements involving nonlinearities and more complex dynamic behavior, such as more detailed models of synchronous machines.

CHAPTER 8

REDUCED SIMULATIONS OF NONLINEAR POWER SYSTEM MODELS

8.1 Introduction

This chapter deals with some practical issues in performing transient simulations for models of real power systems using the time-scale modeling methodology. These issues include the identification of areas for nonlinear models, and the consideration of line resistances and weak connections between the areas. Three simulation schemes are developed, one of which corresponds to the technique used in [41]. A 16 machine system is used to illustrate the different aspects of the methodology described in this monograph. The 48 machine system whose areas have been identified in Chapter 6 is used to illustrate the approximate simulations of a larger system.

The discussion of practical simulation issues is in Section 8.2. The 16 machine and 48 machine examples are in Sections 8.3 and 8.4, respectively.

8.2 Practical Considerations

The model of a power system typically consists of the transmission system as well as the control systems for machines such as voltage regulators and governors. To find the areas, the electromechanical model is sufficient since the areas are determined by coherent machine oscillations. These oscillations are not affected significantly by neglecting the control systems [41]. An analytical support of this observation using weak connections is given in [37]. In addition, the nonlinear oscillations are approximated quite well by the linearized model. Thus, the area partition can be found from the linearized model in which damping and line resistances are neglected and loads are represented by constant impedances. The grouping algorithm in Chapter 5 can be used for this purpose.

The linearization is performed at a particular equilibrium point which is usually the pre-fault equilibrium. Since the area partition obtained from using the slow modes are robust, the same area partition can be used if the equilibrium is only changed slightly. Transient stability studies frequently involve network configuration changes, for example, the loss of a transmission line after a short circuit fault. If the network configuration is not changed significantly, the areas computed for the pre-disturbance network are still applicable to the post-disturbance network.

The conductance terms G_{ij} which reflect line resistances and system loads are assumed to be small. Thus, they do not affect the time-scale separation results even when they are included, as will be shown in the following analysis.

We let the admittance matrix Y be

$$Y = \varepsilon G + jB = \varepsilon(G^I + G^E) + j(B^I + \varepsilon B^E) \qquad (8.2.1)$$

where G^I is the internal conductance matrix and G^E the external conductance matrix. Accordingly, we write P_{ei} as

$$P_{ei} = P_{ei}^B + \varepsilon P_{ei}^G \qquad (8.2.2)$$

where P_{ei}^B is due to the susceptance term B (7.5.5) and

$$
\begin{aligned}
P_{ei}^G &= \sum_{j,j\neq i}^{\alpha} v_i v_j G_{ij}^I \cos(\delta_i - \delta_j) + \sum_{\substack{\beta=1 \\ \beta\neq\alpha}}^{r} \sum_j^{\beta} v_i v_j G_{ij}^E \cos(\delta_i - \delta_j) \\
&= P_{ei}^{IG} + \sum_{\substack{\beta=1 \\ \beta\neq\alpha}}^{r} P_{ei\beta}^{EG}
\end{aligned}
\qquad (8.2.3)
$$

is due to the conductance term G. Thus, the electromechanical model is expressed as

$$m_i d^2 \delta_i/d\tau^2 = -\varepsilon d_i d\delta_i/d\tau - P_{ei}^I - \varepsilon \sum_{\substack{\beta=1 \\ \beta\neq\alpha}}^{r} P_{ei\beta}^E + (P_{mi} - v_i^2 G_{ii}), \qquad (8.2.4)$$

where

$$P_{ei}^I = P_{ei}^{IB} + \varepsilon P_{ei}^{IG}, \quad P_{ei\beta}^E = P_{ei\beta}^{EB} + P_{ei\beta}^{EG}. \qquad (8.2.5)$$

In the aggregate variables (7.5.8)

$$y_\alpha = \sum_i^\alpha m_i \delta_i/m_{a\alpha} \qquad (8.2.6)$$

and the difference variables (7.5.9)

$$z_k = \delta_j - \delta_i - s_j, \qquad (8.2.7)$$

(8.2.4) becomes

$$m_{a\alpha} d^2 y_\alpha / dt^2 = -\sqrt{\epsilon} d_{a\alpha} \, dy_\alpha / dt - d'_{a\alpha} - \sum_i^\alpha P_{ei}^{IG}$$

$$- \sum_{\substack{\beta=1 \\ \beta \neq \alpha}}^r (P_{e\beta}^{\beta\alpha} + P_{e\beta}^{G\alpha}) + P_m^\alpha, \quad \alpha = 1,2,\ldots,r, \tag{8.2.8}$$

$$d^2 z_k / d\tau^2 = -\epsilon(d_j / m_j) d/d\tau(y_\alpha - w_j(z^\alpha - s)) - P_{ej}^I + P_{mj} - v_j^2 G_{jj}$$

$$+\epsilon(d_i / m_i) d/d\tau(y_\alpha - w_i(z^\alpha - s)) + P_{ei}^I - P_{mi} + v_i^2 G_{ii}$$

$$-\epsilon \sum_{\substack{\beta=1 \\ \beta \neq \alpha}}^r (P_{ej\beta}^E - P_{ei\beta}^E) ,$$

$$j \text{ in } J_\alpha, \, j \neq i, \, x_i = x_1^\alpha , \tag{8.2.9}$$

where

$$P_{e\beta}^{G\alpha} = \sum_i^\alpha P_{ei\beta}^{G\alpha} . \tag{8.2.10}$$

The term

$$\sum_i^\alpha P_{ei}^{IG}$$

is the total power consumed in area α. Note that y_α is slow and z_k is fast since the small conductance terms do not change the time-scales.

In simulation studies when good accuracy is desired, it may be necessary to keep the $d'_{a\alpha}$ terms in (8.2.8), the $O(\epsilon)$ terms in (8.2.9) and only partially decouple (8.2.8) and (8.2.9). We develop three approximation schemes using (8.2.7) and (8.2.8). Each of the schemes is suitable for a particular purpose. They will be demonstrated in the next sections.

If only the slow dynamics are of interest, the fast dynamics z_k can be neglected and replaced by the quasi-steady state value z_{ks} which is solved for from

$$0 = -P_{ej}^I + P_{mj} - v_j^2 G_{jj} + P_{ei}^I - P_{mi} + v_i^2 G_{ii} - \epsilon \sum_{\substack{\beta=1 \\ \beta \neq \alpha}}^r (P_{ej\beta}^E - P_{ei\beta}^E). \tag{8.2.11}$$

The term z_{ks} is then substituted into (8.2.8), which accounts for the averaging effect of the power flow within the areas in the slow time-scale. In this slow time-scale, the angles z_{ks} are equivalent to phase shifters which adjust the power flow between the areas. This approximation (A1), which could be simulated with larger time-steps, is suitable for the determination of stability for a longer time-period.

Since the areas are weakly connected, the fast dynamics due to a disturbance within an area, say α, are confined to only the area containing the disturbance. To simulate the fast dynamics we let the fast variables in the other areas be in their quasi-steady state, that is, z_s^β, $\beta \neq \alpha$, are solved from (8.2.11) while (8.2.9) is retained for area α. This simplified model is sufficient for transient stability studies of machines close to the disturbance. Combining the fast variables of area α with the slow variables (8.2.8), this approximation (A2) reproduces the original state variables for the area containing the disturbance and the quasi-steady states for the state variables in the other areas.

Approximation (A2) can be simplified by solving (8.2.11) for z_s^β, $\beta \neq \alpha$, at $\tau = 0$ only. This approximation (A3) fixes the quasi-steady states of the z_s^β variables in the areas other than α, and is basically similar to the equivalencing technique used in [41]. In contrast to approximations (A2), this simulation results in a steady state error since the coupling between the areas is neglected. These z_s^β variables, which represent fixed phase shifters, will not vary with time to account for the power flow within the areas. If ϵ is small, this approximation does not produce a significant error.

Time simulations using approximations (A1), (A2) and (A3) will be shown for two power systems in the next sections.

8.3 16 Machine System Example

The one line diagram of the 16 machine system [9] is shown in Figure 8.3.1. This system is a much less detailed model of the U.S. Northeastern and Ontario system than the 48 machine system which we have studied in Chapters 5 and 6. In the 16 machine system, only the New England system is represented in detail with machines 1 to 9, while the neighboring utility systems in New York, Pennsylvania, Michigan and Ontario are modeled with large equivalent machines 10 to 16. The New England system representation in the 16 machine system is identical to that in the 48 machine system.

To apply the time-scale modeling methodology, we first have to identify the areas in the system. For the time being, let us pursue a purely numerical approach by using the grouping algorithm. Then, we will verify the areas using our knowledge of the system.

To use the grouping algorithm, we linearize the nonlinear electromechanical model and neglect the damping to form a second order dynamic network

$$\ddot{\delta} = M^{-1}K\delta = A\delta. \tag{8.3.1}$$

The first step of the algorithm requires us to specify the number of areas. The objective is to find weakly connected areas. This can be accomplished by examining the eigenvalue gaps in (8.3.1). Thus, we calculate the eigenvalues of A and then their square roots which give the frequencies of oscillations. The eigenvalues of (8.3.1) for the 16 machine system are given in Table 8.3.1. The expression ε_i is a measure of the inverse of the eigenvalue gap. A smaller ε_i results in a wider separation between the eigenvalues and weaker connections between the areas. Table 8.3.1 shows that $\varepsilon_2 = 0.74$ is the smallest ε_i if we disregard $\varepsilon_1 = 0$. For a system with 16 machines, we want to have between four to six areas such that the number of machines in each area is not too large. In this case, five areas seem to be appropriate since $\varepsilon_5 = 0.85$ is smaller than either ε_4 or ε_6. Thus, we apply the grouping algorithm with r = 5.

Table 8.3.1

Separation of eigenvalues of undamped 16 machine system

	Eigenvalues ($\pm jf_i$)	$\varepsilon_i = f_i/f_{i+1}$
1	0,0	0
2	$\pm j$ 2.578	0.74
3	$\pm j$ 3.499	0.77
4	$\pm j$ 4.532	0.89
5	$\pm j$ 5.069	0.85
6	$\pm j$ 5.997	0.92
7	$\pm j$ 6.536	0.91
8	$\pm j$ 7.160	0.96
9	$\pm j$ 7.485	0.94
10	$\pm j$ 7.960	1.00
11	$\pm j$ 7.973	0.95
12	$\pm j$ 8.405	0.91
13	$\pm j$ 9.268	0.96
14	$\pm j$ 9.653	0.99
15	$\pm j$ 9.773	0.85
16	$\pm j$ 11.421	

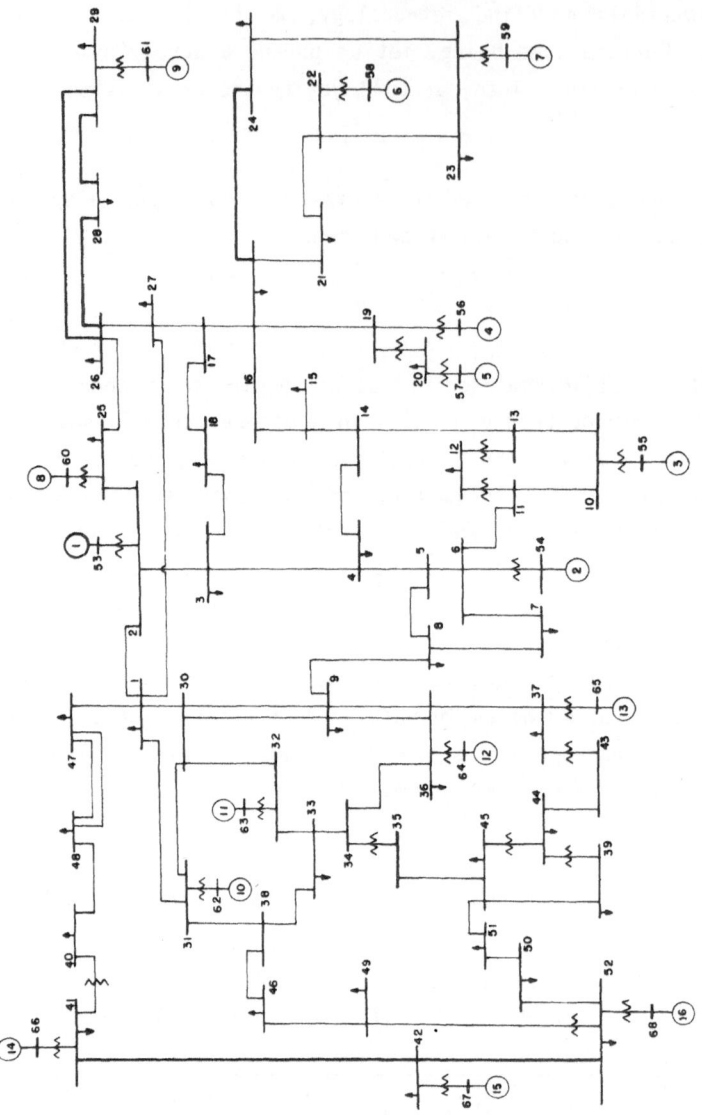

Figure 8.3.1 One line diagram of 16 machine system

In the second step of the algorithm, a basis for the 5-dimensional slow subspace is computed. As a precautionary measure, we may want to compute and store the eigenvectors of the first $r > 5$ smallest eigenvalues. If we decide later on to find an area partition with r different than 5, we can retrieve the appropriate precomputed eigenvectors and go to step 3 directly.

In the third step, Gaussian elimination is performed and the reference machines are found to be 5, 12, 14, 15 and 16. In the fourth step, the L corresponding to this reference set is computed and is given in Table 8.3.2. The largest entry in each row of L, which is underlined, is used to identify the machines in each area. As a result, the following area grouping of machines is obtained:

Area 1:   machines 1-9
Area 2:   machines 10-13
Area 3:   machine 14
Area 4:   machine 15
Area 5:   machine 16.

Note that for machines 1, 2, 3 and 8, the entries in the column under machine 12 are not significantly smaller than those under machine 5. This implies that the responses of machines 1, 2, 3 and 8 are only slightly more coherent with machine 5 than with machine 12.

Table 8.3.2

Matrix L of 16 Machine System

Other Machines	Reference Machines				
	14	12	15	16	5
1	.0599	.411	-.0156	.0222	.522
2	.0335	.422	-.0135	.0014	.557
3	.0320	.387	-.0132	-.000466	.595
4	.0221	.178	-.00818	.00225	.806
6	.0217	.193	-.00971	-.00404	.799
7	.0227	.198	-.00987	-.00312	.793
8	.0585	.377	-.0170	.0186	.563
9	.0372	.215	-.0183	-.00352	.769
10	.100	.618	-.0179	.110	.189
11	.0720	.643	-.000447	.133	.152
13	.00140	.972	-.00116	.0197	.00794

This five area partition groups the nine machines in New England into a single area, four neighboring machines representing New York into another area, and three large machines into single machine areas. This partition is meaningful in terms of weak and strong connections. The same nine machines have been grouped into an area in the 48 machine system.

To illustrate the accuracy of this area partition, we consider the linearized model with damping included. One measure of accuracy is to compare the eigenvalues of the aggregate and local models with the accurate eigenvalues. Table 8.3.3 shows that the worst error is 9.6% for the small eigenvalue approximation and Table 8.3.4 shows that the worst error is 30.1% (in area 2) for the large eigenvalue approximation. The damping is approximated well by all eigenvalues.

In view of the poor approximation by some local modes, we perform an iteration on the aggregate and local models to include the effect of weak connections. As Tables 8.3.3 and 8.3.4 show, the worst error is 3.6% for the pair $-0.08970 \pm j4.531$. Thus, the eigenvalue approximation is excellent despite $\epsilon = 0.85$ not being very small.

The above analysis is based on the linearized model of the 16 machine system. We now demonstrate the validity of this approach on the nonlinear model for several disturbances; that is, we show that the coherency and aggregation results remain valid when applied to the nonlinear model of the 16 machine system.

The first case is a five cycle, three phase fault in area 1 at bus 29 which is subseqently cleared by the removal of the line connecting buses 28 and 29. Figure 8.3.2 shows that the angular differences for machines in area 1 with respect to machine 5 consist mainly of high frequency components, constant offsets and only a small amount of low frequency components. These constant offsets which are denoted by s in (8.2.7) have been eliminated in our previous analysis, but are kept here for illustrative purposes. The response curves for machines in area 1 not shown in Figure 8.3.2 are similar. Hence, these machines are near-coherent with respect to the slow modes.

Time-scale separation can be shown by comparing the aggregate variables y with the difference variables z. The frequencies of the aggregate variables for areas 1 to 5 shown in Figure 8.3.3 are about 0.5 Hz and clearly lower than the frequencies of the angular differences shown in Figure 8.3.2 which are about 1.5 Hz. Thus, the time-scale properties are carried over from the linear to the nonlinear model.

Let us illustrate the approximate simulation method (A2) in Section 8.2 which uses both the aggregate model and the model for area 1 on the 16 machine system. Figures 8.3.4 to 8.3.6 show the close agreement between the exact solution (E) and the approximation (A2) for selected machines in the faulted area as well as in area

2. The differences between these curves are due to the neglected fast dynamics in the external areas.

Table 8.3.3

Slow time-scale approximations of the 16 machine system

Accurate Eigenvalues	Eigenvalues of Aggregate Model	Eigenvalues of Aggregate Model With Weak Coupling Corrections
.0 -.1969 -.1063 $+$ j2.574 -.09877 $\mp$ j3.498 -.08970 $\mp$ j4.531 -.09399 $\mp$ j5.068	.0 -.1944 -.1022 $+$ j2.667 -.09895 $\mp$ j3.491 -.09467 $\mp$ j4.964 -.09325 $\mp$ j5.128	.0 -.1969 -.1058 $+$ j2.589 -.09882 $\mp$ j3.496 -.09097 $\mp$ j4.695 -.09385 $\mp$ j5.075

Table 8.3.4

Fast time-scale approximations of the 16 machine system

Accurate Eigenvalues	Eigenvalues of Local Model	Eigenvalues of Local Model With Weak Coupling Corrections
Area 1: -.1294 $+$ j5.997 -.1162 $\mp$ j6.532 -.1178 $\mp$ j7.159 -.1198 $\mp$ j7.962 -.09360 $\mp$ j7.970 -.1350 $\mp$ j9.267 -.1007 $\mp$ j9.650 -.1264 $\mp$ j9.732	 -.1386 $\pm$ j5.436 -.1093 $\pm$ j5.552 -.1062 $\pm$ j6.557 -.1199 $\pm$ j6.925 -.09720 $\pm$ j6.807 -.1337 $\pm$ j8.821 -.1111 $\pm$ j8.403 -.1263 $\pm$ j9.362	 -.1219 $+$ j5.975 -.1222 $\mp$ j6.445 -.1177 $\mp$ j7.156 -.1195 $\mp$ j7.962 -.09425 $\mp$ j7.959 -.1351 $\mp$ j9.267 -.1025 $\mp$ j9.646 -.1264 $\mp$ j9.732
Area 2: -.07192 $\pm$ j 7.485 -.08926 $\pm$ j 8.405 -.2013 $\pm$ j11.419	 -.07192 $\pm$ j6.557 -.08670 $\pm$ j5.876 -.1945 $\pm$ j8.832	 -.07207 $\pm$ j 7.481 -.08873 $\pm$ j 8.259 -.1986 $\pm$ j11.378

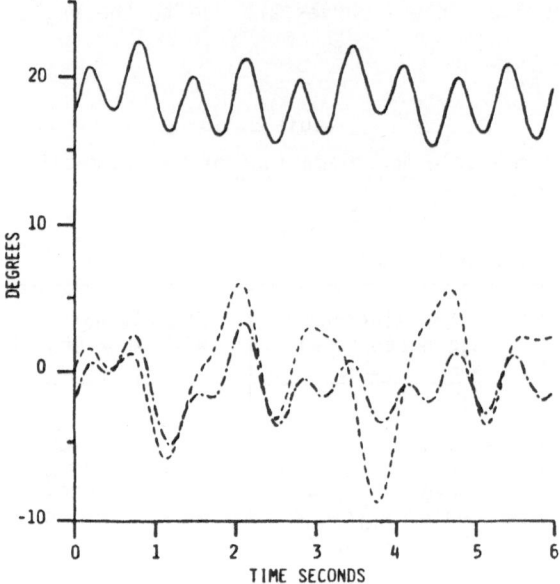

Figure 8.3.2 Difference variables in area 1

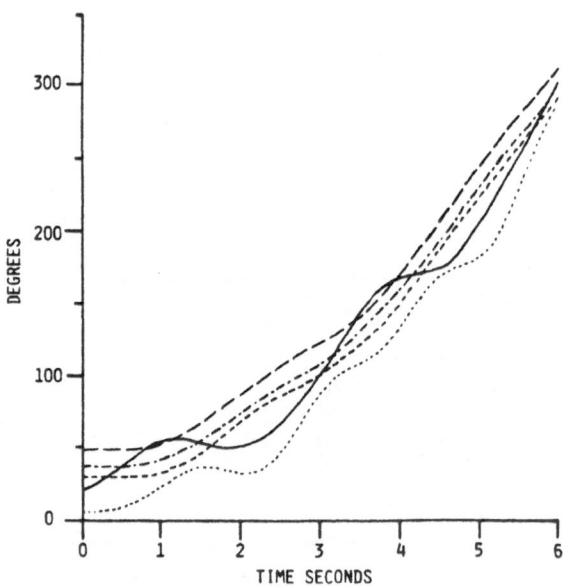

Figure 8.3.3 Aggregate variables for areas 1 to 5

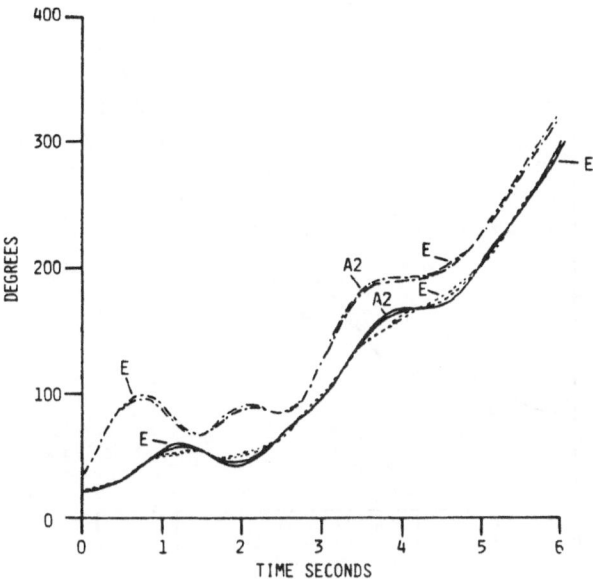

Figure 8.3.4   Individual machine angles in area 1, exact (E) and approximation
(A2)

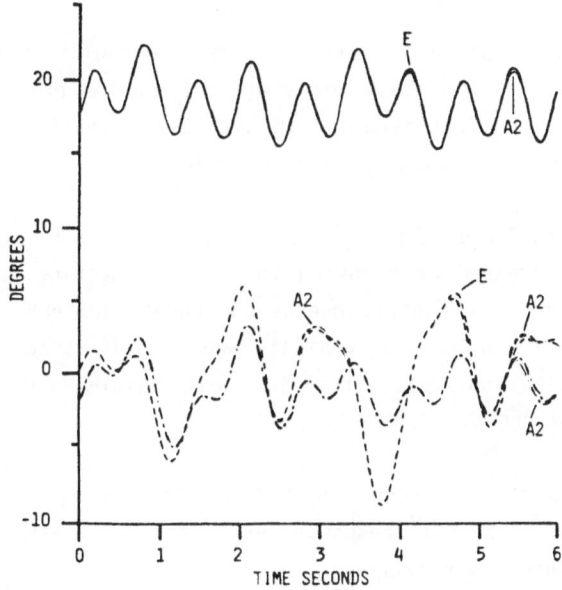

Figure 8.3.5   Difference variables in area 1, exact (E) and approximation
(A2)

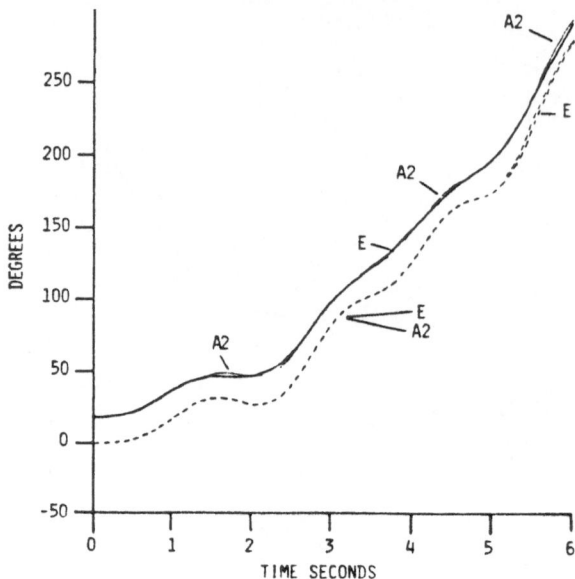

Figure 8.3.6   Individual machine angles in area 2, exact (E) and approximation
(A2)

Figure 8.3.6 shows the response of individual machine angles in area 2 which is adjacent to the faulted area. The close agreement between the exact curves and the approximation implies that the fast dynamics in area 2 are small, thus illustrating the weak coupling of the fast dynamics between the areas.

The second case we considered in the 16 machine system is a 5 cycle, three phase fault on bus 16 which is cleared by removing the line connecting buses 15 and 16. In Figure 8.3.7, we see that the high frequency components dominate in the response of the angular difference curves for typical machines in area 1. Hence, the machines in area 1 are slow coherent, since their differences contain only a small contribution from the slow modes.

To illustrate the time-scale property, we compare the aggregate variables y with the difference variables z. The time response curves for the areas 1 to 5 in Figure 8.3.8 are clearly of a much lower frequency than the angular differences in Figure 8.3.7.

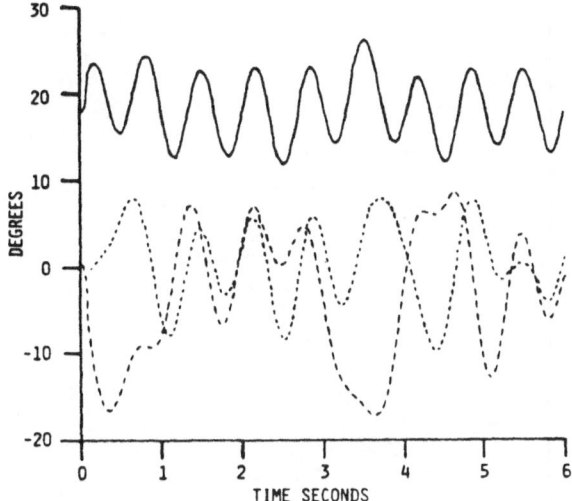

Figure 8.3.7 Difference variables in area 1

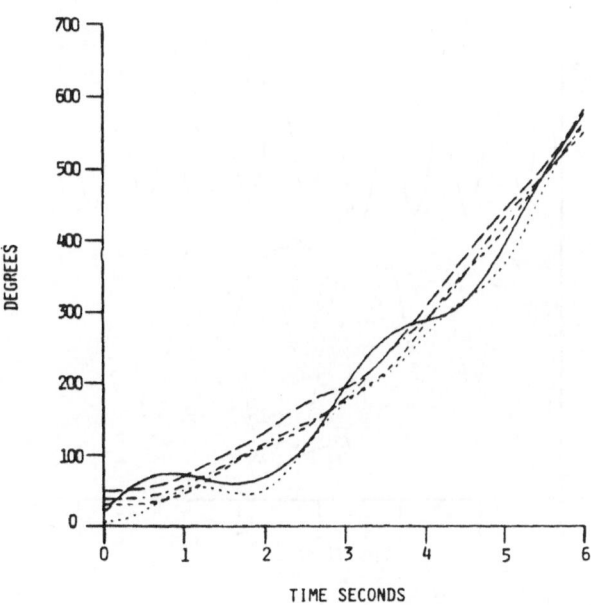

Figure 8.3.8 Aggregate variables for areas 1 to 5

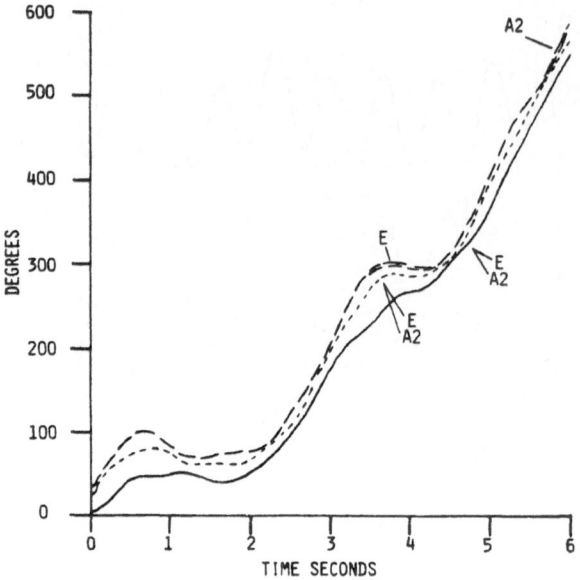

Figure 8.3.9   Individual machine angles in area 1, exact (E) and approximation (A2)

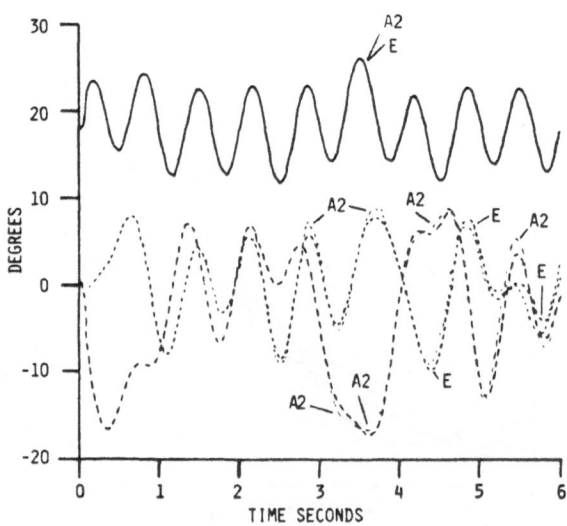

Figure 8.3.10   Difference variables in area 1, exact (E) and approximation (A2)

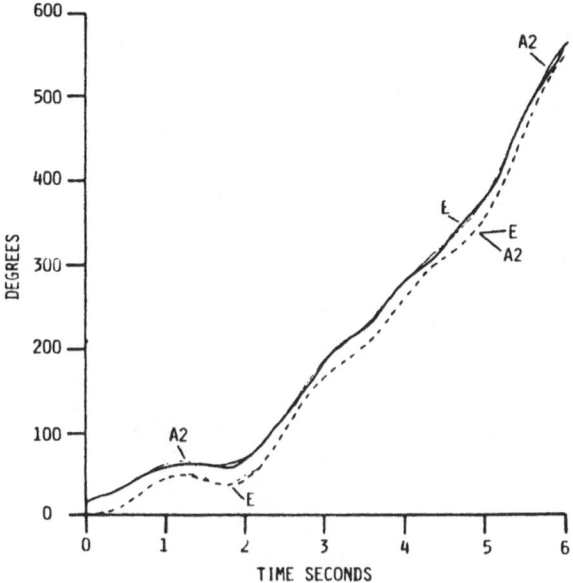

Figure 8.3.11   Individual machine angles in area 2, exact (E) and approximation
(A2)

Applying approximation (A2) to the simulation of this disturbance, we obtain the
results shown in Figures 8.3.9 to 8.3.11.   These figures show the close agreement
between the exact solution (E) and the approximate solution (A2).

The results of these two disturbances show that for the 16 machine system, the
areas obtained from linear analysis are robust, that is, they are valid for
nonlinear simulations and are fault location independent.   The concepts of
aggregation, time-scale, and weak connection properties developed in the earlier
chapters have been demonstrated on this system.

8.4 48 Machine System Example

The 48 machine system is a representation of the Northeastern portion of the
United States and Ontario, Canada, and is basically an expanded model of the 16
machine system.   The coherency grouping of this system has been found in Section 5.7
and the eigenvalue approximations by the subsystems have been examined in Section
6.6.   We now illustrate the applicability of the nine area partition (Figure 8.4.1)
found in Section 5.7 to the nonlinear electromechanical model, and show that for two
different fault locations the same area partition remains valid.

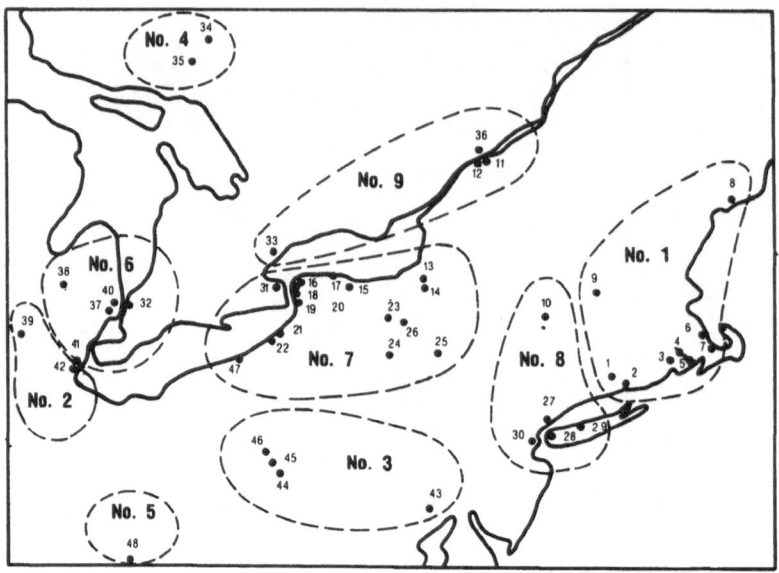

Figure 8.4.1 48 machine system nine area partition

First, a six cycle, three phase fault applied a bus in area 1 is cleared by switching out a line between this bus and an adjacent bus in the same area. Slow coherency is confirmed by Figure 8.4.2 in which the high frequency component dominates in the angular differences for machines in area 1, and hence these machines are near-coherent. These response curves are typical of those in area 1.

Time-scale separation can be shown by comparing the aggregate variables y with the difference variables z. The aggregate variables for areas 1, 5, 6, 8 and 9 in Figure 8.4.3 are clearly of a much lower frequency than the angular differences in Figure 8.4.2. Thus, the time-scale properties are carried over from the linear to the nonlinear model.

To show the validity of this area partition for different fault locations, a 6 cycle, three phase fault is applied to a bus in area 7 and is cleared by switching out a line between this bus and an adjacent bus in the same area. The angular differences for machines 13 to 16 in Figure 8.4.4 show that the fast component is dominant and only a small portion of the slow dynamics is present. Thus, the same area partition is found to be valid.

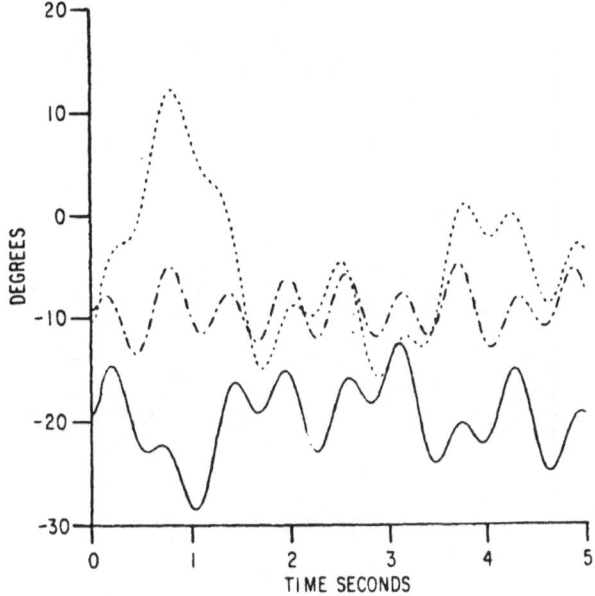

Figure 8.4.2 Difference variables in area 1

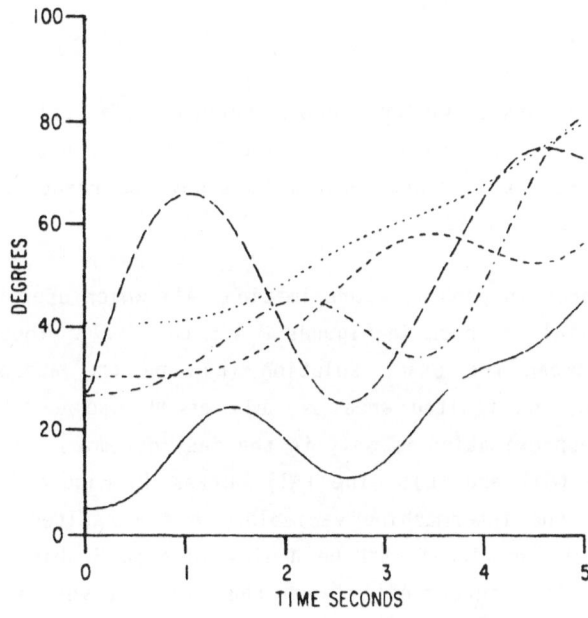

Figure 8.4.3 Aggregate variables for areas 1, 5, 6, 8 and 9

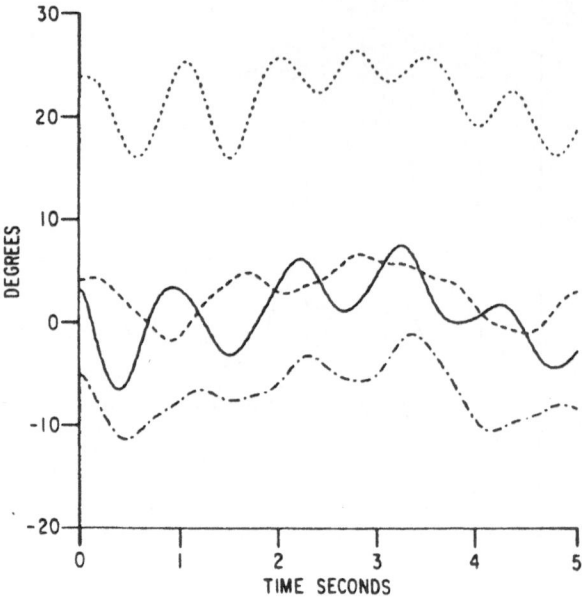

Figure 8.4.4 Difference variables in area 7

From the above discussion we have shown that the time-scale and weak connection properties are preserved in the nonlinear model. Let us now use the approximate simulation schemes presented in Section 8.2 to study the response of the 48 machine system for the two disturbances.

For the disturbance in area 1, approximation (A1) which uses the aggregate model gives responses typical of those in Figures 8.4.5 to 8.4.7. These figures show the close agreement between the exact solution (E) and the approximation (A1) for selected machines in the faulted area as well as the adjacent areas. The error introduced by this approximation is only in the fast dynamics and there is no steady state error between (A1) and (E). The (A1) curves in Figure 8.4.6 show the slow dynamics present in the intermachine variables in the faulted area. Figure 8.4.7 shows the response of individual machine angles in area 8 which is adjacent to the faulted area. The close agreement between the exact curves and the approximation implies that the fast dynamics in area 8 are small even though the fast dynamics in the faulted area are substantial.

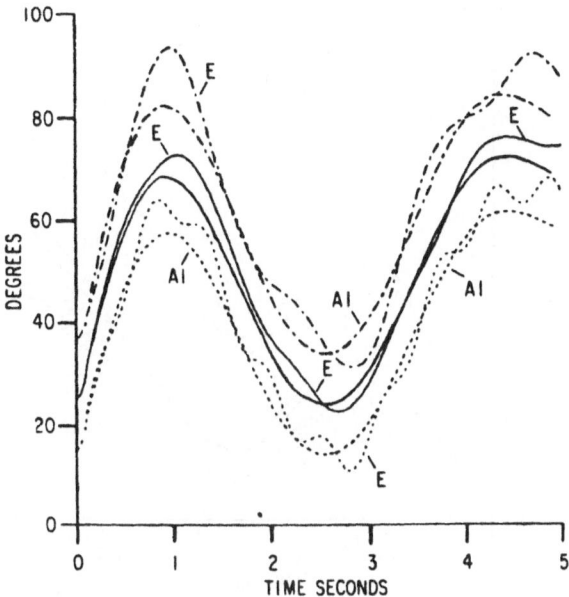

Figure 8.4.5   Individual machine angles in area 1, exact (E) and
approximation (A1)

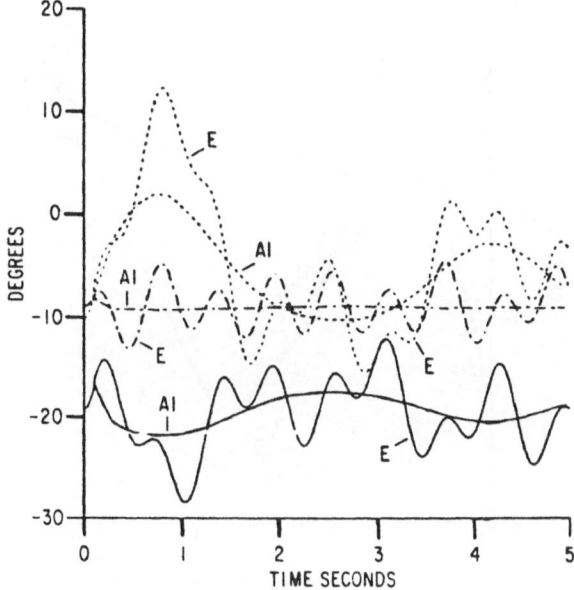

Figure 8.4.6   Difference variables in area 1, exact (E) and approximation
(A1)

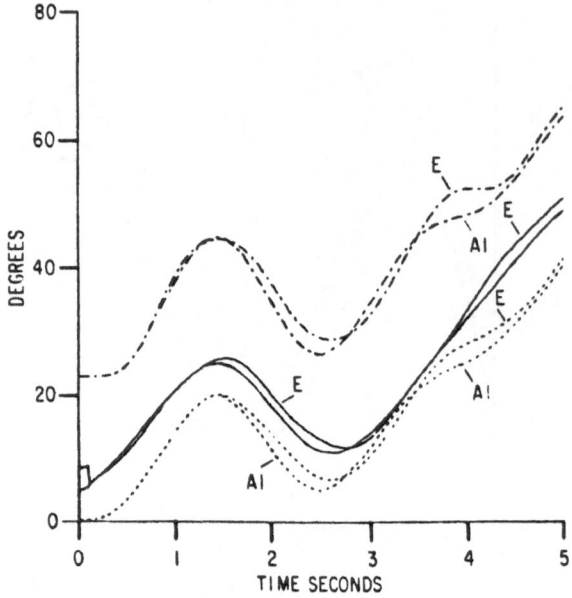

Figure 8.4.7   Individual machine angles in area 1, exact (E) and
approximation (A1)

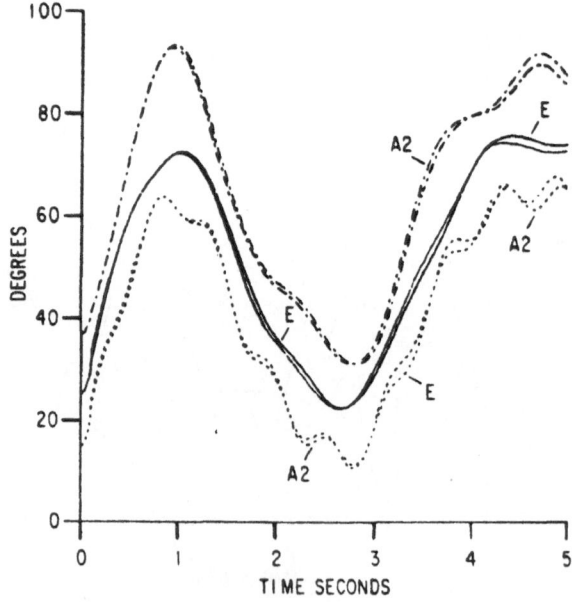

Figure 8.4.8   Individual machine angles in area 1, exact (E) and
approximation (A2)

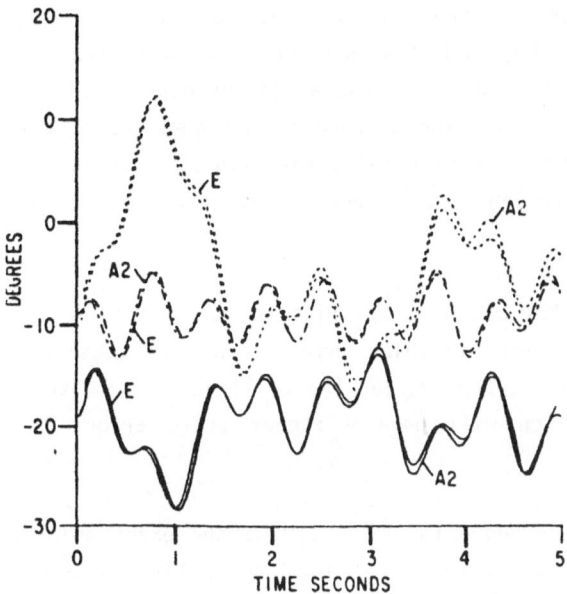

Figure 8.4.9   Difference variables in area 1, exact (E) and approximation
(A2)

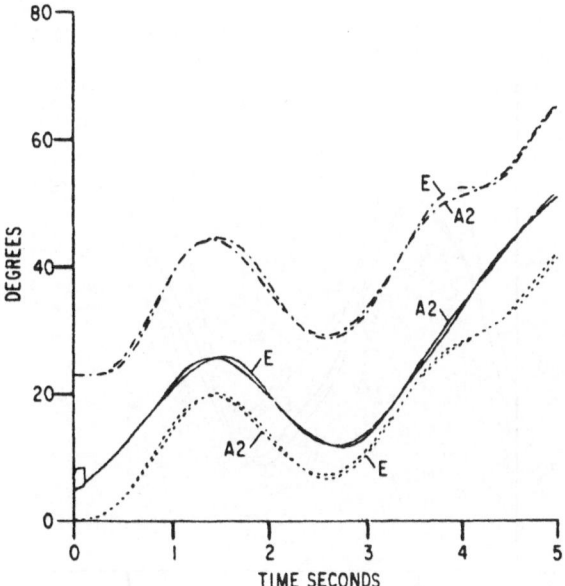

Figure 8.4.10   Individual machine angles in area 8, exact (E) and
approximation (A2)

The localized nature of the fast dynamics demonstrates the weak connections present in the system. Such a phenomenon serves as a motivation for approximation (A2). Figures 8.4.8 to 8.4.10 show close agreement between the exact curves (E) and their approximations by (A2). The differences between these curves are due to the neglected fast dynamics in the external areas. Thus, (A2) curves are more accurate than those of (A1), although both approximations provide the correct steady state value.

The approximation (A2) can be simplified to approximation (A3) by assuming that the intermachine difference variables remain constant outside the faulted area. Errors introduced by this approximation (A3) will be both in the fast variables and the slow variables, which will have a steady state error, as was discussed in Section 8.2.

The agreement between approximation (A3) and the exact solution (E) is shown in Figures 8.4.11 to 8.4.13. Within the study area, Figures 8.4.11 and 8.4.12 show that the agreement is good. However, (A3) curves for area 8 (Figure 8.4.13) do not compare with the exact curve as well as the (A2) curves. This is due to the approximation of the intermachine difference variables as constants.

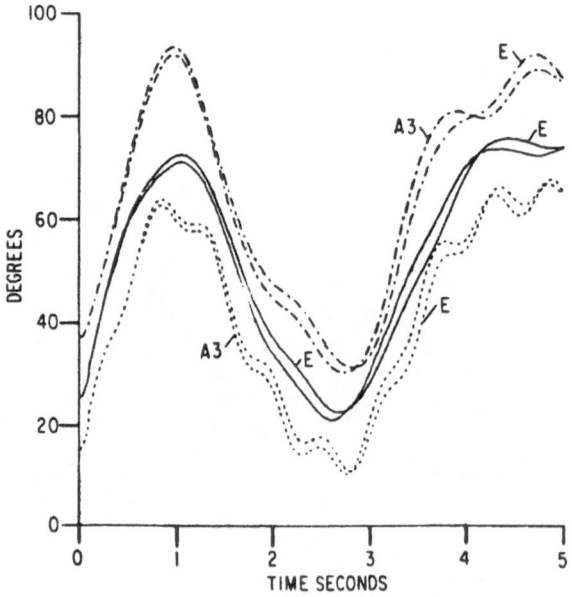

Figure 8.4.11   Individual machine angles in area 1, exact (E) and
approximation (A3)

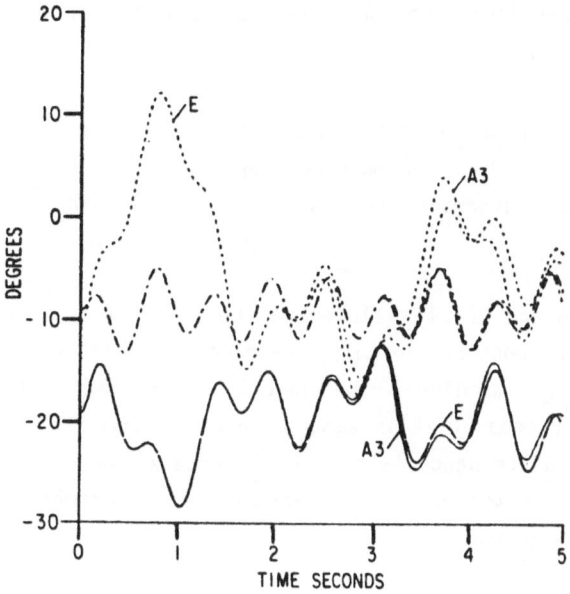

Figure 8.4.12 Difference variables in area 1, exact (E) and
approximation (A3)

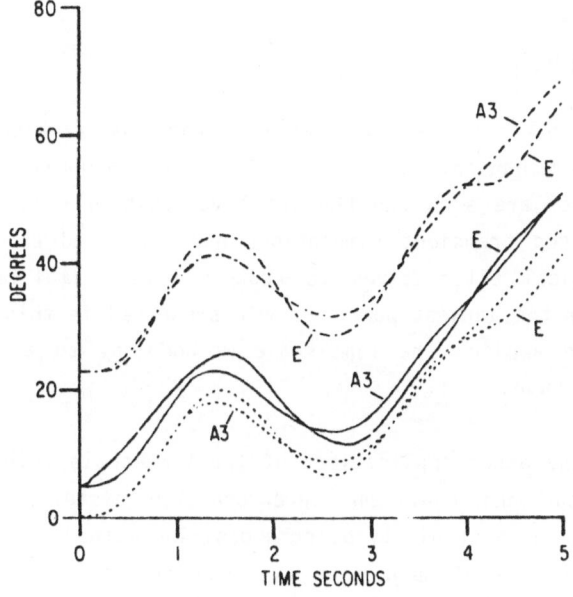

Figure 8.4.13 Individual machine angles in area 8, exact (E) and
approximation (A3)

We now use the approximation (A1) to simulate the machine response to the disturbance in area 7.

For selected machines in the faulted area, Figures 8.4.14 and 8.4.15 show the individual machine angles and machine angular difference variables, respectively. Although the fast dynamics are neglected, the underlying slow dynamics is preserved.

Figures 8.4.16 and 8.4.17 illustrate the response of selected machines in area 8. Note that one machine, namely, machine 10, has significant fast dynamics. Examining the row for machine 10 in Table 5.7.1, we see that although its strongest "attraction" is for area 8, it is also strongly "attracted" to area 7. Thus, we can expect that, if a disturbance is present in area 7, machine 10 will be disturbed to a certain extent. Note that the response of approximation (A1) on the average tracks the exact response (E).

Finally, we examine the response of machines in area 3. Figures 8.4.18 and 8.4.19 illustrate the absolute and relative motion of the machines in this area. Again, it should be noted that the absence of fast dynamics in the (E) curves indicates the weak connections between the areas, resulting in the close agreement between the (A1) curves and the (E) curves.

8.5 Concluding Remarks

The nonlinear power system examples show that the time-scale separation in the linearized electromechanical model carries over to the nonlinear model, and that the aggregate variables are slow and the local variables are fast. The three schemes proposed for reduced transient simulations have provided excellent approximations. They offer practical alternatives to reduced order simulations for power system studies. Although the largest power example presented in this monograph has only 48 machines, we have applied the time-scale methodology to a power system with 400 machines and 1700 buses.

We foresee many other applications of the time-scale methodology in the reduced modeling of linear and nonlinear interconnected systems. It serves as a new framework for examining stability by decomposition methods. A potential application is in the formulation of aggregate Lyapunov functions for power system direct transient stability analysis [35]. The methodology is also a starting point of the multi-modeling approach [24] for decentralized control design. It clearly separates the controls into aggregate and local controls, which is important for robust control designs. In addition, the methodology also simplifies the state estimation and model identification for multi-time-scale systems.

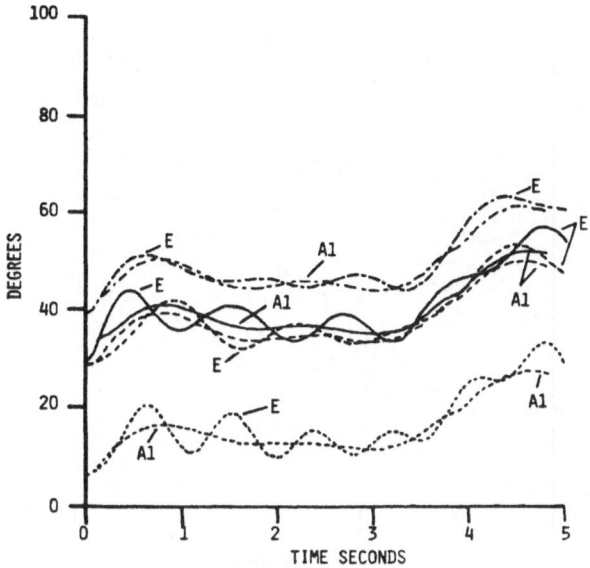

Figure 8.4.14   Individual machine angles in area 7, exact (E) and
approximation (A1)

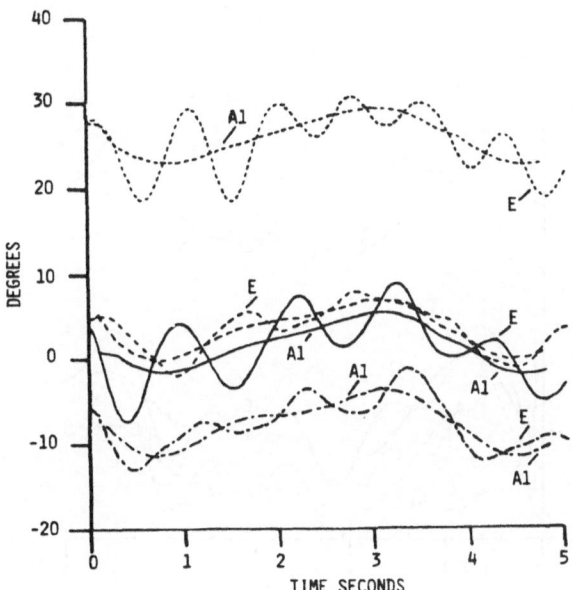

Figure 8.4.15   Difference variables in area 7, exact (E) and approximation
(A1)

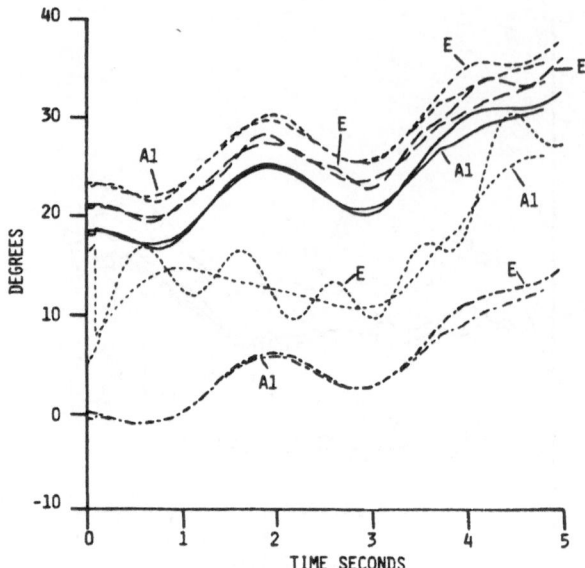

Figure 8.4.16   Individual machine angles in area 8, exact (E) and
                approximation (A1)

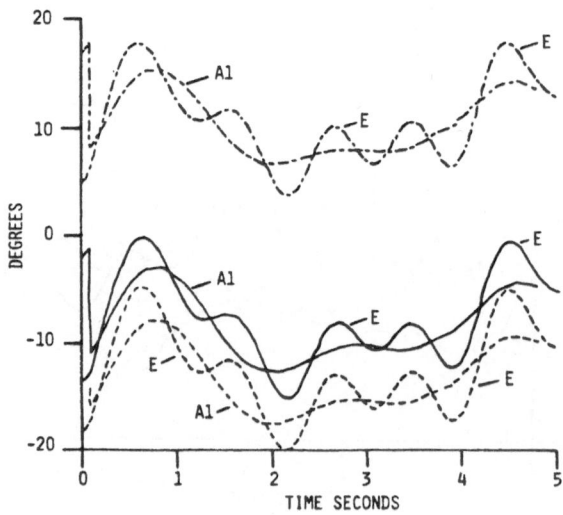

Figure 8.4.17   Difference variables in area 8, exact (E) and
                approximation (A1)

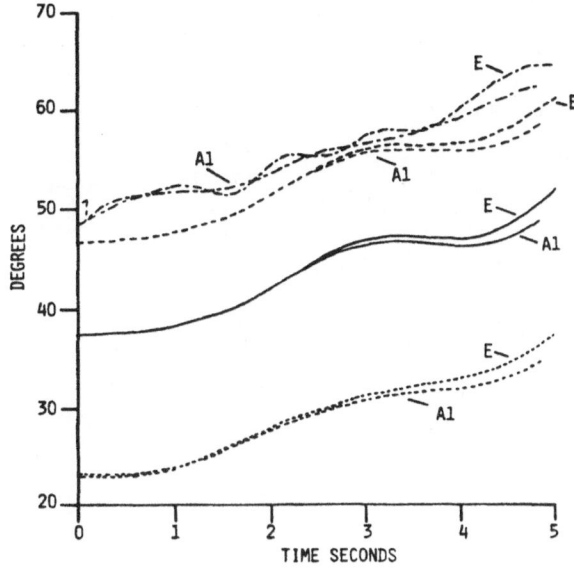

Figure 8.4.18 Individual machine angles in area 3, exact (E)
and approximation (A1)

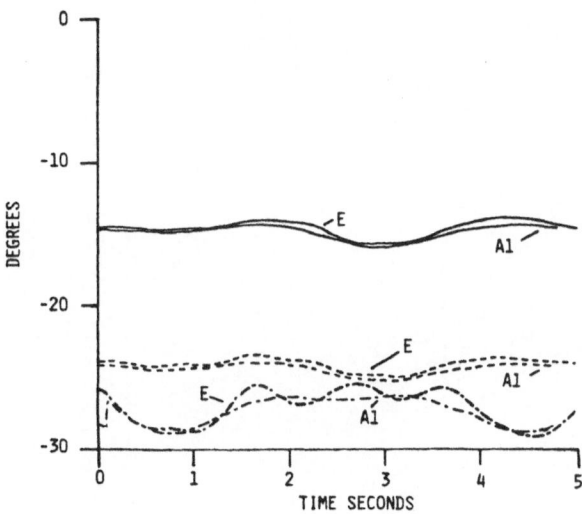

Figure 8.4.19 Difference variables in area 3, exact (E) and
approximation (A1)

MATRIX M⁻¹K FOR 48 MACHINE SYSTEM

MATRIX $M^{-1}K$ FOR 48 MACHINE SYSTEM

	1	2	3	4	5	6	7	8
1.	-0.150	0.037	0.010	0.004	0.003	0.012	0.009	0.009
2.	0.032	-0.148	0.013	0.005	0.003	0.014	0.011	0.010
3.	0.011	0.016	-0.202	0.039	0.025	0.033	0.026	0.014
4.	0.020	0.028	0.166	-0.583	0.172	0.057	0.045	0.025
5.	0.004	0.005	0.035	0.061	-0.142	0.011	0.009	0.005
6.	0.010	0.014	0.026	0.010	0.007	-0.172	0.061	0.013
7.	0.010	0.014	0.027	0.010	0.007	0.080	-0.196	0.013
8.	0.006	0.008	0.009	0.003	0.003	0.011	0.009	-0.089
9.	0.014	0.017	0.016	0.006	0.004	0.018	0.014	0.034
10.	0.007	0.007	0.004	0.002	0.001	0.005	0.004	0.006
11.	0.001	0.001	0.001	0.000	0.000	0.001	0.001	0.001
12.	0.002	0.002	0.001	0.000	0.000	0.001	0.001	0.002
13.	0.002	0.002	0.001	0.000	0.000	0.002	0.001	0.002
14.	0.003	0.004	0.002	0.001	0.001	0.002	0.002	0.003
15.	0.001	0.001	0.000	0.000	0.000	0.000	0.000	0.001
16.	0.000	0.000	0.000	0.000	0.000	0.000	0.000	0.000
17.	-0.000	-0.000	-0.000	-0.000	-0.000	-0.000	-0.000	0.000
18.	0.000	0.000	0.000	0.000	0.000	0.000	0.000	0.000
19.	0.000	0.001	0.000	0.000	0.000	0.000	0.000	0.000
20.	0.000	0.000	0.000	0.000	0.000	0.000	0.000	0.000
21.	0.000	0.000	0.000.	0.000	0.000	0.000	0.000	0.000
22.	0.000	0.000	0.000	0.000	0.000	0.000	0.000	0.000
23.	0.001	0.001	0.001	0.000	0.000	0.001	0.001	0.001
24.	0.003	0.004	0.002	0.001	0.001	0.002	0.002	0.003
25.	0.003	0.003	0.002	0.001	0.001	0.002	0.002	0.003
26.	0.002	0.002	0.001	0.000	0.000	0.001	0.001	0.002
27.	0.005	0.005	0.002	0.001	0.001	0.003	0.002	0.002
28.	0.000	0.000	0.000	0.000	0.000	0.000	0.000	0.000
29.	0.000	0.000	0.000	0.000	0.000	0.000	0.000	0.000
30.	0.000	0.000	0.000	0.000	0.000	0.000	0.000	0.000
31.	0.000	0.000	0.000	0.000	0.000	0.000	0.000	0.000
32.	0.000	0.000	0.000	0.000	0.000	0.000	0.000	0.000
33.	0.000	0.000	0.000	0.000	0.000	0.000	0.000	0.000
34.	0.000	0.000	0.000	0.000	0.000	0.000	0.000	0.000
35.	0.000	0.000	0.000	0.000	0.000	0.000	0.000	0.000
36.	0.000	0.000	0.000	0.000	0.000	0.000	0.000	0.000
37.	0.000	0.000	0.000	0.000	0.000	0.000	0.000	0.000
38.	0.000	0.000	0.000	0.000	0.000	0.000	0.000	0.000
39.	0.000	0.000	0.000	0.000	0.000	0.000	0.000	0.000
40.	0.000	0.000	0.000	0.000	0.000	0.000	0.000	0.000
41.	0.000	0.000	0.000	0.000	0.000	0.000	0.000	0.000
42.	0.000	0.000	0.000	-0.000	0.000	0.000	0.000	0.000
43.	0.000	0.000	0.000	0.000	0.000	0.000	0.000	0.000
44.	0.000	0.000	0.000	0.000	0.000	0.000	0.000	0.000
45.	0.000	0.001	0.000	0.000	0.000	0.000	0.000	0.000
46.	0.000	0.000	0.000	0.000	0.000	0.000	0.000	0.000
47.	0.001	0.001	0.000	0.000	0.000	0.000	0.000	0.001
48.	0.000	0.000	0.000	0.000	0.000	0.000	0.000	0.000

	9	10	11	12	13	14	15	16
1.	0.011	0.002	0.001	0.001	0.003	0.001	0.001	0.001
2.	0.012	0.002	0.001	0.001	0.002	0.001	0.001	0.001
3.	0.013	0.001	0.000	0.001	0.002	0.001	0.001	0.000
4.	0.023	0.003	0.001	0.001	0.003	0.002	0.001	0.001
5.	0.004	0.000	0.000	0.000	0.001	0.000	0.000	0.000
6.	0.012	0.001	0.000	0.001	0.002	0.001	0.001	0.000
7.	0.012	0.001	0.000	0.001	0.002	0.001	0.001	0.000
8.	0.020	0.001	0.000	0.001	0.002	0.001	0.001	0.000
9.	-0.198	0.006	0.002	0.002	0.006	0.004	0.002	0.001
10.	0.011	-0.259	0.009	0.012	0.024	0.020	0.009	0.005
11.	0.002	0.007	-0.185	0.084	0.010	0.006	0.003	0.002
12.	0.003	0.010	0.083	-0.228	0.013	0.009	0.005	0.003
13.	0.004	0.009	0.004	0.006	-0.172	0.027	0.015	0.009
14.	0.006	0.017	0.007	0.009	0.055	-0.289	0.025	0.012
15.	0.001	0.002	0.001	0.002	0.012	0.009	-0.144	0.011
16.	0.001	0.001	0.001	0.001	0.006	0.004	0.009	-0.158
17.	0.000	-0.002	0.000	0.000	0.004	-0.003	0.007	0.020
18.	0.001	0.001	0.001	0.001	0.006	0.003	0.014	0.023
19.	0.001	0.002	0.001	0.001	0.009	0.006	0.015	0.041
20.	0.001	0.001	0.001	0.001	0.007	0.004	0.015	0.029
21.	0.000	0.001	0.000	0.001	0.004	0.002	0.007	0.015
22.	0.001	0.001	0.001	0.001	0.006	0.004	0.011	0.024
23.	0.002	0.004	0.002	0.002	0.014	0.013	0.069	0.015
24.	0.006	0.010	0.003	0.004	0.013	0.013	0.013	0.011
25.	0.005	0.009	0.003	0.004	0.011	0.011	0.008	0.005
26.	0.003	0.008	0.003	0.003	0.016	0.032	0.009	0.005
27.	0.004	0.005	0.001	0.001	0.003	0.003	0.001	0.001
28.	0.000	0.000	0.000	0.000	0.000	0.000	0.000	0.000
29.	0.000	0.000	0.000	0.000	0.000	0.000	0.000	0.000
30.	0.000	0.000	0.000	0.000	0.000	0.000	0.000	0.000
31.	0.000	0.001	0.001	0.001	0.005	0.003	0.008	0.024
32.	0.000	0.000	0.000	0.000	0.000	0.000	0.001	0.002
33.	0.000	0.000	0.001	0.001	0.001	0.001	0.002	0.005
34.	0.000	0.000	0.000	0.000	0.000	0.000	0.000	0.001
35.	0.000	0.000	0.000	0.000	0.000	0.000	0.000	0.001
36.	0.000	0.000	0.005	0.008	0.001	0.000	0.001	0.001
37.	0.000	0.000	0.000	0.000	0.000	0.000	0.000	0.001
38.	0.000	0.000	0.000	0.000	0.000	0.000	0.000	0.000
39.	0.000	0.000	0.000	0.000	0.000	0.000	0.000	0.000
40.	0.000	0.000	0.000	0.000	0.000	0.000	0.000	0.000
41.	0.000	0.000	0.000	0.000	0.000	0.000	0.000	0.000
42.	0.000	0.000	0.000	0.000	0.000	0.000	0.000	0.000
43.	0.000	0.000	0.000	0.000	0.000	0.000	0.000	0.000
44.	0.000	0.000	0.000	0.000	0.001	0.000	0.000	0.000
45.	0.001	0.001	0.000	0.001	0.002	0.001	0.002	0.002
46.	0.000	0.000	0.000	0.000	0.000	0.000	0.000	0.000
47.	0.001	0.002	0.001	0.001	0.006	0.004	0.010	0.020
48.	0.000	0.000	0.000	0.000	0.000	0.000	0.000	0.000

	17	18	19	20	21	22	23	24
1.	0.000	0.001	0.000	0.000	0.000	0.000	0.000	0.000
2.	0.000	0.001	0.000	0.000	0.000	0.000	0.000	0.000
3.	0.000	0.001	0.000	0.000	0.000	0.000	0.000	0.000
4.	0.000	0.001	0.001	0.000	0.000	0.000	0.000	0.000
5.	0.000	0.000	0.000	0.000	0.000	0.000	0.000	0.000
6.	0.000	0.000	0.000	0.000	0.000	0.000	0.000	0.000
7.	0.000	0.000	0.000	0.000	0.000	0.000	0.000	0.000
8.	0.000	0.001	0.000	0.000	0.000	0.000	0.000	0.000
9.	0.000	0.002	0.001	0.001	0.001	0.000	0.001	0.001
10.	0.001	0.007	0.004	0.002	0.002	0.001	0.003	0.002
11.	0.001	0.003	0.002	0.001	0.001	0.000	0.001	0.001
12.	0.001	0.004	0.002	0.001	0.001	0.001	0.001	0.001
13.	0.003	0.012	0.006	0.004	0.003	0.001	0.004	0.001
14.	0.003	0.016	0.008	0.005	0.004	0.002	0.007	0.002
15.	0.006	0.023	0.009	0.007	0.004	0.002	0.017	0.001
16.	0.008	0.030	0.017	0.010	0.007	0.004	0.003	0.001
17.	-0.134	0.031	0.024	0.009	0.010	0.004	0.000	-0.000
18.	0.011	-0.173	0.019	0.023	0.010	0.006	0.004	0.001
19.	0.013	0.054	-0.306	0.025	0.024	0.012	0.005	0.001
20.	0.011	0.081	0.032	-0.289	0.020	0.012	0.005	0.001
21.	0.006	0.027	0.023	0.015	-0.239	0.039	0.003	0.001
22.	0.008	0.043	0.034	0.025	0.110	-0.383	0.005	0.002
23.	0.004	0.026	0.013	0.009	0.009	0.005	-0.279	0.011
24.	0.003	0.017	0.012	0.008	0.011	0.006	0.031	-0.436
25.	0.002	0.007	0.005	0.003	0.004	0.002	0.009	0.019
26.	0.001	0.006	0.004	0.002	0.003	0.001	0.005	0.009
27.	0.000	0.001	0.001	0.000	0.000	0.000	0.001	0.001
28.	0.000	0.000	0.000	0.000	0.000	0.000	0.000	0.000
29.	0.000	0.000	0.000	0.000	0.000	0.000	0.000	0.000
30.	0.000	0.000	0.000	0.000	0.000	0.000	0.000	0.000
31.	0.009	0.028	0.017	0.009	0.007	0.004	0.002	0.001
32.	0.001	0.002	0.001	0.001	0.001	0.000	0.000	0.000
33.	0.002	0.006	0.003	0.002	0.001	0.001	0.001	0.000
34.	0.000	0.001	0.001	0.000	0.000	0.000	0.000	0.000
35.	0.001	0.001	0.001	0.000	0.000	0.000	0.000	0.000
36.	0.001	0.001	0.001	0.000	0.000	0.000	0.000	0.000
37.	0.000	0.001	0.000	0.000	0.000	0.000	0.000	0.000
38.	0.000	0.001	0.000	0.000	0.000	0.000	0.000	0.000
39.	0.000	0.000	0.000	0.000	0.000	0.000	0.000	0.000
40.	0.000	0.000	0.000	0.000	0.000	0.000	0.000	0.000
41.	0.000	0.000	0.000	0.000	0.000	0.000	0.000	0.000
42.	0.000	0.000	0.000	0.000	0.000	0.000	0.000	0.000
43.	0.000	0.000	0.000	0.000	0.000	0.000	0.000	0.001
44.	0.000	0.000	0.000	0.000	0.000	0.000	0.000	0.000
45.	0.001	0.004	0.003	0.002	0.010	0.003	0.002	0.003
46.	0.000	0.000	0.000	0.000	0.000	0.000	0.000	0.000
47.	0.007	0.034	0.029	0.019	0.134	0.048	0.006	0.006
48.	0.000	0.000	0.000	0.000	0.000	0.000	0.000	0.000

	25	26	27	28	29	30	31	32
1.	0.001	0.001	0.038	0.000	0.000	0.000	0.001	0.000
2.	0.001	0.001	0.032	0.000	0.000	0.000	0.001	0.000
3.	0.000	0.000	0.014	0.000	0.000	0.000	0.000	0.000
4.	0.001	0.001	0.026	0.000	0.000	0.000	0.001	0.000
5.	0.000	0.000	0.003	0.000	0.000	0.000	0.000	0.000
6.	0.000	0.000	0.011	0.000	0.000	0.000	0.000	0.000
7.	0.000	0.000	0.012	0.000	0.000	0.000	0.000	0.000
8.	0.000	0.000	0.009	0.000	0.000	0.000	0.000	0.000
9.	0.002	0.001	0.035	0.000	0.000	0.000	0.001	0.000
10.	0.005	0.005	0.075	0.000	0.000	0.000	0.005	0.001
11.	0.001	0.002	0.012	0.000	0.000	0.000	0.003	0.001
12.	0.002	0.002	0.018	0.000	0.000	0.000	0.004	0.001
13.	0.002	0.005	0.023	0.000	0.000	0.000	0.009	0.001
14.	0.005	0.018	0.038	0.000	0.000	0.000	0.012	0.001
15.	0.001	0.002	0.005	0.000	0.000	0.000	0.011	0.002
16.	0.001	0.001	0.003	0.000	0.000	0.000	0.026	0.003
17.	-0.000	-0.000	-0.003	0.000	0.000	0.000	0.023	0.004
18.	0.001	0.001	0.003	0.000	0.000	0.000	0.024	0.003
19.	0.001	0.002	0.005	0.000	0.000	0.000	0.041	0.005
20.	0.001	0.001	0.004	0.000	0.000	0.000	0.029	0.004
21.	0.001	0.001	0.003	0.000	0.000	0.000	0.016	0.002
22.	0.002	0.001	0.004	0.000	0.000	0.000	0.024	0.003
23.	0.007	0.006	0.014	0.000	0.000	0.000	0.015	0.002
24.	0.044	0.028	0.046	0.000	0.000	0.000	0.012	0.001
25.	-0.259	0.036	0.035	0.000	0.000	0.000	0.005	0.001
26.	0.027	-0.208	0.025	0.000	0.000	0.000	0.005	0.001
27.	0.001	0.001	-0.170	0.041	0.017	0.021	0.001	0.000
28.	0.000	0.000	0.239	-0.241	0.000	0.000	0.000	0.000
29.	0.000	0.000	0.194	0.001	-0.196	0.000	0.000	0.000
30.	0.000	0.000	0.300	0.001	0.000	-0.303	0.000	0.000
31.	0.001	0.001	0.003	0.000	0.000	0.000	-0.258	0.025
32.	0.000	0.000	0.000	0.000	0.000	0.000	0.015	-0.169
33.	0.000	0.000	0.001	0.000	0.000	0.000	0.043	0.017
34.	0.000	0.000	0.000	0.000	0.000	0.000	0.007	0.004
35.	0.000	0.000	0.000	0.000	0.000	0.000	0.010	0.005
36.	0.000	0.000	0.001	0.000	0.000	0.000	0.007	0.003
37.	0.000	0.000	0.000	0.000	0.000	0.000	0.006	0.066
38.	0.000	0.000	0.000	0.000	0.000	0.000	0.005	0.048
39.	0.000	0.000	0.000	0.000	0.000	0.000	0.000	0.001
40.	0.000	0.000	0.000	0.000	0.000	0.000	0.003	0.029
41.	0.000	0.000	0.000	0.000	0.000	0.000	0.001	0.005
42.	0.000	0.000	0.000	-0.000	-0.000	-0.000	0.003	0.027
43.	0.001	0.000	0.077	0.000	0.000	0.000	0.000	0.000
44.	0.000	0.000	0.003	0.000	0.000	0.000	0.000	0.000
45.	0.004	0.003	0.007	0.000	0.000	0.000	0.002	0.000
46.	0.000	0.000	0.006	0.000	0.000	0.000	0.000	0.001
47.	0.006	0.004	0.011	0.000	0.000	0.000	0.021	0.003
48.	0.000	0.000	0.001	0.000	0.000	0.000	0.000	0.001

	33	34	35	36	37	38	39	40
1.	0.000	0.000	0.000	0.000	0.000	0.000	0.000	0.000
2.	0.000	0.000	0.000	0.000	0.000	0.000	0.000	0.000
3.	0.000	0.000	0.000	0.000	0.000	0.000	0.000	0.000
4.	0.000	0.000	0.000	0.000	0.000	0.000	0.000	0.000
5.	0.000	0.000	0.000	0.000	0.000	0.000	0.000	0.000
6.	0.000	0.000	0.000	0.000	0.000	0.000	0.000	0.000
7.	0.000	0.000	0.000	0.000	0.000	0.000	0.000	0.000
8.	0.000	0.000	0.000	0.000	0.000	0.000	0.000	0.000
9.	0.000	0.000	0.000	0.001	0.000	0.000	0.000	0.000
10.	0.002	0.000	0.000	0.004	0.000	0.000	0.000	0.000
11.	0.004	0.000	0.000	0.029	0.000	0.000	0.000	0.000
12.	0.006	0.000	0.000	0.045	0.000	0.000	0.000	0.000
13.	0.003	0.000	0.000	0.002	0.000	0.000	0.000	0.000
14.	0.005	0.000	0.000	0.004	0.000	0.000	0.000	0.000
15.	0.003	0.000	0.000	0.001	0.000	0.000	0.000	0.000
16.	0.008	0.001	0.001	0.002	0.001	0.000	0.000	0.001
17.	-0.003	0.000	-0.000	0.001	0.000	0.000	0.000	0.000
18.	0.006	0.000	0.001	0.001	0.001	0.000	0.000	0.000
19.	0.013	0.001	0.001	0.002	0.001	0.001	0.001	0.001
20.	0.009	0.001	0.001	0.002	0.001	0.000	0.000	0.001
21.	0.005	0.000	0.000	0.001	0.000	0.000	0.000	0.000
22.	0.008	0.000	0.001	0.001	0.001	0.000	0.000	0.001
23.	0.005	0.000	0.000	0.001	0.000	0.000	0.000	0.000
24.	0.004	0.000	0.000	0.002	0.000	0.000	0.000	0.000
25.	0.002	0.000	0.000	0.002	0.000	0.000	0.000	0.000
26.	0.002	0.000	0.000	0.001	0.000	0.000	0.000	0.000
27.	0.000	0.000	0.000	0.000	0.000	0.000	0.000	0.000
28.	0.000	0.000	0.000	0.000	0.000	0.000	0.000	0.000
29.	0.000	0.000	0.000	0.000	0.000	0.000	0.000	0.000
30.	0.000	0.000	0.000	0.000	0.000	0.000	0.000	0.000
31.	0.063	0.004	0.006	0.010	0.005	0.003	0.003	0.004
32.	0.013	0.001	0.002	0.002	0.036	0.017	0.016	0.022
33.	-0.172	0.013	0.020	0.034	0.004	0.002	0.002	0.003
34.	0.036	-0.127	0.067	0.006	0.001	0.000	0.000	0.001
35.	0.048	0.057	-0.139	0.007	0.001	0.001	0.001	0.001
36.	0.037	0.002	0.003	-0.076	0.001	0.000	0.000	0.001
37.	0.005	0.000	0.001	0.001	-0.280	0.044	0.042	0.030
38.	0.004	0.000	0.000	0.001	0.068	-0.315	0.064	0.040
39.	0.000	0.000	0.000	0.000	0.002	0.002	-0.013	0.001
40.	0.003	0.000	0.000	0.001	0.021	0.018	0.021	-0.142
41.	0.001	0.000	0.000	0.000	0.006	0.005	0.009	0.008
42.	0.002	0.000	0.000	0.000	0.035	0.028	0.091	0.027
43.	0.000	0.000	0.000	0.000	0.000	0.000	0.000	0.000
44.	0.000	0.000	0.000	0.000	0.000	0.000	0.000	0.000
45.	0.001	0.000	0.000	0.000	0.000	0.000	0.000	0.000
46.	0.000	0.000	0.000	0.000	0.001	0.000	0.000	0.000
47.	0.007	0.000	0.001	0.001	0.001	0.000	0.000	0.000
48.	0.000	0.000	0.000	0.000	0.001	0.001	0.001	0.000

	41	42	43	44	45	46	47	48
1.	0.000	0.000	0.000	0.001	0.001	0.000	0.000	0.000
2.	0.000	0.000	0.000	0.001	0.001	0.000	0.000	0.000
3.	0.000	0.000	0.000	0.001	0.001	0.000	0.000	0.000
4.	0.000	0.000	0.000	0.001	0.001	0.000	0.000	0.000
5.	0.000	0.000	0.000	0.000	0.000	0.000	0.000	0.000
6.	0..000	0.000	0.000	0.000	0.001	0.000	0.000	0.000
7.	0.000	0.000	0.000	0.001	0.001	0.000	0.000	0.000
8.	0.000	0.000	0.000	0.000	0.001	0.000	0.000	0.000
9.	0.000	0.000	0.000	0.001	0.002	0.001	0.000	0.000
10.	0.000	0.000	0.001	0.003	0.005	0.001	0.001	0.001
11.	0.000	0.000	0.000	0.001	0.002	0.000	0.000	0.000
12.	0.000	0.000	0.000	0.001	0.002	0.000	0.000	0.000
13.	0.000	0.000	0.000	0.001	0.003	0.001	0.001	0.001
14.	0.000	0.000	0.001	0.002	0.004	0.001	0.001	0.001
15.	0.000	0.000	0.000	0.001	0.003	0.001	0.001	0.001
16.	0.000	0.000	0.000	0.001	0.002	0.000	0.001	0.001
17.	0.000	0.000	-0.000	0.001	0.003	0.000	0.002	0.001
18.	0.000	0.000	0.000	0.001	0.003	0.000	0.002	0.001
19.	0.000	0.000	0.000	0.002	0.006	0.001	0.004	0.003
20.	0.000	0.000	0.000	0.001	0.005	0.001	0.004	0.002
21.	0.000	0.000	0.000	0.004	0.021	0.003	0.021	0.011
22.	0.000	0.000	0.000	0.004	0.021	0.003	0.020	0.011
23.	0.000	0.000	0.001	0.005	0.011	0.002	0.002	0.002
24.	0.000	0.000	0.005	0.025	0.059	0.011	0.006	0.007
25.	0.000	0.000	0.002	0.012	0.032	0.006	0.003	0.003
26.	0.000	0.000	0.001	0.005	0.013	0.002	0.001	0.001
27.	0.000	0.000	0.009	0.022	0.002	0.005	0.000	0.003
28.	0.000	0.000	0.000	0.000	0.000	0.000	0.000	0.000
29.	0.000	0.000	0.000	0.000	0.000	0.000	0.000	0.000
30.	0.000	0.000	0.000	0.000	0.000	0.000	0.000	0.000
31.	0.002	0.002	0.000	0.001	0.002	0.000	0.001	0.002
32.	0.012	0.011	0.000	0.001	0.000	0.001	0.000	0.008
33.	0.002	0.001	0.000	0.000	0.000	0.000	0.000	0.001
34.	0.000	0.000	0.000	0.000	0.000	0.000	0.000	0.000
35.	0.000	0.000	0.000	0.000	0.000	0.000	0.000	0.000
36.	0.000	0.000	0.000	0.000	0.000	0.000	0.000	0.000
37.	0.024	0.026	0.000	0.002	0.000	0.002	0.000	0.025
38.	0.031	0.032	0.000	0.002	0.000	0.001	0.000	0.016
39.	0.002	0.003	0.000	0.000	0.000	0.000	0.000	0.001
40.	0.022	0.014	0.000	0.001	0.000	0.001	0.000	0.006
41.	-0.060	0.006	0.000	0.002	0.000	0.001	0.000	0.016
42.	0.036	-0.264	0.000	0.001	0.000	0.001	0.000	0.009
43.	0.001	0.000	-0.478	0.267	0.010	0.064	0.000	0.049
44.	0.000	0.000	0.005	-0.052	0.003	0.034	0.000	0.005
45.	0.000	0.000	0.004	0.070	-0.228	0.057	0.015	0.021
46.	0.002	0.000	0.011	0.325	0.022	-0.405	0.001	0.032
47.	0.000	0.000	0.003	0.034	0.203	0.025	-0.769	0.115
48.	0.003	0.000	0.001	0.006	0.001	0.003	0.000	-0.020

REFERENCES

1.   P.M. Anderson and A.A. Fouad, Power System Control and Stability, Iowa State University Press, Ames, Iowa, 1977.

2.   M. Aoki, "Control of Large Scale Dynamic Systems by Aggregation," IEEE Transactions on Automatic Control, Vol. AC-13, pp. 246-253, 1968.

3.   B. Avramovic, "Time Scales, Coherency, and Weak Coupling," Ph.D. Dissertation, Report DC-40, Coordinated Science Laboratory, University of Illinois, Urbana, 1980.

4.   B. Avramovic, P.V. Kokotovic, J.R. Winkelman and J.H. Chow, "Area Decomposition of Electromechanical Models of Power Systems," Automatica, Vol. 16, pp. 637-648, 1980.

5.   M.J. Balas, "Trends in Large Space Structure Control Theory: Fondest Hopes, Wildest Dreams," IEEE Transactions on Automatic Control, Vol. AC-27, pp. 522-535, 1982.

6.   A.D. Bhatt, H.G. Kwatny and V.E. Mablekos, "A Coherency Concept for Construction of Power System Equivalents," presented at the 1976 International Conference on Information Sciences and Systems, Patras, Greece, 1976.

7.   S.L. Campbell, Singular Systems of Differential Equations, Pitman Advanced Publishing Program, 1980.

8.   J.H. Chow, J.J. Allemong and P.V. Kokotovic, "Singular Perturbation Analysis of Systems with Sustained High Frequency Oscillations," Automatica, Vol. 14, pp. 271-279, 1978.

9.   J.H. Chow, B. Avramovic, P.V. Kokotovic and J.R. Winkelman, "Singular Perturbations, Coherency and Aggregation of Dynamic Systems," Final Report, U.S. Department of Energy Contract DE-AC05-77ET29104, July 1981.

10. J.H. Chow and P.V. Kokotovic, "A Two-Stage Lyapunov-Bellman Feedback Design of a Class of Nonlinear Systems," IEEE Transactions on Automatic Control, Vol. AC-26, pp. 656-663, 1981.

11. J.D. Cobb, "Descriptor Variable and Generalized Singularly Perturbed Systems: a Geometric Approach," Ph.D. Dissertation, University of Illinois, Urbana, 1980.

12. P.J. Courtois, Decomposability: Queueing and Computer System Applications, Academic Press, New York, 1977.

13. R.L. Cresap and J.F. Hauer, "Emergence of a New Swing Mode in the Western Power System," IEEE Transactions on Power Apparatus and Systems, Vol. PAS-100, pp. 2037-2045, 1981.

14. J. Cullum and R.A. Willoughby, "Lanczos and the Computation in Specified Intervals of the Spectrum of Large, Sparse Real Symmetric Matrices," Sparse Matrix Proceedings 1978, (I.S. Duff and G.W. Stewart, editors), SIAM, Philadelphia.

15. J. Cullum and R.A. Willoughby, "Fast Modal Analysis of Large, Sparse but Unstructured Symmetric Matrices," Proceedings of the 17th IEEE Conference on Decision and Control, pp. 45-53, San Diego, 1979.

16. F. Delebecque and J.P. Quadrat, "Optimal Control of Markov Chains Admitting Strong and Weak Interactions," to appear in Automatica.

17. U. DiCaprio and R. Marconato, "Structural Coherency Conditions in Multi-machine Power Systems," Proceedings of IFAC 7th Triannual World Congress, Helinski, Finland, pp. 35-45, 1978.

18. N. Fenichel, "Geometric Singular Perturbation Theory for Ordinary Differential Equations," Journal of Differential Equations, Vol. 31, pp. 53-98, 1979.

19. F. R. Gantmacher, The Theory of Matrices, Chelsea, New York, 1964.

20. L. Grujic, M. Darwish and J. Fantin, "Coherence, Vector Liapunov Functions, and Large-Scale Power Systems," International Journal of System Science, Vol. 10, pp. 351-362, 1979.

21. J.K. Hale, Oscillations in Nonlinear Systems, McGraw Hill, New York, 1963.

22. F. Hoppensteadt, "Properties of Ordinary Differential Equations with Small Parameters," Communications of Pure and Applied Mathematics, XXIV, pp. 807-840, 1971.

23. F. Hoppensteadt, "Asymptotic Stability in Singular Perturbation Problems, II," Journal of Differential Equations, Vol. 15, pp. 510-521, 1974.

24. H.K. Khalil and P.V. Kokotovic, "Control Strategies for Decision Makers Using Different Models of the Same System," IEEE Transactions on Automatic Control, Vol. AC-23, pp. 289-298, 1978.

25. A.I. Klimushev and N.N. Krasovskii, "Uniform Asymptotic Stability of Systems of Differential Equations with a Small Parameter in the Derivative Terms," Journal of Applied Mathematics and Mechanics, Vol. 25, pp. 1011-1025, 1962.

26. P.V. Kokotovic, "Subsystems, Time Scales, and Multimodeling," Automatica, Vol. 17, pp. 789-795, 1981.

27. P.V. Kokotovic, B. Avramovic, J.H. Chow and J.R. Winkelman, "Coherency Based Decomposition and Aggregation," Automatica, Vol. 18, pp. 47-56, 1982.

28. P.V. Kokotovic, R.E. O'Malley, Jr., and P. Sannuti, "Singular Perturbations and Order Reduction in Control Theory - An Overview," Automatica, Vol. 12, pp. 123-132, 1976.

29. O. Lange, "The Stability of Economic Equilibrium," Appendix to Price Flexibility and Employment, Cowles Commission Monograph, 8, Bloomington, Indiana.

30. J. Lawler, R.A. Schlueter, P. Rusche and D.L. Hackett, "Modal-Coherent Equivalents Derived from an RMS Coherency Measure," IEEE Transactions on Power Apparatus and Systems, Vol. PAS-99, pp. 1415-1425, 1980.

31. S.T. Lee and F. Schweppe, "Distance Measures and Coherency Recognition for Transient Stability Equivalents," IEEE Transactions on Power Apparatus and Systems, Vol. PAS-92, pp. 1550-1557, 1973.

32. J.R. Luini, R.P. Schulz and A.E. Turner, "A Digital Computer Program for Analyzing Long-Term Dynamic Response of Power Systems," IEEE PICA Conference Proceedings, pp. 136-143, 1975.

33. R.E. O'Malley, Jr., "Boundary Layer Methods for Nonlinear Initial Value Problems," SIAM Review, Vol. 13, pp. 425-434, 1971.

34. R.E. O'Malley, Jr. and J.E. Flaherty, "Singular Singular-Perturbation Problems," Lecture Notes in Mathematics, No. 594, Springer-Verlag, pp. 422-436.

35. M.A. Pai, Power System Stability, North Holland, Amsterdam, 1981.

36. M.A. Pai and R.P. Adgaonkar, "Identification of Coherent Generators Using Weighted Eigenvectors," IEEE Paper A79 022-5, presented at PES Winter Meeting, New York, 1979.

37. G.M. Peponides, "Nonexplicit Singular Perturbations and Interconnected Systems," Ph.D. Thesis, University of Illinois, 1982.

38. G. Peponides and J.H. Chow, "Area Aggregation of Network Systems," Proceedings of the 20th IEEE Conference on Decision and Control, pp. 206-214, San Diego, 1981.

39. G. Peponides and P. Kokotovic, "Weak Connections, Time Scales, and Aggregation of Nonlinear Systems," to be presented at the 1982 IEEE International Large Scale Systems Symposium, Virginia Beach, Virginia, October, 1982.

40. R.G. Phillips and P.V. Kokotovic, "A Singular Perturbation Approach to Modeling and Control of Markov Chains," IEEE Transactions on Automatic Control, Vol. AC-26, pp. 1087-1094, 1981.

41. R. Podmore, "Identification of Coherent Generators for Dynamic Equivalents," IEEE Transactions on Power Apparatus and Systems, Vol. PAS-97, pp. 1344-1354, 1978.

42. W.W. Price, "A Study of the Accuracy and Computational Savings of Modal Analysis Dynamic Equivalents," report to NPCC-10 Working Group, 1974.

43. M. Ribbens-Pavella, "Transient Stability of Multi-machine Power Systems by Lyapunov's Direct Method," presented at IEEE Winter Power Meeting, New York, 1971.

44. F. Saccomano, "Development and Evaluation of Simplified Dynamic Model for Multi-machine Electric Power Systems," Proceedings of 4th PSCC, Grenoble, France, paper No. 3.1.22, 1972.

45. S. Sastry and P. Varaiya, "Coherency for Interconnected Power Systems," IEEE Transactions on Automatic Control, Vol. AC-26, pp. 218-226, 1981.

46. C.H. Sauer and K.M. Chandy, "Approximate Solution of Queueing Models," Computer, pp. 25-32, 1980.

47. R.P. Schulz, A.E. Turner and D.N. Ewart," Long Term Power System Dynamics," EPRI Report 90-7-0, Palo Alto, California, 1974.

48. D.D. Siljak, Large Scale Dynamic Systems, North Holland, New York, 1978.

49. H.A. Simon, "The Architecture of Complexity," Proceedings of the American Philosophical Society, Vol. 104, pp. 467-482, 1962; also reproduced in The Sciences of the Artificial, MIT Press, 1969.

50. H.A. Simon and A. Ando, "Aggregation of Variables in Dynamic Systems," _Econometrica_, Vol. 29, pp. 111-138, 1963.

51. K.N. Stanton, "Dynamic Energy Balance Studies for Simulation of Power Frequency Transients," _IEEE PICA Conference Proceedings_, pp. 173-179. 1971.

52. G.W. Stewart, _Introduction to Matrix Computation_, Academic Press, New York, 1973.

53. G. Strang, _Linear Algebra and Its Applications_, Academic Press, New York, 1976.

54. C.J. Tavora and O.J.M. Smith, "Characterization of Equilibrium and Stability in Power Systems," _IEEE Transactions on Power Apparatus and Systems_, Vol. PAS-91, pp. 1127-1130, 1972.

55. A.N. Tihonov, "Systems of Differential Equations Containing a Small Parameter Multiplying the Derivative," _Mat. Sb._, Vol. 73, N.S. 31, pp. 575-586, 1952.

56. E.C.Y. Tse, J.V. Medanic and W.R. Perkins, "Chained Aggregation of Linear Time Invariant Systems," _Proceedings of JACC_, San Francisco, California, pp. 550-555, 1977.

57. A.B. Vasileva, "Asymptotic Behavior of Solutions to Certain Problems Involving Nonlinear Differential Equations Containing a Small Parameter Multiplying the Highest Derivative," _Russian Mathematical Surveys_, Vol. 18, pp. 13-81, 1963.

58. A.B. Vasileva, "Singularly Perturbed Systems Containing Indeterminacy in the Case of Degeneracy," _Soviet Math. Dokl._, Vol. 16, pp. 1121-1125, 1975.

59. G.C. Verghese, B.C. Levy and T. Kailath, "A Generalized State Space for Singular Systems," _IEEE Transactions on Automatic Control_, AC-26, pp. 811-831, 1981.

60. J.B. Ward, "Equivalent Circuits for Power-Flow Studies," _AIEE Transactions_, Vol. 68, pp. 373-382, 1949.

61. J.H. Wilkinson, _The Algebraic Eigenvalue Problem_, Oxford University Press (Clarendon), New York, 1965.

62. J.H. Wilkinson and C. Reinch, _Linear Algebra_, Springer-Verlag, New York, 1971.

63. J.R. Winkelman, J.H. Chow, J.J. Allemong, and P.V. Kokotovic, "Multi-Time-Scale Analysis of a Power System," _Automatica_, Vol. 16, pp. 35-43, 1980.

64. J.R. Winkelman, J.H. Chow, B.C. Bowler, B. Avramovic and P.V. Kokotovic, "An Analysis of Interarea Dynamics of Multi-Machine Systems," _IEEE Transactions on Power Apparatus and Systems_, Vol. PAS-100, pp. 754-763, 1981.

65. F.F. Wu and N. Narasimhamurthi, "Coherency Identification for Power System Dynamic Equivalents," Memorandum No. UCB/ERL M77/57, University of California, Berkeley, 1977.

66. G. Peponides, P.V. Kokotovic and J.H. Chow, "Singular Perturbations and Time Scales in Nonlinear Models of Power Systems," _IEEE Transactions on Circuits and Systems_, Vol. CAS-29, No. 11, 1982.

Lecture Notes in Control and Information Sciences

Edited by A. V. Balakrishnan and M. Thoma

Lecture Notes in Control and Information Sciences

Edited by A. V. Balakrishnan and M. Thoma